THE GREAT AMERICAN BUS RIDE

IRMA KURTZ writes a regular column for *Cosmopolitan*.
Her most recent books are *Mantalk: Tough Talk from
a Tender Woman* and *Jinx*, a novel. She was born in
Jersey City, New Jersey, and is a graduate of Columbia
University. She lives in London.

D0291468

ALSO BY IRMA KURTZ

The Grand Dragon

Beds of Nails and Roses

Loneliness

Mantalk

THE ★ GREAT

AMERICAN

BUS ★ RIDE

IRMA KURTZ

FOURTH ESTATE • *London*

First published in the United States of America
in 1993 by Simon & Schuster Inc.

First published in Great Britain in 1994 by
Fourth Estate Limited
289 Westbourne Grove
London W11 2QA

A catalogue record for this book is
available from the British Library.

ISBN 1–85702–185–1

Printed and bound in Great Britain
by Cox & Wyman Ltd, Reading, Berkshire

To my son, Marc

CONTENTS

CONTENTS

THE ★ GREAT
AMERICAN
BUS ★ RIDE

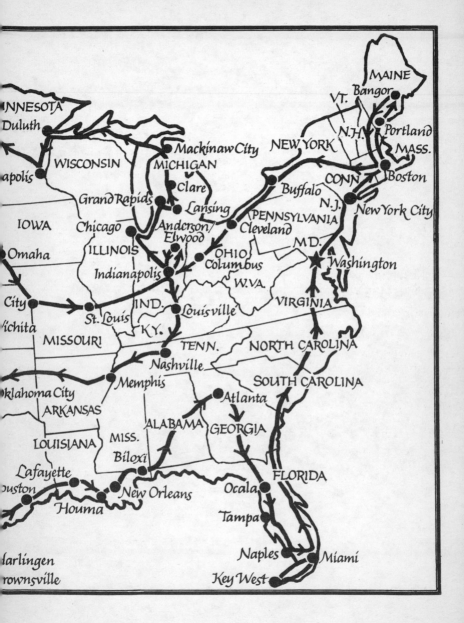

— · — · — · — · — · — · — · —

*You road I enter upon and look around, I believe you are not all
that is here,
I believe that much unseen is also here.*

*Here the profound lesson of reception, nor preference nor
denial. . . .*

"Song of the Open Road" by Walt Whitman

THE FIRST BUS

The first bus stop, Jersey suburbs

—·—·—·—·—·—·—

On a Thursday in October I packed an overnight case and set out to see America. I could have left a day earlier, or the previous week, or the next day. I could have waited until the weekend. I chose that Thursday as a baby will get itself born after months of highly exacting preparation more or less around the time it was expected, and for no good reason. Thursday chose me, and suitably enough my departure was unmarked by anyone but my mother. She stood in the doorway waving me off wistfully. Where the path turns out of sight of her house, I looked back one last time and I thought the words "Good-bye again" rose in a phantom bubble over her head.

My mother grew up in a flyspeck called Elwood, Indiana. New York was the last stop for all her Hoosier dreams and it is no surprise she fell in love with a New Yorker. But they ended up living across the river in Jersey City, and she never altogether lost her postulant's awe of Manhattan. Now she is in a retirement community she calls "Geriatric Gulch" near Princeton, New Jersey, about an hour from New York by bus. Not that Mother or her neighbors use the bus. Not unless it is absolutely necessary. Buses and bus depots scare the wits out of genteel Americans (*America* scares the wits out of genteel Americans) and the Greyhound depot defines the wrong side of the tracks. Even Mother, no chicken-hearted octogenarian, would have her bladder cast in bronze before she'd use the ladies' room at the Port Authority bus terminal.

The day before I hit the road, Mother and I bumped into one of her little old neighbor ladies on the path outside our front door. Mother introduced me, her daughter who lives in London.

"Irma is going to spend the next few months traveling all over the United States."

"Well, well," said the mauve-tinted neighbor, "isn't that nice?"

Whereupon Mother, who loves to shock, added slyly: "On Greyhound buses!"

"Oh, dear, oh dear!" cried the little old lady. "Not with all the nut cases!"

Four lanes of highway separate "Geriatric Gulch" from the stop for the Suburban Transit bus to New York. Near where I waited for a break in the traffic, a well-dressed old man made several false starts into the road before he finally drew himself together like a shrinking hedgehog and risked a dash to the median strip. When I arrived a few paces behind him at the bus shelter, he was perched on the narrow bench, puffing and triumphant. I paced, and twitched every time a branch heavy with coagulating fog scraped the transparent roof of the shelter, while the old man cast anxious sidelong glances my way. To be frank, I looked a trifle sinister for a nice people's bus from the suburbs. I wore sneakers and thick socks, jeans, a black T-shirt under a baggy lime-green pullover, a scarf from Indonesia printed with two bug-eyed demons, and open over this ensemble the Australian raincoat they call a Driza Bone, ankle length, in brown oiled cotton with a cape that converts into a hood, an unbuttoning rear vent, and optional thigh ties for leaping onto horses and motorcycles. It's a garment that possesses a tough roadworthiness—just the ticket for Greyhound, though viewed with disapproval, even alarm, by Mother's fastidious neighbors of the "Gulch." In spite of bus protocol, which is purely democratic and always gives priority to the first person at the stop, when the bus pulled in, the old man moved back a few steps to make sure I boarded first so he could keep an eye on me. I moved back to a place near a window. Wisely, he opted for a quick seat on the aisle up front before the bus began its jolting passage onto the Jersey Turnpike.

*　　*　　*

October landscape streaked by, blurred in mist. When I would come that way again in three months' time, the rusty leaves would have fallen, and the bare gray branches that always remind me more keenly than summer foliage of my American childhood would be starting to stir and swell. Those months while the trees slept and began to wake again, what surprising encounters did they hold for me? I had lived most of my life in foreign lands, and never could I recall wanting as deeply to make any trip as the one just beginning. My first idea had been to travel America by train. When I was a kid, sturdy old pufferbellies still chugged into the boondocks whistling in the night to small-town poets. These days, however, little more than the rails remain. Nailed fast to earth at untold expense of human life, silently they track the immense western spaces. I soon discovered American trains would not take me anywhere obscure, or anywhere much at all it seemed, unless I kept going to Chicago first.

America is a road country. To be without wheels in America is to be lame. My countrymen, I know, believe an abundance of choices is one definition of freedom, but I am not so sure. The driver is a prisoner of choosing, like the shopper who frowns at the labels of fifteen varieties of dill pickles in the supermarket while outside a million adventures are going to waste. Besides, I learned to drive late in life and I'll never learn to enjoy it. When the lady from next door had asked why I did not drive myself around America, Mother replied with the quirky pride she has always taken in my eccentricities: "Irma is anti cars."

Suburban Transit buses are not made for distance: the seats are badly sprung, the windows are small, and short-run drivers tend to be sunk in self-pity, resentful if they must bestir themselves to open the hold for luggage or outsize packages. Between commuters' buses like the one I was on and Greyhound's Americruisers there was a world of difference, I knew. A year earlier, when the idea of traveling around America on the bus had occurred to me, I made a trial run from Ocala, Florida, to San Diego. I survived.

And more: thanks to my fellow travelers, every mile of the journey had been a discovery—mostly they *were* the journey.

"But the discomfort!" Mother's worried neighbor had cried.

"Nothing like it," I told her.

The truth is, I am a hussy of low appetites who always yearns shamelessly for rough travel, and I grab the chance whenever I can to arrive at my destination exhausted, knowing I've earned my goal the hard way. Greyhound and I were made for each other. "It had to be you," I whispered as I watched a great big Americruiser zip past us effortlessly, homing in on the Port Authority after what vast and thrilling distances?

"Port *of* Authority" is what my father used to call the Manhattan depot, and what he thought it was until the end of his days: the one, the only Port *of* New York City's Universal Authority! He had grown up on the Lower East Side, but he was the firstborn son of an immigrant couple, and he never altogether mastered the local language or customs. Sometimes I think it was from his uncertainty and alienation that I inherited my wanderlust, or perhaps it came from a flaky chromosome, or a genetic fluke, and I'm a throwback to some crazy pilgrim from the Pale. For whatever reason, from practically the day I was aware, I was outward bound, and outward for me was eastward. When I finally shipped out for Europe, I was pretty sure I'd be back as soon as I felt the need to settle down. That was more than thirty years ago. Since then I've traveled all over Europe, in Asia and Australia, and a little in Africa, and I've made my home in London. Whenever I returned to my native land it was for quick visits to one coast or the other. Expatriatism turned out to be like middle age—it sneaked up on me and accumulated stealthily until one day it was complete—and when I thought about America it was tenderly, with astonishment that I had ever been so young. But life is a circular journey; as soon as my son turned nineteen and I could plan on open-ended travel for the first time since his birth, it had to be west at last, to the most baffling of all places, my unknown homeland.

*   *   *

Through the grimy window of our bus, New York's stunning skyline was suddenly to be seen in the distance. It disappeared as we started the twisting run down to the Hudson, then there it was, back again and this time big as life, leaving us nonentities from the Polyester Belt in no doubts about our unimportance. As we joined traffic inching toward the tunnel, people around me began to wake up and bring their coats and briefcases down from the overhead rack. In the dim light of the tunnel they moved forward to be first off when we pulled into the bay. My overnight case was on the empty seat beside me, and my tapestry handbag was on my lap. For the nth time that morning I checked its contents: wallet; camera; inflatable pillow; hip flask; passport; comb; Chap Stick; two pens; notebook; three Greyhound Ameripasses bought in London, each good for one month's unlimited travel. In one big pocket of my coat was the second volume of Anthony Burgess's autobiography, *You've Had Your Time*, in the other a small packet of Kleenex and Saul Bellow's *Something to Remember Me By*. There was also a folded piece of paper.

"I want you to read this and think about what it says," Mother's little old lady neighbor had said when she'd thrust it into my hand. At that moment the telephone rang—it was my brother calling from California—and afterward, between one thing and the other, I had forgotten all about her missive until I came upon it folded up in the pocket of my Driza Bone just as the Suburban Transit bus was emerging from its burrow into New York. I figured it was a prayer she wanted me to take to heart, or a religious tract. It was crudely printed on green paper. "Protect Yourself from Attack" was written in big letters at the top; underneath was a line drawing of a woman fending off a big black man, and a postal address for ordering Mace sprays.

BUSES 2 TO 6

BOSTON — BUFFALO

Making the most of the waterfront in Portland, Maine

BUS 2 to BOSTON

There are no flashy shops downstairs at the Port Authority, no hawkers, no saloon where the thirsty commuter can grab a quick one. Down there, travel is a serious business, and the people crouching in corners are not panhandlers, but weary passengers from Chicago or New Orleans between stints on the road, waiting for their buses out. A cosmopolitan group had already gathered when I arrived at the Boston gate. First in line were two women, tourists from northern Italy, dressed in buttery wools and suede. Behind them were a couple of latter-day hippies, he and she, both long-haired, wearing socks and sandals and fringed denim jackets. They sat back-to-back on the floor; clearly they were seasoned hands—each of them cuddled a big feather pillow. Next to them was a Japanese woman holding a sleeping baby. A group of Haitian men and women speaking their French patois fell in behind me, and in front of me two old women chatted in Russian. Everyone was surrounded by luggage except for the hippies and me.

I had learned on my previous trip that luggage has a way of traveling on a different bus from its owner, and the only hindrance to impulsive bus-hopping is a suitcase in the hold. This time I intended to make the entire journey with only my tapestry handbag and a weekender small enough to fit in the overhead rack or under my seat. It contained a change of underwear, a toiletry kit, my old black bathing suit, thick black tights, a black cashmere pullover, a print skirt, black flats, three pairs of silk socks as recommended by arctic explorers, and a small photograph of my son in a heart-shaped frame out of a Christmas grab bag. I had base coat, mascara, and a lipstick, but no fancy extras. In spite of a lifetime of received wisdom, I intended to wash my face in soap and water.

* * *

It is a peculiarity of the solitary woman in her fifties that she can for long periods of time believe herself to be invisible. I count anonymity as a chief virtue of middle age, so when one of the babushkas turned suddenly and addressed me in English—"Can you speak Russian?" she asked—I was taken aback.

"I know how to say, 'More vodka and caviar,' " I told her. "And I can say, 'Yes,' 'No,' and 'Thank you.' "

The older of the two, it turned out, was fresh from Moscow and traveling alone to Boston, where relatives were going to meet her at the depot. The other asked me, please, to keep an eye on her during the journey. Keeping an eye on an old lady and permuting my little bit of Russian for five long hours on the road was not something I really wanted to do. Fortunately, the little dumpling felt the same way. When I dutifully went to sit next to her on the bus, she glared at me and folded her arms, and made me know she too preferred to be alone.

From the seat right behind the Russian woman I imagined myself to be seeing Manhattan through her eyes. Words, words, words, everywhere high and low. Words in neon waiting to blaze, words embossed, hand painted, words picked out in reflecting studs, words scribbled on walls: warnings, descriptions, names, jokes, enticements, profanities. In Moscow there is a stone-gray visual silence everywhere; her old eyes must have been deafened by central Manhattan. Even if she could not understand any of the words, words, words, she had to see the racket they made until they were finally lost in the battlefields of the island's upper reaches.

We moved practically due north into a late flash of chrysanthemum colors that only near the Massachusetts border gave way to bare branches; even there, golden oak and copses of fiery maples held out against winter. "There you go again," my son says whenever I start to babble about autumns of my childhood in America, "overstating the case." I wanted him next to me to see for himself the blaze of his mother's memory through the window of the

Greyhound. I had headed first for New England simply because that is where autumn rules at its best in the world. My travel plans were loose after that. I was going to take America pretty much as she came.

Aside from the gang who boarded at the Port Authority, the bus acquired a number of boys and girls going to and from colleges of the Ivy League. They buried their noses in textbooks the moment they boarded. The man in the seat next to me was in his early to middle thirties. Like every last adult male on board, he wore a baseball cap, and like nine out of ten of them, he was bearded. Beards in my American generation were considered affected and somehow unpatriotic; nowadays northeastern American men appear to grow them as soon as they are old enough not to shave. My seatmate wore a sweatshirt embossed with the seal of Yale University that none of the genuine students on board would have been caught dead wearing. When he raised his arms to scratch the back of his neck, a stale smell rose from his armpits. I had heard him tell the neo-hippies diagonally across the aisle that he had been on the buses for three days and nights.

"Three days? Four days? I can't remember ever being *off* it," the girl said, and turned her face to the pillow propped against the bulkhead.

While the New England towns slipped by, and fields of cars like shiny mushrooms sprouted around suburban railway stations, the two men compared travel notes. I listened enviously. Mostly, they talked about road surfaces and highway numbers: 80, smooth through Nebraska, 70, twisting through Colorado.

"I can take desert as much as the next guy," the man next to me said, "but Nevada felt like it was never gonna end."

A car passed on the road to Boston carrying the plate "549 TEA." When I looked back to my neighbors, the younger one had collapsed on the pillow against his girlfriend's shoulder. Fatigue takes people in funny ways, as I was certainly to discover in the miles ahead; my seatmate went on a gabby jag, and without preamble he turned, talking, to me.

"Been helping my mother move to Nevada with her number three husband. Been unemployed for four months before that up in Maine. I like Maine good enough; like to hunt; love the sea. But things are bad right now. Might move to Nevada for work. I dunno. They are real short of 'wah-duh' there. Got this little bitty lake near my mom's place. Drove her there with a boat hitched on the trailer. A boat crossing the desert. That was a sight to see. Took this here trip to think things over. My wife and me might get together again, but things will have to change. Dunno how. Just change. Can't go on the way we've been. Married four years. Got a little girl from this one. Boy from the time before."

It has been several years since smoking was prohibited on all buses, yet smokers persist in sitting near the back. When we stopped for a rest not far from the Massachusetts state line, they shoved their way forward, tugging cigarettes out of their pockets, then stood shoulder-to-shoulder like a firing squad next to the bus and lit up. On my way out to stretch my legs, I offered to fetch the old Russian lady a coffee from the vending machine inside the storefront station, but she said, "Naah, naah," and shooed me away. On her lap was spread a feast of bread, cheese, sausage, chocolate, and fruit.

Traffic increased enormously in the afternoon, most of it out of central Boston to the suburbs that were thickening around us. My neighbor continued his agonized dithering: Nevada, Maine, maybe California. There was supposed to be work in California. One thing was for sure, his wife was going to have to change her ways, or he was going to have to change wives. The young hippie across the aisle woke, yawned, stretched. "Hey man, did you bump into an Australian dude called Barry?" he asked my neighbor. "He drives a bus east out of Cheyenne, Wyoming."

Cheyenne, Wyoming. I liked the sound of it. As we were pulling into Boston, I added Cheyenne, Wyoming, to my list.

—·—·—

* * *

My old lady was swept up by a mob of Russians at the depot. As I was turning to leave, she called out: "Hey! Hey!" She was beaming and holding out an apple. My father's mother used to keep big red apples like it in the fruit bowl for visiting grandchildren: they have mealy yellow flesh that tastes ancient, as if they have been carried in a suitcase from some other country where fruit is rare and valuable. "Tanks," said the old lady. "You good kid."

One lesson I have learned from traveling is to encounter a city exactly as you do an individual, open to its personality and its intent. Cities can mean a newcomer good or ill—I'd stake my life on it. Boston came across to me as a wily old charmer, decidedly masculine in temperament, and a little bit two-faced. But Boston and I go back a long time. It is saddled with memories from the days when I was doing my rounds for college entrance. I rejected Boston then, took New York instead, and I could be too defensive of my choice to see it fairly even now. After all, great cities can be recognized among other things, by efficient public transport, food, and how much they make you laugh: Boston certainly has the first two. As for laughs, I had checked my bag at the depot for the afternoon bus to Portland, Maine, and was snooping around town on foot when I turned a corner into a narrow street and there was a tall blond policeman leaning against a wall, flossing his teeth.

"You caught me flossing," he said, and winked. "Think how much worse it coulda been."

And rarely have I seen a more resonant historical joke than a bunch of English tourists being inveigled by a madly upbeat guide into acting the part of rebels dressed as Indians at the site of the Boston Tea Party. "How!" he made them shout, and with feathers in their hair. How, indeed?

"Dear student," said a hand-lettered sign in the Chinese restaurant near my bed and breakfast where I had dinner, "in order to find stolen items we reserve the right to examine your changing clothes."

BUS 3 to PORTLAND, MAINE

Back in London I had daydreamed for hours over the Greyhound map and studied the blue lines of the bus routes, thick and tangled from the eastern seaboard all the way to a central division that runs roughly from Minneapolis to Houston, where the knot relaxes, and then meanders out to the Pacific. To start on a bus in New York and travel from the bunched and varicose routes of the East to the long lithe routes of the West I thought would be like starting out old and growing younger. As eager as I was to jump into the spacious oblongs of Greyhound's romantic western trails, there were a few things I wanted to see first in the Northeast. For instance, back in the 1950s at Barnard College a lot of the upper-crust girls used to summer in Maine; the way they had talked about Bar Harbor lodged in my mind like a jazzy tune, and I had always wanted to have a look at the place.

The white-haired man who sat next to me on the Portland bus was handsome, but with a damaged quality, like a piece of antique furniture in need of restoration. He didn't speak until we were pulling out of Portsmouth, New Hampshire, a posh little town where the only passenger to board was a young man seen off by a very fat older woman who kissed him twice on the mouth. "Ah, mother love," said my neighbor. I wasn't all that sure.

"Nice weather," he said. "Been funny weather. But this is nice weather. . . ."

Manhattan was strong enough in his voice so it surprised me when I realized he was English: the British as a rule do not surrender their accents without a mortal battle. He came from Bristol, he told me. And when I asked him if he was ever homesick, he looked at me with mild surprise, and said in a puzzled way: "Homesick?"

"Were you a merchant seaman?" I asked, as Bristol is a seaport.

"I was in the restaurant business in London. One of our regular customers was a man who worked for the American embassy, and he arranged to get me my visa. That was a long time ago, just after the war, and a visa to America wasn't easy to get. The funny part is, I didn't want the bloody thing. I only took it because he was so happy to fix it for me. I didn't want to hurt his feelings. Then when the visa was running out, one of my friends said to me, 'Mate, you'll never get a chance like this again. Why not give it a go?' And I did. And I haven't been back there since."

We had come to the edge of the great northern wilderness. The hills were turning into mountains and snow lingered in the shade of thickly wooded forests. So immediate had been the change of contours and colors from Massachusetts to Maine, it was as if nature marked man's frontiers in her own way.

"I am an expatriate by accident," my neighbor said in his dull, flat way.

"And you stayed in New York?" I asked, coaxing. "Most European expats go west."

"Accident," he said.

Gradually traffic had been slowing and growing congested. Blue lights were flashing ahead of us and we passed a group of figures in yellow slickers gathered on the median strip. In the oncoming lane next to ours was a huge truck in segments, like a hard-shelled bug. The cabin was erect, but the trailer had fallen on its side, and under it lay a crumpled car. "Someone's not gonna walk away from that," our driver said over the microphone.

"My God," I said to my seatmate. "Look. Isn't that dreadful?"

"A man starts out one morning like any other morning . . . ," the driver said. He was a big man, and when he sighed his shoulder lifted high over his seat.

"How terrible," I said to my neighbor.

His face was turned resolutely away from the window, and from me. He spoke into the air: "When I was a kid in Bristol," he said, "you could go to a movie for two shillings. When I was a kid we paid for a loaf in pennies. Back then a pair of shoes left you change from a pound note. . . ."

The other passengers were all talking about the accident. I heard some of them speculating on the popping noises, like gunshots, as we were passing the scene. However, from the moment of the accident all the way into Portland I could get nothing out of the man in the seat next to me except a litany of British prewar prices delivered in a monotone. I was already out of the depot hunting for a taxi when I realized he must have been a boy in Bristol during the war, when the Germans were bombing the heart out of the place.

Eavesdropping is a longtime avocation of mine. Most of America is an eavesdropper's paradise, which puts it as close as a whisker to hell: anyone who has tried to sleep on a bus, then watched the sun rise up in glory over the Central Plains, must know that heaven and hell are only the blink of an eye apart. Until I arrived in the open spaces of America, where people no longer shout over each other's voices to be heard, eavesdropping was more often inadvertent than by choice, and it nearly drove me nuts. When I stopped for a drink that evening in the bar of my Portland motel, I was stunned by the level of noise and by the conversations I had to overhear, some of them quite intimate. Near me sat a tall young man with another man about twice his age.

"She made the best chili I ever tasted," the young man said. "She didn't make the sauce, she bought the sauce ready made."

"Since I started looking at statistics," said the old man, "I seen our divorce rate is so high, it's an epidemic."

"Unh-hunh," said the young man, and though they did not look alike, something in his tone made me think they must be father and son.

"Now, in the old days, you got pissed off. But divorce was a disgrace."

"Unh-hunh."

"Nowadays we make it too easy. The system is gonna hold you financially responsible, you know. She's gonna get the lot, tax free. And she can go out and get herself a job. See, back when the man had the job, it was all different."

"Anybody could make that chili," the young man said. "Only you need to know what brand of sauce it was."

"We have all these broken homes nowadays, kids getting pregnant. There is only one way for kids to develop and that is in a man-woman relationship."

"Unh-hunh."

Next morning at breakfast, two men who resembled each other except in age, both pale and thin-lipped, took a table at the far end of the dining room. I heard them order two New England Specials, one with decaf. When the food arrived, the young man bent his head and roared out: "For what we are about to receive . . ." His prayer was long and comprehensive, and when it was over both men glared self-righteously at us benighted souls before they tucked into their eggs and bacon, and talked about the sales figures of holy books and videotapes.

On the front page of a morning paper I picked up in the lobby was a photograph of the crash my bus had passed the day before. The headline read: "Driver Crushed by Cattle Truck." We had been among the first at the scene, and local roads afterward had been impassable until midnight due to backed-up traffic. Emergency crews had to cut the roof off the car to remove the crushed body of the driver. The popping noises we'd heard were state police shooting a dozen of the animals injured when the two-tier truck tipped over. The driver of the truck was being treated in a local hospital for minor injuries.

"Life's fulla bad surprises," said the off-duty desk clerk who gave me a lift to the depot in a motel van. He was impressed to learn that I had been at the scene of the accident. However, he was infinitely more impressed to find out that many years earlier I had interviewed the Monty Python team for a magazine article.

With my bag checked in a locker at the depot, ready for the afternoon bus to Bangor, I went down to visit the port. Henry

Wadsworth Longfellow wrote a pretty tribute to his "dear old town" of Portland; but the coastal towns of New England, once rich and thriving on "the beauty and mystery of the ships," seem to rely these days on summer tourists, and the port in October was curiously quiet. Only the lobster fisheries set up a little bustle around the docks. And the ferry over to Peaks Island had a view of Portland, sparkling through the northern air. Beside me two strapping young women were comparing the price of oxygen in hospitals and the rates of their heartbeats while they were being delivered of their babies. "The doctors had never seen anything like my blood pressure," said one of them, and she yanked her two-year-old, who was on a leash, back from the rail.

The depot was small and countrified. Only one other person was in it when I arrived early for my bus, a young soldier who was on the telephone to his girlfriend, arranging for her to come and pick him up. He glanced my way briefly in automatic sexual appraisal, then he sat in one of the plastic bucket seats with his back to me and opened a morning paper someone had left behind. After a few minutes, a stocky man in his early forties entered and looked around wildly, as if he had mislaid something there earlier. He was very pale and the skin around his lips was bluish. I heard him ask the girl behind the ticket window for the times of the buses to New York. Then he stood at the door, shifting from foot to foot.

"Hey, see that?" he said, pointing to the front page of the soldier's newspaper. "That was me. I was driving that truck. I was the driver." His accent was out of central Texas, or just north of there.

"Well, I'll be darned," said the soldier. "How'd it happen?"

"It wasn't drink. I never drink. The wee-ind. It was the wee-ind did it. The way it happened was, he hit the right rear of my tractor, I couldn't see, and he come over into my lane, and he just kept going with me. Just kept going with me. And the speed of the tires kept pushing him ahead. And the wee-ind and everything, that wee-ind, carried him right around the front, right around the front of the truck. And he just kept going with me. They hadda shoot a whole lot of the cattle. Fifteen years I been driving. I got a wife and two little girls. Not sure I'm ever gonna drive agin. I know I'll never drive a truck agin." He looked around the station frantically, this way and that. "Gotta get out," he said. "Gotta eat something." And he bolted for the door.

"Ain't that life for you?" the soldier said. "A guy gets up one morning . . . Here today, gone tomorrow."

Reports from the Portland District Court were itemized in the paper. I had read about some petty theft, some lobster fishing without a license and operating of unregistered boats; one dog owner was fined $27.50 for letting his pet run at large. I had chatted with people in a bookstore, at the ferry port, and at a restaurant, and they had all assured me drugs were no problem in Portland. When I asked a taxi driver why he thought Portland was immune to the problems of other cities, he said: "We only got a handful of blacks. And we know where they are." It was a surprise, therefore, to see a sniffer dog appear in the bus depot, led by a short bald man in blue. The bus from Boston had pulled in and a crowd of youngsters off it were milling around in the sunshine, smoking and drinking Cokes, waiting for the driver to call them back to their seats for the trip to Bangor. The dog and his handler were a lackadaisical pair and struck no apparent fear in the crowd. Only one woman just ahead of me in the line of the boarders said: "Geez, I hope he don't go for my medication." I looked up and found myself face-to-face for the first time with Vera from Detroit.

When I say Vera and I were "face-to-face," that's not quite how it was. Her proportions came from an age when doorways were cast out of boulders and everything was big and basic. "Are you a nurse?" I asked, for in my experience women of such large, earthy dimensions are often nurses or nuns. But she was already wafting her duffel bag in hands the size of shovels and swinging herself on board the bus. By the time I climbed in after her there were no window seats remaining and the only space up front was on the aisle next to her.

"I guess you'll just have to sit here," she said.

Her voice was gruff and begrudging, but her button-bright eyes were full of loneliness. Throwing my lot in with hers for a while, I took the seat she was offering me, trying to look as if she didn't care.

BUS 4 to BANGOR

"Now, that's funny, I'm going to Bar Harbor too," said Vera, and as if she had heard the alarm sounding between my ears, she added: "I'll bet I thought of it before you did."

Like many very big women, Vera had a trilling voice, and she was dainty in other ways too: her duffel bag was pink; her hair was artificially streaked and curled; her nails, though bitten close to the quick, were done in opalescent polish. And she let me know right away that one of the reasons she had chosen Maine for her holiday was that she'd seen a film on TV about the state, and she thought the Maine men were gorgeous.

"Look at that guy," she said. She pointed to a big young man who was nodding off in the seat across the aisle. "Isn't he a doll?" She leaned across me and said: "Hey, I was just telling my friend, I'd sure like to take you home for Christmas." He smiled, then laughed and stroked his beard, pulled his baseball hat down over his eyes, and went back to sleep.

Vera said she would be driving her own car if they let her. "They let rapists and anyone drive. But not me. It makes me boiling mad. My seizures only last a second."

When I asked what kind of seizures, she said she had been epileptic since birth.

"What does it feel like to have a seizure, Vera?"

"Like a seashell," she said. "Like my brain is a seashell, and an electric shock is buzzing around it. But it could be happening to me right now and you'd never notice. You might think I was looking into space for a second or two."

"Gee, Vera," I said, warming toward her, "maybe we *all* have epilepsy."

It took a moment, then she laughed and punched my arm so hard I nearly tumbled into the aisle.

Behind us was a little boy of about three with his mother. They had come a long way together: the plastic bag she stuffed into the overhead rack carried the name of a store in Nashville. At the Portland depot, when he had played at hitting all the buttons on the Coke machine, she had barely the strength to whimper: "Cordel, oh, Cordel, for pity's sake, honey, simmer down." Cordel had been playing with a little plastic figure out of a cereal box—it looked like a troll or a garden gnome. Several times he'd thrown it into the aisle and scrambled after it. This time he overshot. The creature flew over Vera's shoulder and into her lap.

"I'll bet you want this back," she said, squirming around to talk to him. "But I have it. And I want it. And you can't have it back."

Cordel was not a kid to cry easily: he'd had a rough life. But he looked awfully worried and made a swipe at the toy. Vera held it easily beyond his reach.

"Can't have it," she said. "It's mine now."

He grabbed for it again. She pulled it away with one hand while making a rough pass at his head with the other. If he hadn't ducked fast, he would have been clobbered. Desperately, he went for the toy again. His face had turned very red. She pulled the figure out of his reach.

"Vera, please," I said. "Give the child his toy."

"Well, of course," she replied, and handed the plastic figure to the boy. "It's just my way," she said. "Kids understand. They like it."

The incident, and the fact that I'd intervened, made an intimacy between us, and she began to tell me about herself. She was the last of five daughters, "an accident," and her childhood had been so devoid of tenderness and fun and freedom it could have been the sentence of a harsh judge who held no brief for innocence. Her father was drunken and abusive; her mother was cold and critical. Vera'd had no friends; she didn't need to tell me how cruelly the other children must have treated their weird, outsize classmate. None of her family had spoken to her in years. She didn't know why they shunned her—she figured it must be because of her epilepsy.

"But that doesn't make sense—" I began.

"Who makes sense?" she said sarcastically.

"I mean, Vera, there must be some other reason—"

"Look at those trees," she interrupted, pointing to a stand of giant firs, snow dusted and serene in the dusk. "I like trees. They remind me of people."

She was on a disability pension, which she augmented with part-time work.

"I'm a caretaker," she said, and our Englishes crossed lines, so she had to explain that she did not take care of property, as I assumed, but she took care of people who didn't want to go into a hospital or home because of age and disability.

"That must be a hard job."

"Well, I'm practically retired," she said, and a shadow crossed her broad, open face.

As we were nearly at the end of the journey, I felt I owed Vera a few facts about myself. But when I started out by telling her I lived in England, she showed an indifference so complete that I quickly said, "Maybe you'll travel abroad someday."

"No. I'd be scared. Their potatoes, say, aren't like our potatoes, and they might make me constipated." We were pulling into the station, our parting was imminent, and Vera was suddenly sulky. "Besides, you could be pretending to live in England. How would I know? You could be a drug smuggler or something."

"Don't you trust your own impressions, Vera?"

"Well," she said, "I could be anyone, too."

"Are you a leaf peeper?" the taxi driver asked me.

We were pulling away. I was watching Vera push through the door of the station carrying her pink duffel bag and another big bag that had been in the hold. Her needy, hurt gaze drilled into my back.

—·—·—

"A leaf peeper?"

"Ee-yup. We get 'em every year. They come to watch the leaves turn color."

It was late in the season for leaf peepers, and soon he was at a loss to explain why every one of a half-dozen motels and hotels we tried in Bangor was booked up solid, not a room to spare. Finally, we crossed the river to the twin town of Brewer, where in a row of old houses was one that advertised a bed and breakfast. With twelve dollars on the meter, and a sinking feeling at images of spending the night in a plastic bucket chair at the bus depot, I rang the doorbell while my taxi waited. A woman of about my own age, who was very shy for an innkeeper, whispered that, yes, there was a single available for the night, and I was saying that, yes, I'd take it, oh, yes, when suddenly from the hall behind her a soprano voice rang out: "Don't give that woman a room! She's a wanted criminal!" My heart sank, and with strange premonition, I saw that the figure who stepped out from the hall was Vera from the bus.

We went together for lobster at a restaurant our landlady recommended. It was a walk of four or five blocks, and Vera radiated good humor beside me in the dark.

"Now, I have a funny way of eating," she told the waitress, whose professional smile faded immediately. "I'll have the coleslaw and the baked potato. But I don't like anything on the same plate, okay? Don't put the coleslaw in one of those paper cup things. I don't like that. And don't bring the potato until I've finished the lobster. Is your decaf freshly brewed? I want decaf with the meal, but only if it's freshly brewed. . . ."

When I ordered a glass of white wine with my lobster, Vera shook her head sadly and said she used to drink until she'd had a terrible experience with a guy she met in a bar, and after that she'd sworn off drink, and hadn't touched a drop since.

"He slipped a mickey in my drink."

"Oh, come on, Vera, people don't do that, not in the real world," I said.

"They do in Detroit," she replied.

*   *   *

After dinner, we plunged back into the crispy dark and Vera started to tell me about her work. At first she spoke in general terms; soon she narrowed her monologue down into a specific story. She spoke with increasing speed and heat. For several months before her trip she had been in charge of an aged couple in a prosperous residential section of Detroit. The wife was a depressive who wanted to die, according to Vera, but before she went, she wanted her husband dead too. He was mildly demented but sweet tempered, and the only trouble Vera had was persuading him to take his pills before every meal.

"His medication. He had to take his medication or he'd die. I had to get him to swallow those pills. So I'm in the kitchen trying to get that medication down the old man, and all of a sudden she leaps on my back. Like a monkey or a raccoon or a giant spider, or something. And she's yelling, 'You're killing him! You're killing him!' But she's the one, not me. She's the one who won't let me give him his medication. It's her that wants him dead. Believe me, believe me. It's her."

"I believe you, Vera," I said, and she was quiet for a little while. Then, in a calmer tone, she told me how she had designed restraining cuffs for the old man, made them herself out of Velcro.

"Just like the kind they use in hospitals on violent patients."

"*Are* you a nurse, Vera? *Were* you a nurse?"

She did not answer. She stood stock-still for a moment.

I nearly put out my hand to touch her, a trembling monolith darker than the night, then I thought better of it. We stood that way for ten seconds or so, until she started to move on. In the light over the porch of our bed and breakfast I could see that her big, archaic face was covered with anger and real hatred. That night, uncharacteristically, I locked my door from the inside.

The local bus from Bangor left late and did not stop within a mile of Bar Harbor. Resignedly, I agreed to share a taxi from Brewer. The driver said we were going to be his last fares, as hunting season opened next day and nothing on earth could stop a good

Maine man from heading for the woods. He was bearded and big; he wore a hunter's fluorescent orange cap and smoked a pipe.

"Oh, wow, I love pipe smoke," said Vera. She sat in the backseat next to me. "I'd like to take you home for Christmas."

"Do women hunt?" I asked, cutting her off.

"Well, we got this one old Indian woman of ninety-plus who still hunts pretty reg'lar. Once when this Indian lady was about eighty-four, I guess, she was driving another little old lady into town when the door flies open on the driver's side and the Indian lady was throwed out into the road. Well, that little old lady, she picked herself up, ran to where her car had stalled nose first in a ditch, and did she ever chew out the other little old lady. 'When you seen me fall outta the car, why didn't you slam on the brakes, you silly old fool?'"

Vera and I were lucky to find a motel with rooms in Bar Harbor. The season ended officially on the very day of our arrival and the place was shutting up around us like a gigantic bivalve. We walked the pretty streets, thick with leaves. In the old cemetery around St. Saviour's Episcopal Church lived a family of feral cats, descended perhaps from familiars that fled north three hundred years ago when life got too hot for them in Salem. Vera rolled those wild pussycats in her big hands and kneaded them against the wet grass until they nearly burst with purring. As we were leaving the graveyard, a dozen lean tabbies hopped up on the wall to see her off. Further on, a man in his late fifties stepped out of a shop on the main street where we were window-shopping. He was every inch the weekend sailor. Vera bellowed, "Hey, Irma, get your camera out. Here's a genuine old sea dog for you!" I strode ahead, cursing under my breath. But she was so contrite and frolicsome and clumsy, she made me feel guilty for my embarrassment, so I invited her to lunch.

"These tourists came in the other day," our waitress said, "and they asked me, 'Is your fish sent down from Boston?' So I says that no, we fish them right here. So then they say, 'Even in winter?' And I says, 'Why, sure.' So they nodded over that way"—she nodded her own head toward the steel-cold Atlantic. "And they asked, real puzzled, 'But what do you do when it freezes over?' "

Vera laughed so hard she choked on the piece of bread she'd been chewing. She thumped the table very hard.

"Where did they come from?" I asked the waitress.

"Oh, Michigan, of course," she said. But she was watching Vera nervously.

Bar Harbor is no longer the country seat of exclusivity and style it once was. I did not see a McDonald's or a video arcade, true enough, but there were a lot of T-shirt and souvenir shops, all in the throes of their end-of-season sales. Only the Bayside Walk was reminiscent of what I imagined the old days to have been. It followed the coast in the shade of grand summer houses built for the views and comforts of another age, and empty in the gathering fogs of winter. Vera did not see the point of walking to no ostensible destination—very few people do—so I left her behind on a tarry little beach where she pretended to look for shells while impatiently waiting for me to return. Remembering why most of my life I've had to travel alone, blaming myself, not Vera, but annoyed with her for making me do it, I turned back from the Bayside Walk much sooner than I would have had I been free to go my own way.

That evening we went to a bar called the Thirsty Whale. I had a bourbon and water. Vera had a decaf, freshly brewed. In spite of being teetotal, she seemed very at ease in the murky bar, and flashed glances at some local boys drinking beer in a corner. After a while another story started emerging, and pretty soon she was telling it with the same angry speed of the previous night. A girl had turned up at Vera's door with unimpeachable references to take a room Vera had advertised to let.

"I didn't search her boxes when she moved in. How was I supposed to know she had a gun? Then one night she comes in late, and I'm in bed, and all of a sudden she's standing in my door with a gun pointed right at me. I felt like I was a duck, you know?

In a carnival. She shot me twice. When the cops found me I was out in the yard—the neighbors had called them. And the first thing, they ask me if I'm left-handed. When I said no, I was right-handed, they said that was okay then. Because she had told them I'd gone for her with a knife, see? But the knife wound on her arm went from left to right. And they knew that meant she must have done it herself." She put her left forearm on the table and rolled up the sleeve of her anorak to a few inches above her elbow. "That hole there is where I put my arm up to stop the bullet. It didn't hurt at the time. There's another hole in my shoulder. That didn't hurt either, not until later. What's the matter? Haven't you seen anyone who was shot before?"

"Only in a war."

"Oh, it's a war," she said. "It's a war, all right."

Vera saw me off next afternoon in Bangor and hugged me enormously. There were tears in her eyes. I waved until her taxi was out of sight, then sank back into the delicious anonymity of the depot. I felt bruised, and happy to be on my own again. The man in front of me for the bus to Boston and beyond took off his baseball cap, scratched his head, and turned his light blue eyes my way.

"I have just spent five days camping out in the woods," he said. "On my own."

"There is nothing I would rather do," I told him.

"Well, I was living with this girl for two years. We were both alcoholics. I went into AA. That was six months ago. I haven't had a drink since. She was supposed to come on this trip with me. But she drank herself to death last month."

BUS 5 to BOSTON

I planned to retrace my road as infrequently as possible, and there was probably a circuitous route to Buffalo through Burlington, Vermont, and down to Albany, but the Bangor ticket clerk hadn't suggested it, and I was too green to ask for it. So it had to be back to Boston and a two-hour wait there before the night bus to

Buffalo. Carefully not catching the eye of the recovering alcoholic, I chose a seat two rows back on the right: bus-right, I mean, which is to the left of boarders. Restless during the nights with Vera, I had read Burgess until after midnight and left his book, highly recommended, in the motel. Now, Saul Bellow's book was under way.

"Public life in the United States," I was reading as we pulled away, "is a mass of distractions. By some this is seen as a challenge to their ability to maintain internal order. Others have acquired a taste for distraction, and they freely consent to be addled. . . ."

The bus driver was speaking. Out of the blue, he said: "High school bored the you-know-what outta me." I looked up. He was young and cocky; he didn't mean to be driving a bus for long. No way. "For all practical purposes you could say I graduated high school, I guess. I was just too busy to show up for graduation." I closed the book and put it back in my pocket. He was addressing himself mostly to the woman in the front seat, but anyone who cared to listen was welcome. From where I sat behind her I could see only a tidy bun of gray hair resting on a nest of hand-knitted scarves. "I believe in the school of life," said the driver. "I always say, what can school teach you that life don't teach you better?"

"Do you know anything about bugs?" the woman asked him.

The lad was too full of himself to be easily nonplussed.

"Had a lady get on in New York once, she sat in the back of the bus. All of a sudden, outside Boston she comes tearing down the aisle ripping off her clothes, hollering, 'Get 'em off me! Get 'em off me!' I guess that was bugs."

"Well, I got these whiteflies on my lilacs," the passenger continued. "They're real pretty."

"Whiteflies? Don't know about whiteflies. I know blue flies, but I don't know whiteflies."

"Oh no, these ain't blue flies. These are whiteflies. Whenever I open the door, there they are, like a cloud, millions of 'em, swarming right in, big as you please. Last year they disappeared, then this year there they were again. They seem to be getting more and more. It's a mystery. Like earwigs. We didn't have any of them neither once. And then all of a sudden there they were. That was in the paper. Earwigs was the name they gave them. They love to eat roses. They just thrive on roses. August back a few years ago was hot and rainy. I'd planted flowers, and there they were. Earwigs. Didn't know what they were then—they were just like wormy things. Earwigs. Everywhere. The way to get rid of them is they freeze, see? They don't hibernate. They've got taillike things on 'em. I woke up once and had one in bed with me. Now that almost drove me crazy. . . ."

We passengers exchanged looks, shrugged, shook our heads. But she did not stop for breath until Portsmouth, where she disembarked, and she was still talking while she waited beside the bus for her suitcase, and occasionally swatting her hand at the empty air.

When we pulled away the driver dared to try once more.

"Hey, anybody read how that truck turned over outside Portland?" he asked over the microphone. "Well, I had the guy on the bus the other day going to New York, the guy what drove the truck. You folks oughtta seen that poor guy. He was in a bad way. Not physically. Emotionally. I told him it coulda happened to anyone. You never know what the day will hold, right?"

But after the bug lady, nobody on board had spirit left to rise to his bait. And in silence we entered Boston.

BUS 6 to BUFFALO

We left for Buffalo after dark. My overhead reading light was broken, but I was realizing I had no great taste for reading on the bus. At night I preferred to watch the whitish hulks of houses and silhouettes of hills and trees slip smoothly by, as if the countryside were being rolled past our rocking machine, the way they used to draw scenery past the stagecoach in old westerns. There was less traffic as the hour progressed; no people were out in the towns, and no lights, only here and there in sleepless windows the purple flicker of a late-night TV show. I dug into my bag for the inflatable pillow, and I stretched my legs out onto the empty seat next to mine. In New York State the road gulps and flows in a peristaltic motion; it was like being in the digestive tract of a huge beast, and not at all unpleasant. Behind me a woman was saying: "And then they stuck this tube down my throat...." I dozed.

Only the youngsters in the back rows could be bothered to disembark at the poky stations where we stopped every two hours or so. Each time I half woke, it was to the same scene: a girl with long blond hair who was underdressed for the cold night air stood in a puddle of light near the door, smoking a cigarette and casting long-eyed looks at the rear windows of the bus. In no time, two or three young men disembarked to join her. But as soon as they circled in close, off hopped the stocky fellow she was traveling with. He put his arms around her while she cuddled up to him, whispering in his ear; then she tilted her head back and laughed flirtatiously at the suckers, who never seemed to learn.

Across the aisle eight rows down from me was the first black passenger I had seen on a bus since leaving New York. He couldn't have been much more than eighteen. I heard him tell the man next to him that he was going to stay with relatives in Buffalo, and he had never been out of Georgia before.

"Oh, yeah? How long you gonna stay?"

"Dunno. A month or two. Or maybe for keeps."

At every stop the boy went through the plastic bag at his feet, then stood and searched in all his pockets in a growing panic until he found his ticket again. He always put it back somewhere different, so he'd be bound to have trouble finding it next time. Our driver was black too, and a woman. Her name was Frieda. She was gentle with the nervous boy: she came back herself to warn him his personal stereo was too loud, instead of telling him off publicly over the microphone. Long after midnight, when we were all sunk into degrees of sleep, Frieda suddenly pulled up by the side of the road, and without a word, not even bothering to turn on the overhead light, she patrolled the central aisle. In spite of the warning she had given on departure that smoking was no longer tolerated anywhere on Greyhound buses, some culprit was polluting our airspace. Whoever it was soon extinguished his smoking material, believe you me.

Even the nervous boy from Georgia was snoring rhythmically before we arrived in Buffalo. And the blonde was curled up on her own, asleep on two empty seats near the rest room. Frieda was a great bus driver; her presence at the wheel was security personified.

My brother was an intern at Buffalo General Hospital, and I had always wanted to see the place about which he'd had so many gruesome medical tales to tell. Buffalo must once have been a city of great show-offs. The hotel I stayed in had been built for a carriage trade that is no more: it still had marble floors, real radiators, and windows that could actually be opened. Its restaurant was shut down, however, and the clerk directed me to a fast-food place next door. Big houses on the boulevards, even the modest houses on Buffalo's side streets, are ostentatiously clever in design. None of the mansions appear to be privately owned any longer—as far as I could tell, they all belonged to corporations. There were few signs of life on streets deep in fallen leaves, and quiet except for rattletraps in boudoir colors that zoomed back and forth with music blaring. Buffalo, on the everyday weekday I was there at least, lacked all bustle. Shops were empty or for rent. A church with the pretensions of a cathedral had a "For Sale" sign on it, parking lot included. When I tried the big front doors, they were locked.

One place I found doing business in Buffalo was the Haunted Book Shop, which specializes in the occult and the generally creepy. I slipped in next to a couple of customers browsing in "Magic and Witchcraft," and we started to chat. They turned out to be not locals, but members of a touring theatrical company on the road.

"Oh, we never ride the Greyhound, dear," said one of them. He was an aging junior with eye whites like fried egg whites.

"We thespians rate a bus of our own."

"Golly," I said. "I wanted to be an actress when I was young." He raised his brows, shrugged, opened his hands wide.

"But you're riding the Greyhound instead, aren't you, sweetie?"

CLEVELAND —
CHICAGO

*A Klumpp in Elwood, Indiana,
where my mother was born*

BUS 7 to CLEVELAND

An item on the early news concerned a bungee jumper who had plunged to her death somewhere in upstate New York. I heard about it while I was dressing for the bus to Cleveland.

"What caused the accident?" asked the interviewer.

"We believe," replied the policeman, "there was a disconnection between the bungee cord system and the principal."

A disconnected principal falling into the gaping spaces of the United States: that was precisely how I felt. Every journey imposes its rhythm after a while and becomes its own reason, with no purpose but itself. And every journey, soon after the excitement of departure, has deadly mornings, mornings of bad surprises and disconnections, sick mornings, mornings when you know you're not getting any younger and you wonder what possessed you to leap out of your comfortable bed one day and go to where the telephone always rings for someone else. In the last moments of resistance, in my Buffalo hotel room, as the strands of my cord were parting, I would have given a lot to be back where it had all begun.

"I just got my divorce," said the black Adonis driving my taxi to the depot. "But next week's my birthday, and she says she wants to come out to Buffalo to spend it with me. Can you beat that? After what we been through. What goes on in a woman's head? What I want this time, after my whatcha might call marital defeat, is a nice English woman from overseas, with an English accent."

"Sorry," I told him. "I'm not English." The Buffalo morning was dim and mouse gray. Homesickness, or something, had me tight by the throat. "I'm American," I said.

*   *   *

The cafeteria at the depot was full of teenaged girls squealing about movies and clothes, just the way we used to do back when teenagers were first invented. They were waiting for a local bus to school and through the plate-glass window they kept an eye on the boys, who preferred to wait outside. The boys were smoking and punching each other, except for one or two who stood apart, scowling at passing cars. Across from me sat a woman suffering from a neurological disease that had turned her face into a swollen mask. She watched the noisy girls, not much younger than herself; it was impossible to read the thoughts behind her rigid features. A small suitcase was beside her on the floor. What new loneliness was she traveling to? I looked away before she noticed me staring, and when I turned her way again she was waving happily at a man carrying a tray on which were two steaming cups of coffee. He sat down facing her, blocking from my view all but the pretty flow-ered scarf that covered her hair. I started to feel a little better.

In the main waiting room near the gate for the bus to Cleve-land, a young man stepped out of the crowd and made straight for me.

"Excuse me," he said, "do you speak Hebrew?"

Behind him stood a plump, sharp-eyed old lady wearing a ratty fur coat. She glared at me and bared her teeth.

"My mother," he said, "is going alone to Cleveland, where my brother is going to meet her, and . . ."

An experienced mama-watcher, I took the seat diagonally be-hind hers, and whenever she whipped around to catch me out, I made sure I was studying the signs around us in the departure bay. Stop. Sound Horn. Proceed Slowly. Drinking Intoxicants on the Coach Is Prohibited. No Smoking. No Exit. Danger. The driver came on board, surveyed us all, counting us under his breath, then removed his uniform jacket and hung it carefully on the hook behind his seat before he stowed his dispatch case in the overhead rack.

"My name is Harold. Call me Harry," he said over the mike.

The great bus lurched, got into gear, and we were on our way. Instantly, my mood lifted. Not far outside Buffalo the road

changed tempo to something like a rhumba. I wondered what the
Israeli woman was making of signposts to Hamburg, Eden, An-
gola, Dunkirk, Fredonia, and Geneva. "Welcome to Pennsylva-
nia," said a sign by the side of the road. "America Starts Here."
My yo-yo spirits rose utterly and slammed into the palm of the
Lord. Hallelujah! I was on top of the world.

At a rest stop before Cleveland where everyone filed off to buy
burgers and chips, dutifully I asked the mama: "Can I get you
something?" She shook her head—her mouth was full of honey
cake—and signaled "No" with a waving forefinger. A flask was
upright between her plump ankles and she held a red plastic cup
full of tea, a slice of lemon floated on top. In Cleveland I watched
from a safe distance until a graying middle-aged man ran breath-
lessly into the waiting room, and they fell into each other's arms.
Before she left with him, she turned and walked over to where I
stood.

"Good girl," she said, and reached up to pat my cheek.

At the far side from where I waited for my connecting bus in the
enclosure for ticketed passengers sat an Amish family. I watched
them from behind my copy of the Cleveland *Plain Dealer*. The
young man was talking quietly to a whitebeard in the seat next to
his; the wide brims of their black hats and their spade-shaped
beards were practically touching. At the younger man's shoulder
with her back to him, as if they were on a Victorian love seat, sat
a woman in cloak and bonnet. She held an infant swaddled in dark
cloth, and leaning against her knee was a beautiful little girl, about
five, dressed in blue to her ankles and wearing a miniature of her
mother's bonnet. The younger man held two brown paper bags.
He offered them in turn to the old man, who dipped in deeply for
carrots from one, melba toast from the other. Then the young
man helped himself to food. Finally, without a break in his conversation with the elder, he held the bags one at a time over his
right shoulder. His wife reached in and passed a carrot and some
toast down to her daughter before she nibbled a little herself, head

down and hidden by her bonnet. The horde of common passengers left a space around the dark-clad family.

Suddenly, a little boy with hayfield hair, in jeans and a bright striped T-shirt, pranced into the central space. He was throwing a ball in the air, dropping it, chasing it on his hands and knees.

"Travis!" a woman wailed behind him. "Travis, you are trouble! You get back here! Where's your hat at, Travis? Where's your coat at? Travis, you are real trouble!"

The red ball struck the little Amish girl on her knee and landed against her foot. She started, and her eyes sparkled with laughter. But the Amish mother did not need to say a word: in less time than it took for Travis to grab the ball and run, the little girl had turned her head away.

BUS 8 to COLUMBUS and INDIANAPOLIS

In the tight knot of Ohio towns, Greyhounds are practically local buses and run full to capacity. Hoping for a seat to myself, I coughed, and pulled out my pen and notebook. Both coughing and scribbling, I was starting to notice, put prospective seatmates off. But I was twelve rows back, right at the point where genteel passengers panic and take the first empty seat they come to rather than move on any closer to the back, where the habitual smokers, and goodness knows what else, congregate.

"Do you mind?" said a woman's voice, "if I visit with you?"

She was gray and comfortably frumpy. She had a lot of trouble lifting her bag into the overhead rack, so I got up to help.

"I was fifty-six last birthday," she said, settling in heavily next to me. With all my heart I hoped she was lying about her age. Her name was Grace and she told me she lived in a mobile home in a park south of Buffalo. When I was a child in America, trailer parks were few and far between, and the proliferation of them I was seeing through the windows of the bus was a surprise, especially as trailers these days are like urban houseboats, plumbed into the land and never actually on the move. They have a bleak glamour, like photographs of America during the Great Depression, and when Grace said she had bought hers secondhand for under eight thousand dollars, I found myself thinking I could buy one too, and keep it as a permanent American mouse hole.

Grace was on her way to Tulsa to visit her daughter. She expected to arrive late the following night. She had four children, and she wasn't sure how many grandchildren—"oh, fourteen or fifteen," she said. "Now let me see. My son in California, his first wife has his two back in Pennsylvania. I don't get to see them hardly at all now she's married again. But he had another one with his new wife, and she has three from before that live with them. Then, my daughter in Tulsa, now, she has one from her first marriage, another one from her second marriage, and one on the way from the marriage she's in now. And then there's his kids from before; they spend a lot of time with them because their mother is unstable. Then I've got my youngest down in Florida. . . ." There was a thoughtful pause. "Of course, I was married three times myself," she said after a while. "Not that the third one was what you'd exactly call a marriage, not blessed in church and all. He was a lot younger than me: a liar, a cheat, a drunk. But I loved him better than the other two put together. Can you beat that?"

While we were passing through downtown Columbus I admired the local architecture.

"These Ohio cities have some world-class buildings, it seems to me."

"Why, yes," said Grace. "Just look at the *heighth* of them." If a diphthong can be said to grate, that "th" really put my teeth on edge. I hadn't heard anyone say "heighth" in thirty years, not since my Grandma Annie died. I had never liked my Grandma Annie, and the feeling was mutual. True enough, the purpose of the detour I was making to Indiana was to find the town where she had been born and lived most of her life. But I was doing it for my mother, not for her.

*   *   *

Before we pulled out of Columbus, I gave Grace the inside seat so she could put her head against the window and nap a little in the slanting light of late afternoon. Across the aisle from me sprawled a long-haired blond girl, taking up two seats and sleeping deeply, as only the young can do on a moving bus. In front of her on the aisle was a plump young man in a baseball cap with an "NY" logo and windbreaker embroidered "Gene's Auto Repair—Springfield." On the aisle behind the girl was an older man who had an aura of wisdom and goodwill that put me in mind of the actor Fred MacMurray. It was a congenial bus. Passengers were talking to each other in friendly groups up and down the aisle. After a few minutes, the two men told me separately that they were truckers, and before long we had set up a three-way conversation. The senior driver listened smiling while the starry-eyed youngster told me about the comforts of the big cab: "Some of 'em got a double bed, TV, a refrigerator. I know this one got a waterbed. . . ."

He had to agree when I said it must be hard on family life when a man spends so many hours on the road.

"I've been married twenty-four years without a hitch," the older trucker said. "There's some women can take it. Others just can't stand being so much on their own. You can't really blame them."

"Hell, I'm only a rookie," the younger man said.

"You've done real well to get through the training," said the other. "A lotta trainees drop out."

"I figure on seven, eight years to get to top money. I've never ever been in a wreck yet."

"You will, son," said the older man. "You haven't really started until you've had a wreck."

The older driver was a member of the union, so he was being paid while traveling to his next job.

"Probably getting more right this minute than the bus driver," he told me. "Greyhound being nonunionized at this moment in time, he's probably making about twenty cents a mile. I beat that just sitting here."

The rookie shook his head and nodded to his senior colleague. "I really admire him," he said to me. "I don't mind telling you, I hope to be in his spot someday."

"We have a college professor makes more money driving a truck," said the old hand. "We have a doctor, too, a certified doctor."

"Do women drive?" I asked.

"You bet. They're damned good, too. Any woman who can pay for the training course—that's gonna cost ten thousand—and not drop out is gonna be as good as any man," said the younger fellow.

"Better," said the other.

The pretty blonde stirred, sat up, rubbed her eyes.

"We there yet?"

"Depends," said the older man, "on where you're going."

"I'm going to see my grandma. She lives in Reno. She wants me to come out and take over her business. She runs a big apartment complex, but she is not feeling so good these days, and she's gonna put me in charge of the whole thing. She feels like she owes me on account of my daddy. That's her son, you know. He's serving five life sentences in North Carolina. He's innocent, too. Just because of an outfit he happened to be wearing that day, they identified him for armed robbery. If he'd a wore something different, they'd never have identified him. I haven't seen my daddy in three years. I can't visit him. I'm not allowed. I'm only seventeen."

The sun had set.

"I have a seventeen-year-old daughter," the older trucker said thoughtfully, out of the dark.

"My only real family ever has been my boyfriend's family," the girl said. A middle-aged woman on the aisle in front of me turned, frowned, caught my eye, and shook her head: what are the young coming to? "They took me in when I was fourteen. 'Honey,' they said, 'we want you. You just come right on in and live with us.'

There's my boyfriend, his dad, his mom, his sister, Leena May, and her little boy, Elmo, she had going on for two years ago. My boyfriend's brother is there too, only not all the time. His name's Ray, only everybody calls him Big Tee, I don't know why. These guys come looking for him once, and they called him Big Tee. Only he wasn't there then. The best family I ever had. Only my mom can't see me anymore, because my boyfriend is black, and her new boyfriend, he doesn't want to know, because he hates black people. I'm going to get to Reno and take over that apartment complex my grandma is gonna give me. Only first I wanna get a suntan, so when my boyfriend comes out to join me, I'll look real good. See where my lip is all swoll up?" She leaned forward into the aisle. Night had drawn in and all I could see was her pale hair, swinging. "That is where I bit it, 'cause I was crying so hard when my boyfriend saw me off at the depot. I always bite my lip when I cry. But he's coming to Reno to be with me. We're gonna start a new life. Just as soon as his court case is done. They came busting in our house with their guns and everything. You wouldn't believe it. I said, 'You'd better let me get to that baby you can hear crying, because he's got asthma real bad, and if he dies, you'll pay for it.' That was Elmo. He's got asthma real bad. I don't know how those police think they can come into anyone's private house like that. They pushed my boyfriend's sister around. They took my boyfriend's father out into the street and they beat him up. When he came back inside, his hand left a trail of blood along the wall beside the stairs."

She was wholesome to look at, fresh faced and curvy. You could have cast her as the girl behind the soda fountain or the prom queen. Those of us sitting near her fell into a troubled silence, and no other voice but hers was heard all the way to Indianapolis.

The aged black taxi driver in Indianapolis said he knew a clean, cheap place out past the speedway. I sank back, too tired to argue as the miles ticked up on the meter.

—·—·—·—

"Where do you live?" he asked me.

"London," I said.

"Uh-huh, London. I see," he said, and after a pause he asked: "Are you a missionary?"

In my room, I let the ubiquitous Bible fall open on the dressing table and searched the page for an omen, the way my sweet old taxi driver had confided he did every night and morning. Come to think of it, the bus had passed a "Church of the Open Bible" not far inside the Indiana border. But II Chronicles, chapter 26, concerns Uzziah, who destroyed Ashdod, then became a leper for presuming to priestly powers. And a fat lot of good that did me.

BUS 9 to ANDERSON and ELWOOD, INDIANA

Strictly speaking, buses do not go within thirty miles of Elwood. First, I had to take an American Line bus to Anderson and then, as Elwood has neither bus nor taxi service, I had to arrange to continue in a shared van called the "Tram" that went everywhere in the county for three dollars, and had to be booked in advance. The Tram did not run on Sundays or public holidays, when Elwood, like much of the state, was effectively closed to anyone without a car. By the time I'd made my travel arrangements and found a locker in which to check my bag, there were barely two hours left to have a look at Indianapolis, and get the feel of it.

My father always complained that the only place on earth more boring than Indianapolis was Elwood, Indiana. I found the city pleasant, however, though rather dozy, and with a tempo much more southern than I had expected. Admittedly, I have a vested interest in Indianapolis: it's where my parents met when they were both at university there. I owe the place a favor, and I'm glad I had a chance to show my appreciation.

"Well done," said a passerby. He looked like a CPA or a bank official. I had been photographing some noteworthy art-deco interior design, and he had seen me go out of my way to drop a film wrapper in a public receptacle. "You're a good citizen. We need more like you in Indianapolis."

The single aspect of Indiana my father never mocked or criticized was the countryside, and looking out of the bus at the gentle land spread with thickets and streams, it was easy to see why long walks had been the basis of my parents' courtship. My mother was charmed by my father's past in New York, and by his family's memories of Eastern Europe, which in many places has the same made-for-summer, windswept look of Indiana. The stories Mother liked best to tell and write derived from my father's childhood instead of her own. But for me, it was different: I sometimes felt I knew my father's past to a point further back than he himself remembered. It was all familiar to me and bred in my dreams. My mother's roots, on the other hand, out of Elwood, Indiana, were as alien as they could be. Mr. Longerbone, the grocer; Mr. Sneed, who kept the drugstore; Elbert Cotton, Mr. Cute, and Mr. Snodgrass; "King" Leeson, who founded the department store on Main Street, and his daughter, "Missy": what names were those? They had a Yankee Doodle ring, too blue-eyed to be believed, and utterly foreign to me.

When my mother was barely seven, her father died of TB in Denver, and her vain, pretty, stupid mother, my Grandma Annie, who was herself an only child, came back to live with her parents in Elwood. They were a displaced and moody couple with big problems of their own. In my mind's eye, they are all dark figures while the other Elwood folks are pale as bedclothes, windblown through empty streets. My mother I see as a vivid child among them, and so are her chums, the offspring of a few Syrian families, as ill-placed as Jews in Elwood. A pair of Syrian brothers who used to hang on every word of my little mother's made-up tales of ghosts and the headless dead were the dazzling Zemurod and Osman. They left town as soon as they were grown, and then came back not very long afterward to open a whorehouse down the road. It prospered, too. Those Elwood outcast kids had a serious gift for vengeance.

The Tram was waiting for me when my bus pulled into Anderson. As we rode to Elwood, I held the image of a little hotel in the middle of Main Street, with aspidistras in the lobby, and in its bathrooms big tubs on lions' feet. There was bound to be an oaken bar too, where traveling salesmen in flashy suits stood each other cold beers and compared notes on local trade. But Elwood, though left behind indeed by time, as must be countless American towns where Greyhound doesn't stop, had not been left intact. Anyhow, men traveling in ladies' underwear, and notions, and dry goods, are probably no more to be found on the back roads. And the only accommodation for visitors turned out to be two motels face-to-face across a highway about three miles before Elwood could be said properly to begin. One of them was open for business, but I asked the driver of the Tram to drop me off at the other; I couldn't have said why, unless it was the lazy look of the scrawled sign on the door, "Back in 5 mins," that put me in mind of Hoagy Carmichael.

Big clouds were rolling in from the horizon, racing against night, and already rain fell in streaks on nearby fields. I could barely make out the words "Welcome to Elwood" on a sign at the corner where the highway met the road that led straight into town. Only the big *M* of a McDonald's nearby hung on to the remaining sunlight and contrived to turn the whole scene into an ad for fast food. At last, the proprietor drove up in a noisy old car. He looked surprised to see a customer, and in a slightly bemused way he opened his office and waved me inside. He was in his early sixties, a local man, born and bred in Elwood. He told me "King" Leeson's daughter "Missy" was still alive, though well into her eighties, and had only a little while earlier given up managing the family store. Oh, yes, the old place was still there, though the rumor was it would soon be turned into a public library. I couldn't miss it when I went into town next day. Fancy someone coming from so far away who knew about Leeson's and old Mr. Longerbone.

"What was your mother's name?" he asked as we walked to the chalet I'd rented in a row of ten.

"Her name was Auerbach," I said. "But after her father died and they came back here, she was probably known by her mother's family name."

"And that was?"

Big raindrops were splattering the path around us and forming instantaneous puddles.

"My grandmother's family name?" I felt a queer reluctance to tell him, almost shame. "The name was Kessler."

"Ah, I see," he said. "Yes. Kessler. Oh, yes. I don't recall folks by that name myself. But I don't suppose your mother's memories of Elwood are very happy."

In the 1920s, when Wendell Willkie spent a few days back home in Elwood, he was feted all over town, but his driver had to find lodgings somewhere else, because he was black. Back then, when Mother was a girl, the KKK ran Elwood and most of the state. Now on the fence at the town limits are welcoming plaques from the Kiwanis club, the Optimists, the Lions, the Veterans of Foreign Wars, and a couple of local churches. The Klan is no longer represented. Although I'm sure the Moose, and Elks, and Optimists, and Knights of Pythias, and Masons, and women of the Moose, and Elks, et cetera, do fine things for some of the community, the evident taste for secret societies throughout Middle America gave me the whim-whams, and no place more than in Elwood, Indiana, where, how well Mother remembers, the KKK used to march regularly down Main Street. Sometimes the morning afterward she'd find their obscenities scribbled on the front gate.

Early next morning I accepted a lift from my host to the main cemetery on the opposite side of town from his motel, a trip of four or five miles. No sooner had his car rattled away and left me than the skies, which had been swollen since dawn, broke open and let fall a deluge of rain set to wash Elwood off the face of the earth. With the cape of my blessed Driza Bone converted into a hood, I fled past headstones and mausoleums to a small office building at the far side from the entrance. The door was locked and there was no sign of anyone behind the streaming windows. A big open-sided shed leaned against one wall, and I made for it fast. Two men were already sheltering in there. One of them was wearing a suit and had probably come to pay his respects at a grave. The other was dressed in working clothes; I took him to be a grounds keeper. They were both in their late fifties and clean shaven. The businessman had a glum, clever Hoosier face. The other fellow was fat and jowly. They nodded my way and went on with their conversation.

"Now, I'm one of those guys, I always talk over what I'm gonna do with the wife before I do it," the big man said. "Been married thirty-two years. That's why there's so much darned dee-vorce these days. He does what he wants. She does what she wants."

"Used to be," said the other man, "trends came from the East. Now they appear to be coming in mostly from California."

"Anyways they come, Indiana's in the middle. . . ."

"Drugs. . . ."

"Dee-vorce. . . ."

We stood in a row, me a little behind the men, looking out at the rain falling on stones and bare trees.

"Ever wonder," said the man in the suit after a while, "how come no good trends ever seem to come our way?"

"If I was young . . . ," said the big guy.

". . . I'd get out," the other one said.

The office of Elwood's main cemetery could be put as is into a provincial museum to show what offices were like at the turn of the century. Against the back wall was a big safe, black and rimmed in gold leaf. It was set on wheels. Deadly spindles on the ancient desk were onion-packed with papers, and the telephone was an upstanding prototype of its kind. In summer, flypaper strips are tacked to the dark beams overhead, I'll bet, and the ancient fan inside a cage of chicken wire is no doubt switched on to blow the dust around.

"Her name was Small, you say?" the old fellow asked. He'd shuffled through first one cedarwood box, then another, full of yellowing cards covered in cellophane. "What was her first name, do you know?"

"I'm afraid not. She was my mother's teacher a long, long time ago."

Wheezing and bent, he reached down a huge leather-bound book from the top of a filing cabinet. For a long time he turned pages where I saw names once written in black, now faded and coppery. After a lot of dry, rustling pages and drip, drip, drip from outside where the trees where shaking off rain, he stopped with his finger on a name. He turned the book so I could read the entry. Mary Small had been born in 1873 and died in 1940.

"She's the only female Small interred in this here graveyard," he said. "She's gotta be the one."

"To be a good American," Miss Small announced to her fourth-grade civics class, "a person's got to be Protestant, white, and born here." Whereupon she'd whirled around and pointed at my mother and said, "Minnie Auerbach, you wipe that grin off your face!"

Thus, seventy-odd years later, I stood at the foot of the former teacher's grave, with the mud sucking at my heels, and, pointing to her headstone, I said aloud: "Miss Mary Small, Minnie's girl has come all this way to tell you, wipe that grin off your face!"

No sooner had the words left my mouth than the downpour began again.

The man in the suit offered me a lift from the cemetery into town.

"I'd recommend you take a look at our Catholic church," he

said. "Only thing is, they keep it locked ever since somebody stole items off the altar."

I asked him to drop me off at Leeson's so I could buy an umbrella for the walk to the house on Nineteenth Street where my great-grandparents used to live with my Grandma Annie, and where my mother had grown up. But Leeson's didn't sell umbrellas anymore, or much of anything useful. There were candies, T-shirts, china swans, ormolu clocks, nests of bonbon dishes, and other items not quite fine enough for a wedding gift. At the back of the ground floor was a pretty extensive toy section. A sign tacked on the display rack said irritably: "PLEASE DO NOT PLAY ON OR WITH TOYS!" There wasn't a customer to be seen, only a long-haired boy wearing one earring, who pushed his broom around the aisles ferociously and glared at me when I asked about umbrellas. The elderly staff member who finally told me Leeson's no longer sold umbrellas assured me it was a groundless rumor that the place was closing down. "Why, no such thing!" she cried when I said I'd heard it was to be turned into a library. And with a flash of inspiration she pointed to a cardboard box labeled: "ANY BOOK FOR A DOLLAR." "But we do have some paperbacks if you're interested."

Accretions of repairs and ambitious taste lay like barnacles on the house where mother used to live. Only one of the neighboring houses still looked pretty much as they all must have at the turn of the century: stingy with windows, and with a mean little porch tacked on like a miser's afterthought. Although the rain had stopped, a spattering of drops fell from the trees, and the street ran like a small river; from the other side a woman with stringy yellow hair watched me snap a picture for the record. She leaned on a battered stroller in which was a little girl chewing on a lollipop. When she pulled it out of her mouth, it turned out to be just a frayed white stick.

"My mother grew up in that house," I said to them.

Mother and daughter looked at me with a total lack of interest, only a kind of blank hunger in their eyes that made me ill at ease.

I turned and started back the way I'd come on the empty street, slick with wet leaves. For just an instant I thought I could see saplings within the old trees, like stems in transparent vases. Old-fashioned smells of coal tar and woodsmoke passed in the air, and a girl's voice near me laughed in bright surprise.

It was a good few miles to walk in the damp twilight past empty shops and derelict houses, some of them big and once splendid, until I came back to the major crossroads and the pseudocivilization of McDonald's, Arby's, and Captain Bob's Catfish. As soon as I was in my room, I telephoned Mother. She was already in Southern California, where she prefers to spend the winter months near my brother and his family.

"Well, honey, here I am in Elwood. And I have to tell you, the place is half dead."

"May the other half not linger," said my mother.

"I remembered the story you used to tell about your civics class. And do you know what I did? I went out to the cemetery and found the grave of your Miss Small. And I told her from you to wipe that grin off her face."

There was a tiny pause.

"Well, that was a very nice thought, Irm," my mother said. "And I don't suppose it makes any difference, seeing as it's all in a good cause. But that teacher I used to tell you about? Her name was Little."

BUS 10 to INDIANAPOLIS

"You got your moonshine," the driver of the Tram was saying, "your good corn whiskey, and it's always clear, it doesn't have the color that regular whiskey would have. It does have a taste of its own. It's hard to describe. Corn mash is what it is. It's got the sugar in it, of course, and it's, oh, about two hundred proof, you know? And it will knock your socks off. I recall my twenty-first birthday—I was visiting my uncles in Kentucky and they gave me a baby-food jar full of your good old moonshine. And I thought, 'Well, hell, this here is nothing special.' And I sat there. And I drank it right down. And I was sittin' there, thinkin' it wasn't too bad, you know? And they're all sittin' there, watchin' me. And they says, 'Go get yourself some more, boy.' And I stood up to go get it. And I fell right over on my face. And that is how they make moonshine in Kentucky."

A car passed us heading out of Anderson, a pair of rifles on a rack in the rear window.

"Do you do any hunting?" I asked.

"Yeah, I do. But with great caution. The farmers in Indiana still see it as their God-given right to shoot trespassers."

He was a broad-shouldered boy with longish curly hair and full blond beard.

"Where do your people come from originally?"

"Well, now," he said, flashing me a big grin, "I guess I'd have to say I'm one-quarter German and three-quarters hillbilly."

One other customer was waiting in the Anderson depot. She lay the book she'd been reading to one side the moment I came in, and looked up, ready for a visit.

"What are you reading?" I asked.

She raised her book so I could see the title: *Devices and Desires* by P. D. James.

"Cannot get enough of her," she said.

I toyed with the idea of letting her know I'd met Dame Phyllis once when I was a panelist on her TV book program. But I recalled in time the fall of Ashdod. Besides, BBC palavering was so removed from the spot I was in, I was not sure even I would have believed me.

"I like good reading," my companion said. "I walk a mile every Sunday morning just to get the *Chicago Tribune*. Reading is my only vice. I used to smoke too, until the good Lord took the craving from me."

The woman in charge of the station was on the telephone trying to instruct someone who apparently did not speak English very well.

"There is no other way," she was saying. "Anderson is not a

center of continental transport, I hate to be the one to tell you. You are gonna have to go to Indianapolis first."

The reader listened and shook her head.

"This here town is dead," she said. "They just forgot to bury it. They were going to build an arts center, but they wanted us to give money for it. That'll be the day. You can't hardly afford to go out anymore, everything's got so expensive. I don't like for people to tell me what to do with my money. The really rich people don't put anything into the town. Well, if they aren't putting anything in, I'm not about to put anything in."

The depot manager was off the phone. She came forward, leaned across the wooden counter, and the two women greeted each other as old friends.

"We got us a drug problem here as good as anywhere," the manager said. "Some DEA guy out of Fort Wayne was telling a bus driver who comes in here sometimes that Anderson is the crack capital of the Midwest. When you see kids coming in wearing Rolex watches, real gold, with a big roll of money, you gotta figure they must be doing something. They're not going to school, that's for sure. They go back and forth on the bus to Detroit. Back and forth all the time."

She was small, with a terrier quickness about her. The accent was ninety percent local, but I thought I detected fuzziness around her *R*'s, and sure enough, she turned out to be the daughter of a coal miner from West Virginia.

"I've been robbed in here about five times. But they bred us tough back in West Virginia, and it is not going to happen again. I told the police, next time they try it, they're gonna be dead." She disappeared for an instant under the counter, and reemerged swinging a baseball bat.

"Now, don't you go risking your neck," said the reader. "It is just not worth it."

"It's the principle of the thing," replied the manager. She leaned the bat in a corner near her desk. "Last time they came in, there was one of them just got out of prison. I guess he wanted to go back real bad. Middle of the day, too. The police picked him up about fifteen minutes after he did it."

The reader nodded her head sagely.

"Black," she said.

The manager's eyes gave a little flash.

"Used to get whupped at home for serving a black cleaning lady right at our own table. 'Well,' I told my daddy, 'you'll have to whup me agin, 'cause I'm gonna do it agin.' "

If the reader felt rebuked, she did not show it.

"Gee, I wish that Elmore Leonard would hurry up and write a new one," she said.

"Isn't he wonderful?" said the manager.

Then they talked about weather. Although I live in England, where talking about the weather is practically a folk art, the level of the Indiana conversation left me speechless.

"Next time there's a twister," said the manager, "I'll hustle myself and anyone who happens to be here right over to that fast-food place across the street. I've had that in my mind since the last time, on account of they have a big, deep cellar, and this here isn't much more'n a shed."

"Remember that ice storm last March?" the reader rejoined. "I'm laying in bottled water and plenty of canned food in case there's another one."

"But wasn't it beautiful?" said the manager. "Didn't it just make you gasp at the beauty? Like another planet."

Back at the depot in Indianapolis a bus for St. Louis was boarding next to the gate for my bus to Chicago, and that St. Louis crowd looked so ornery, I figured on the spot to give the place a miss.

BUS 11 to CHICAGO

"My name is Donald Brown, and I'm gonna be your motor-coach operative tactician all the way to the Windy City. . . ."

While I had been looking up my past in Elwood, the Greyhound staff had changed into their winter uniforms. Mr. Brown looked dashing in his royal-blue Russian-style hat with the Greyhound logo gleaming in front. It surprised me how good and right it felt to be back on the bus. I settled down in a state of high contentment and watched Indianapolis slide by my window. At the northern limits of the city was an entire block up for sale, including a boarded-up church and a public school with every window smashed. How crafty of The Director to have them name the road out of town Kessler Boulevard. Wasn't that a neat twist of the plot, and one in the eye for Elwood?

At two-thirty in cool sunlight we crossed the Wabash River, and almost immediately afterward the Tippecanoe. At three fifteen we pulled up to a fast-food place where the smokers leapt out to light up while the rest of us rushed inside to grab a coffee or cold drink in the ten minutes we were allowed. Only one till was working and the girl behind it looked with horror at the sudden mob.

First in line was a woman I'd noticed in the front seat of the bus. She was grossly overweight and her little girl, about knee-high and skinny, had not stopped whining since Indianapolis.

"Tiffany," said Big Mama to the child, "do you want juice, Coke, or Seven-Up?"

The child pulled a shriveled thumb out of her mouth and scuffed her feet.

"Dunno."

"Oh, come on, Tiffany, I don't wanna ask you again," said Big Mama, and she asked again: "Juice, Coke, or Seven-Up?"

The others of us exchanged glances, looked at our watches, looked away.

"Dunno," said Tiffany.

Big Mama's face wore a look of helpless martyrdom often seen on the faces of mothers when their kiddies cut up: see, it said, what a hard job I've taken on for the future of humanity.

"Tiffany," she said, "I haven't got all day." Not a word about the rest of us hanging on Tiffany's decision.

"Juice," said Tiffany at last.

"No," replied her mama. "You don't want no juice, Tiffany. You know you never finish your juice. She'll have a Seven-Up," said Big Mama to the counter girl.

As soon as we crossed into Illinois, it seemed to me the look of the land became sophisticated: twin towers of coppery glass rose out of the prairie, and a big billboard advertised a clinic for "Anxiety Depression Addiction." The great cities of America are magnets, drawing into themselves everything that moves for miles along the road and overwhelming the countryside in a web of bridges and freeways. During the approach to Chicago, passengers on Greyhound grew quiet and preoccupied. Each of us was being submerged to some degree, just as the bus itself was, and diminished a little in the widening streams of urban traffic. This must be the way cities create their personalities: by levying a tax on everyone who enters them.

My kind of town, Chicago is. I like the way people use the center of it, lots and lots of them, and on foot. I like the way it respects pedestrians and gives us time at crossings: no great city will ever give cars priority, or put the rights of the road before the pavement. The people in the streets looked good-humored too, and with more than a fair share of handsome old men in evidence, laid on, no doubt, for us Saul Bellow fans. I like being touched to the quick by the cold wind off Lake Michigan. There will never be an important place without weather, and what can call itself a great city if it doesn't have a waterfront? My hotel was old-fashioned, cheap, and right in the center of town, all qualities I admire in hotels. Chicago's modern architecture especially knocked me for a loop, though it was a little disconcerting to see it from the top of a double-decker London bus imported for tourists. When the time came to leave, I knew that if London were to vanish on the morrow, and Manhattan were to be washed away by a tidal wave, Chicago would be a strong contender for my hand in marriage.

GRAND RAPIDS —
DULUTH

*Cafe in the Park, Duluth:
lunch was not being served*

BUS 12 to GRAND RAPIDS

The bus depot in Chicago is just what Mother's neighbor had in mind when she recommended a Mace spray. And it was not all that bad. True enough, the streets around urban bus stations are generally sinister; it is there influx meets outflow of bad guys—not very successful bad guys, either, or why are they traveling by bus? Particularly in depots that are open all night the staff will sometimes turn a blind eye when vagrants stumble in off the streets, but panhandling had been cut back a lot since my first Greyhound journey a year earlier, and the presence of police or armed security guards had increased. Evildoers hang around bus depots, to be sure, but probably because they need to get out of town fast, and have every reason to keep a low profile. I'm not saying I'd invite someone I wanted to impress, even with my originality, to a Greyhound depot for lunch, and only a fool would wear Grandma's pearls on the bus, or pull out an expensive camera and expect to go unnoticed, or deserve to. However, for the most part, varieties of pathology that my kid brother never saw during all his years of medical training, as well as poverty, madness, and exhaustion, are more in evidence at urban bus depots than violence and evildoing.

Around 6:00 A.M. in the cafeteria of the Chicago depot: four black boys wearing their caps with the bills to the back were beating out rap rhythms on the tabletops. Day-Glo graffiti for the ears, I thought, just right for the venue. But an old man, also black, in the uniform of a security guard, planted himself in the aisle and scowled at them.

"Now," he said, "where do you guys think you're at?"

"We know where we're at, man," one of the boys said. He rose to his feet, standing tall and splendid in satiny black with touches of scarlet. "What do you think we are? Retarded?"

"Now, now, you guys," said the weary old fellow, "just you all keep it down, okay?"

A tall American Indian stood between my table and the entrance, where anyone coming in or going out had to walk around him. His eyes were as blank and unblinking as slate chips; only the rise and fall of his denim jacket showed he was breathing. Young men milled around him and stopped, nose-to-nose.

"Where you been, man?"

"Been travelin' thirty-six hours straight, man."

"Where you goin', man?"

"Nashville, man. Where you been?"

"Seattle, man."

"Where you guys goin', man? Where you guys been?"

Four girls, barely women, sat at the table next to mine. They were stubbing out cigarettes in ashtrays of reinforced tinfoil and passing bottles of juice to dazed infants. With tired eyes, streaking mascara, they watched the men. A fifth girl appeared, carrying a tray of coffee cups; she maneuvered around the Indian.

"Hey, you guys," she said, "I got you guys' coffee."

She put the tray on the table, then sat down next to the others, and fell straight into their condition of inertia.

I finished my coffee, detoured around the Indian, and went to sit near the gate for the Detroit bus. I was only going as far as Grand Rapids, there to change for Lansing, and then change yet again for Mackinaw City, where I hoped to arrive before midnight. Overhead in the waiting room a big banner was suspended; gold letters on it said: "Greyhound Celebrates 75 Years in Chicago." The public-address system was piping in "Somewhere Over the Rainbow." Five seats along from me in the row was a black bag lady. She wore a nylon wig à la Nefertiti; atop it was a black hat trimmed in yellowish fur. Outsize clear glasses with white plastic rims and one lens cracked straight across sat down on the end of her nose. Her fur-trimmed boots had long ago seen better days. Two worn plastic shopping bags, full to the top, were on the seat beside her, and a third was at her feet. Muttering complaints, she went for water at a drinking fountain under a framed poster from the Art Institute of Chicago. Although the fountain was only a few paces away, she took all her bags with her and hung on to them while she drank. Still complaining, she shuffled back to her seat and put the bags carefully back in their original positions.

The sharp-faced middle-aged woman who sat down two seats from me and three from the bag lady was a suburbanite whose car had broken down, I was pretty sure. She was not happy at all to find herself between buses in the Chicago depot. She darted hostile glances from under her smart little hat. Suddenly, the bag lady turned and glared at her.

"Keep your hands off my bags, you hear?"

The suburbanite drew herself up; she clutched the collar of her navy-blue cashmere coat.

"You keep your motherfucking hands off my bags," shrieked the bag lady, and threw herself across the two shopping bags on the seat next to her.

"Now what," said the suburbanite, "would I want with your bags?"

"Jus' you keep your hands off my bags, or I'll kill you," snarled the bag lady.

The suburbanite lady jumped to her feet and stomped away.

"That'll show her," the bag lady said. "Ain't nobody messes with my bags."

But in no time the suburbanite was back, and with her was an armed security guard.

"There she is, officer," said the matron. "That woman threatened my life."

The old bag lady folded her arms and stuck out her lower lip. "Did not," she said.

"Why, you did too!" said her accuser.

"Now, now, ma'am," said the officer gently to the bag lady "you cannot go around threatening people's lives. It's a crime to threaten life."

The bag lady remained seated, but she put her hands on her hips.

"I did not threaten nobody's life. I certainly did not. No such thing, officer, man. I jus' said if she didn't keep her hands off my bags, I'd kill her."

A girl of about nineteen sat down next to me.

"Do you mind if I sit next to you?" she asked.

She was fair and very pretty, but her big baby blues looked scared.

"This guy's been following me around asking if I want a coffee." Behind us was a young man in a green windbreaker with "Godfrey's Boatyard" on it, and a green baseball cap embroidered "Ajax." The moment he caught my eye a blush rose swiftly from under his beard, and he turned away.

"He's gone," I told the girl. "You know, you've got to get used to that kind of thing when you're young and pretty. God knows at my age," I told her, "a woman has to get used to doing without it." She looked at me blankly. "What I mean is, young people, when you travel, well, you are bound to be seen by the world. Later in life you can travel and see the world without anyone paying much attention to you." Blink, blink. "I mean to say, I know unwanted attention from men can be infuriating. But most of the time, remember, men are more scared of you than you realize." Blink, blink, blink. "I'm trying to say, if you don't trust yourself to defuse situations like that, well, you're never going to be free to travel, or go anywhere on your own."

"I can't wait to get home to Grand Rapids. I'm so homesick I could die. They can keep Chicago."

"How long have you been away?"

"Four days."

Finally, they announced the departure of our bus, which had been delayed due to the brake fluid having frozen. The homesick girl stayed behind me in the line at the gate, then sat herself next to me on the bus, though it wasn't crowded and there were seats to spare. Immediately, she launched into what soon became a recitation of every Thanksgiving dinner she could remember since she'd sprouted teeth enough for turkey. In spite of the droning at my elbow, I felt the customary lift when the city fell behind us and our bus started to cover new ground. The trees were bare, and derelict nests were snarled in their upper branches. Lake Michigan steamed in the cold morning air. Winter was an austere presence on the land. A billboard stark against the tarnished sky said, "Socrates drank the hemlock. Jesus died on the rood."

"Isn't that curious," I said to my neighbor. "I wonder, is it an argument for capital punishment, or against it?" But she continued telling me how her mother added pecans to sausage meat for stuffing.

An hour out of Chicago, a sudden snowstorm hit the right side of the bus while through the windows across the aisle were glimpses of blue skies. We traveled half in, half out of the blizzard that way for a mile or two before we committed ourselves to it utterly. Snow whirled around us, hanging in a curtain off to port over a gray-green space that I took on faith for Lake Michigan—it could as well have been the place where dragons be. Our bus slowed right down. The outsize windshield wipers worked hard against big flakes that were falling fast and clinging. For moments at a time nothing was visible, only the opaque film of cataracts, and I stared out at the absolute absence of all I had ever known, or knew for sure.

BUS 13 to LANSING

The homesick girl and I disembarked together. I gave her a hand with a heavy suitcase out of the hold, but as soon as she spotted her mother I was instantly forgotten. Off she went without so much as a "So long" to pursue her destined allotment of turkey dinners and think no more of traveling or the terrors of the road.

I had to hang around the station for the bus southeast to Lansing in order to end up due north in Mackinaw City. It was my first experience of the illogic sometimes imposed on Greyhound's scheduling, by weather, by roadwork, and occasionally, I suspect, by ignorance, laziness, or just plain mischief. We few passengers who were transferring from the incoming Chicago bus to the northern route exchanged travelers' complaints before we settled down for a short wait until departure. The bus for Lansing was bound ultimately for Detroit and it was certainly a gloomy bunch, with no banter or laughter, not even in the back rows, where the young people sat frowning and isolated between the hissing earpieces of their personal stereos.

Moments before we pulled out, a late passenger leapt on board. He was a skinny black man in his late fifties or early sixties. An etiquette applies to seating on Greyhound that is pretty strictly enforced, though voluntarily. Race with race, sex with sex: this is the basic tenet of bus manners. And when no seat is vacant next to a same-sex member of the same race, it is preferable to sit with a same-sex member of another race than with an opposite-sex member of any race including one's own, unless the age difference is vast, and even then with circumspection. Countless times I saw these simple rules enforce themselves on buses; they were broken only when bold young men fancied their chances with young girl travelers, usually in the back rows. There were only three seats left empty when the latecomer boarded, and he had to make up his mind quickly. After perceptible hesitation he chose to sit next to me rather than a flamboyant redhead, or in the single remaining seat, next to a male member of his own race, who was talking to himself and patently mad. As soon as my neighbor was seated, he fell asleep, or pretended to, and we made the short trip to Lansing in silence.

BUS 14 to CLARE and MACKINAW CITY, MICHIGAN

The bus left the Lansing depot with its dour cargo for Detroit, and we northbound passengers settled down to wait for our own departure. It was a small place with the usual plastic seats designed for minimal comfort to discourage layabouts and street people. Among the dozen or so of us waiting for the bus north was a woman I had noticed out of the corner of my eye in Grand Rapids. Her profile was strong and hawklike. I guessed her to be well into her sixties; she was tall, and her hair was iron-gray. She wore mannish clothing and she carried a shooting stick. A pillow on a homemade halter was slung across her back. When the bus stopped for a coffee break, she was the only passenger ready with a collapsible umbrella against the snow. She carried only one bag, and it was smaller than my own.

"Clean underwear and a pound of trail mix is all you need to get most places you'd ever want to go," she said while we were waiting in Lansing. Then she told me she came originally from—"Soo Saint Marie" is how she said the name of the town that shares Michigan's border with Canada: Sault Ste. Marie. I had thought about going there to mark the northernmost point of my journey, but it lies more than one hundred miles above the main route across upper America, and there was a real danger that even if Greyhound got me in, it would not be able to get me out again. I imagined my son's reply when London friends asked where his mother was. "Oh, Mom's slingin' hash in Soo Saint Marie till after the spring thaws."

"Been on the road one month practically to the day," Hawk Woman said. "Got myself one of them month tickets, and got up on the Greyhound, and went to see a few things."

"What did you see?"

"Saw Chicago, Texas, Los Angeles," she said, giving it a hard g the way lots of people used to do back in the 1950s. "Saw enough to know I like it best in northern Michigan. Still and all, I'm glad I went. And if the notion strikes me, I'll do it again." She tapped her forehead. "My folks think I'm nuts. I probably am nuts. But most of 'em have hardly seen a thing excepting the U.P."

"The U.P.?" I asked.

She looked at me: she was wondering where I'd been all my life.

"Why, Upper Peninsula," she said.

"Is that where you're going now?"

"I'll be changing buses up in Clare for Traverse City, where I got some folks to see on my way home."

A man sitting in the plastic bucket seat next to mine leaned over.

"Traverse City! Now, isn't that something," he said. "That's where I'm going to, too!"

He was astounded at the coincidence, though to tell the truth, there are not that many stops to choose from on Greyhound's route through northern Michigan. He said he had been born in Traverse City and lived there until he had to go to Lansing to find work. Every year he went back home for the hunting.

"What do you shoot?" I asked.

"Why, mostly deer," he said, frowning at such an idiotic question. "Still see moose once in a while. Even black bear. But mostly it's deer."

"Do you eat the deer?"

"Do we eat the deer! Oh, my gosh," Hawk Woman cried. "Well, of course we eat the deer."

"My wife and me, we cold-pack the venison," the Hunter said.

"How do you do that?"

"Well, you boil your venison, and then you boil everything else, and you cold-pack it." He stroked his beard and frowned again. "It's called cold-packing."

"It's a process," Hawk Woman said, "called cold-packing."

"And then you got your venison sausages," the Hunter continued. "We make our own. More or less knead it with spices and all, then put it in a cold room for three days before you gotta roll it out."

"We go ice fishin' in the winter," Hawk Woman said. "In northern Michigan ice fishin's still the best there is. That ice gets so thick you can build a fire on it for your coffeepot."

"Perch," said the Hunter.

"Pike," said Hawk Woman. "And that whitefish smokes up real good."

Suddenly it seemed to me everything had grown brighter, and the snow that had been falling wet and sticky since just outside Chicago acquired flecks of crystal: they sparkled in the air and on the ground outside. My spirit stretched its toes to the hearth. I was snug in the presence of two who slew for the pot, and I thanked America's lucky stars for diversity.

The bus to Clare and Mackinaw City was half empty. In spite of conversations begun in the waiting room we all sat separately, the way travelers met by chance probably would in England. For a while, I watched the snow quilt the cut-off octagons of red barns, and cover the fields softly. There is a part of every one of us, even lifetime urbanites, that looks enviously on tilled land after the harvest, when the main house and outbuildings of the farm are well stocked and drawn in against winter. I pulled my pen and notebook out of my bag to jot down a few words about nostalgia, and about cold-packing venison. And that was when I saw him: a lean and hungry-looking fellow across the aisle from me. He was smiling to himself in a smug way and, Lord have mercy, he was scribbling. With a fountain pen, yet. In a notebook twice the thickness of my own. He must have known himself to be the object of hostile interest—his kind usually does—for he looked up, and if he'd been a rat or meerkat his ears would have stiffened in alarm. He looked this way, that, and saw me: *my* pen, *my* notebook.

"Well, well, well," said he and I in concert, watching each other with suspicion.

"I am writing a novel," he said at last. "And you?"

I put the cap on my pen and threw it negligently into my bag.

"Oh, just a journal sort of thing, you know," I replied, and I asked casually: "Been working on your novel long, have you?"

"Three years," he said. "It's about half done. I had a business in Grand Rapids, but I'm not getting any younger, and I figured it was now or never to devote myself to what I really want to do. So I'm on the Greyhound, traveling to clear my mind. And whenever the impulse takes me, don't know where exactly, and don't wanna know, I'll stop for a while. And write."

We exchanged final looks of distaste, then turned to our opposing windows and pretended to be absorbed by the view. But I could not recapture my mood of deep contentment, not until we arrived in Clare, where I stayed put for the trip to Mackinaw City, and I saw him run in the swift descending dusk for the bus to Traverse City.

Greyhound's routes run like litmus paper throughout America, reacting without judgment to what they find: when we pulled out of Clare with new passengers on board, for example, there was not a black person among us, and we had a white driver too. A clutch of hunters were on board, all bearded and wearing orange billed caps, and a few women with packages, no doubt bound for home and families in the U.P. Every Greyhound driver's automatic response to snow or ice on the road, or even just a chill in the air, is to turn the thermostat up as far as it will go, and pretty soon the intense heat inside the bus was stupefying. But it is perilous to be on wheels when freezing night is closing in and the snow is falling fast on patches of ice; nobody wanted to complain to the driver, not while he needed every bit of concentration for the road. We slipped out of our coats, and those of us sitting next to the windows moved to the aisle seats, away from the heaters that were hot enough to raise welts on bare skin.

"I remember when I was a girl . . . ," the woman across from me began tentatively, and I nodded at her silhouette in the dark, to encourage her. "When I was a girl in the U.P. we often used to have snowfalls of ten, twelve feet, when we'd wake up and find the snow piled right up past the windows. It was like . . . ah, I don't know. There was no TV back then. We were really thrown on our own devices, as they say. You don't get snowfall like that anymore." Although I was leaning into the aisle to hear her, she spoke too softly for me to be sure over the noise of the engine: I think what she said next was: "We loved each other better in the winter."

"I'm on my way up to the U.P.," said a young man sitting behind me. He had taken off his hunter's hat and was fanning himself with it. "Going up to Detour. Do you know Detour, ma'am?" he asked the woman next to him.

"Oh, my, yes. That is remote."

"Go up every year. Got friends with a cabin. Hunt black bear with the crossbow."

Heads close together, we watched the road with the driver for a while. There was little traffic; oncoming lights were diffused and softened by the blizzard. The only sound was our hardworking motor and the clickety-clack, clickety-clack-clack of the big windshield wipers.

"They say up in Detour there's this bear roaming around," said the hunting man out of the dark, "only he's not a living thing, you know? He's a spirit, or a ghost. Something like that."

"Do you know anyone who's ever seen him?" I asked.

"Well, my friends have this dog they used to take hunting. Mad Dog, we used to call him, because he used to be so fierce, you know. There was nothing this dog was a-scared of, nothing on two legs or four he wouldn't tackle, given the chance. Well, one night it was snowing about like it is now, only there was a wind blowing, too. And we were inside, sitting around, and this dog, all of a sudden, he jumps up sniffing at the door and growling. You oughta seen this dog, the hairs are all up on his back, like he's throwing a fit or something. So my friends, they get up and they let him out, 'cause this here animal won't quit once he's got it in his head to chase something. Off he goes like a shot, out of sight into the trees. And we go back to what we were doing, just sitting around. And pretty soon we hear a noise, like a-scratchin' and a-cryin' at the door. And we open it up, and there's Mad Dog, only he's a-whimperin' and a-crawlin' on his belly. I mean that dog was seriously cowed, you know. And he slides himself straight under this big chifforobe they got. And that dog didn't come out from under there for a day and a half. And when he did, he was all changed and good for nothing. He sure as heck saw something in the woods. Something he had never seen before."

"Well, well," said the woman from the U.P after a while. "Who's to know what all there is out there?"

In summer, Mackinaw City is popular with tourists for its access to the Great Lakes and the holiday homes of Mackinac Island. In winter, however, it's not much more than a sparsely populated base for the southern foot of Mackinac Bridge in its stunning leap across the straits to St. Ignace on the U.P. Mackinaw City has no bus depot—no shelter, no telephone, no local taxi, no anything at all, just an unmarked stop in the middle of somewhere or other—and I was the only passenger to get off. No sooner had my feet touched the ground than the bus pulled away. I watched the leaping greyhound on its back become a noisy shadow in the night, then it was gone. Of course it was illogical to expect Greyhound to care what happened to a single passenger like me. Yet for all the many times I had left home in my life, never before had home left *me*. And for a moment or two on that forsaken road, as snowflakes collected rapidly in my hair and covered my shoes, my feelings were hurt.

A block east and across the road from where the bus dropped me I found the only motel in town that was open out of season. One of the genuine delights of rough travel is the way it takes a simple luxury like a hot bath from so far down the scale that westerners barely count it as a luxury at all, and raises it to the level of a glorious immersion, a baptism into normal society, an epiphany. ("There you go again," I can hear my son say.) That is how it felt to me in Mackinaw City after seventeen hours on the buses, when I sank into a tub of hot water. On the floor, where I could reach it easily, was a paper cup containing two inches of neat bourbon out of my hip flask. Afterward, there was bed, the word itself redolent of roses. Before I fell asleep I had just presence of mind to find the remote control and switch off the television. An unctuous voice-over was recommending a toning machine that "replicated the act of cross-country skiing," guaranteed to keep a body in better shape than similar machines that "replicated bicycle riding, stair climbing, and treadmilling."

A general plan was taking shape in my mind: to go west across northern America, stopping here and there, on a more or less straight line over the top to Seattle, and then to zigzag, like the brushstrokes of an action painter on stretched canvas, only I'd be doing it by Greyhound, mile by mile, across the United States. In that case, Duluth had to be my next stop, arrived at by skirting the top of Lake Michigan. It looked easy enough to do on the map, and in theory the trip was straightforward. But it snowed. It snowed. And it snowed. Greyhound has no agent in Mackinaw City; numbers listed nearby in the region rang without any answer. I had the idea that across the bridge in St. Ignace the northbound bus for Sault Ste. Marie was bound to dovetail with the westbound bus. Therefore, all I had to do to make the connection I wanted was catch the same bus that had dropped me off.

After a good night's sleep and a day of rest, I went out to wait for the bus at the very spot where it had left me. But it snowed. How it snowed! And the bus was very slow in coming. Before I allowed myself to turn again and look once more down the desolate road for the Greyhound's headlight, I made myself count in how many languages I could say "Thank you" (fifteen). The next time I had to think of six girls' names beginning with Z (Zoe, Zelda, Zipporah, Zenobia, Zizi, Zinnia). Then I trampled out the word HELP in letters three feet high. For two hours I played waiting games, until well after midnight. And it snowed. All it did was snow. The bus never came. I spent the next day pleasantly doing very little. The following night, after I had been waiting for an hour, and it was snowing, the proprietor of the motel drove his pickup out to where I was pacing, and trying to remember the entire score of *Pal Joey*. Kind though it was of him to offer me a place to wait in the warmth, the fact is, I had begun to enjoy being out alone in the night, singing, thinking, and brushing snow off my shoulders before I became one with the landscape. City folks don't often have the chance to stand by themselves in wondrous star-pricked darkness and breathe air as chaste as pure silver. When the bus failed to turn up again, I decided to give it one more chance before I tried to reconcile myself to flagging down the southbound bus, which was still running, so I could go all the way back to Chicago.

Three days in Mackinaw City may not be much in ordinary time, but they became a major episode of my journey. I ought to have been fretful and champing at the bit, and if I were still a youngster I probably would have been. But for a lone woman, no longer pressed by domestic cares or heartsick for a lover, it wasn't bad at all to be snowed in. By merely the second day, a pleasant routine was established, and I could have continued happily, for who can say how long, spending time without rough edges. The single restaurant that remained open for winter trade was an upscale diner and bar called Audie's, out toward the end of town. Making my way the half mile or so to Audie's for breakfast in the morning, I let the crunch of fresh snow take me back in memory to the house of my earliest days—only a summer house on a lake fifty miles from the city, but unlike our neighbors we used it on winter weekends too, and for the long Christmas holiday. The woman on the bus was right: there used to be blizzards every winter back then, and the snow drifted against the windows, muffling us up like things of great value in cotton wool. My brother and I went wild with joy every winter of our childhood that the heavens delivered such a colossal and endlessly miraculous plaything as snow. And my father used to be good-tempered on those short, bright days. Patiently he stomped up and down the big hill next to the house and flattened the snow for our sleds. What had I heard the woman on the bus say? We loved each other better then. Yes, memories of winters in the country are the best I have of classically American memories, and they came back whole in Mackinaw City as soon as I felt the clean snow underfoot.

I ordered poached eggs and toast, and kicked off my shoes so they would dry against the heater. Through the window next to my booth I saw that Audie's was receiving delivery from a truck on which was written "Blarney Castle Oil." There were a dozen or so men in the place, though whether it was always the same batch as on the first morning, I cannot say. They all had beards, they all wore fluorescent hats, they were all massive in anoraks or thick lumber jackets, and I watched them every morning check out the waitresses with such evident cupidity that I had to ask myself, as I had before in bus depots and at rest stops, if there were anywhere animals so restlessly keen to mate in every season as young American males. An enormously fat man squeezed himself into the booth in front of me. On the back of his windbreaker was written: "Michigan Rabbit Breeders Association." Then the waitress brought my eggs and toast. She said she was expecting more snow. I said, yup, it sure did look that way. And winter closed a silky-soft cocoon in which a body could safely snooze until the pangs of spring.

Snowfall during the second night wasn't bad in the end, just enough to cover gently the playground next door to my motel, and to hide patches of ice that made the going on foot slippery. A single one of the tourist stores was open on Main Street. When I opened the door, a bell rang and a gray-haired woman wearing glasses appeared from the back. I had the impression I'd interrupted her knitting, or some other busywork. After browsing among the T-shirts and china plates, and looking over the trays of fudge and nutty candies that appeared to be mainstays of Mackinaw City's economy— they were on sale even in the lobby of my motel—I chose a few postcards from a rack, and we entered into conversation. As usual when I spoke to anyone much over the age of forty, we began by talking about drugs and crime in the cities. "It started with taking God out of public life," she said. "From then on it has been getting worse and worse. They failed in a sacred trust when they took God out of public life. You've got to remember, America is the forward movement of keeping the world sane."

A fleeting image of the bus station in Chicago passed through my mind. She leaned very close. Her blue eyes snapped.

"That's how come they're out to get us," she said.

"But the Communists are all finished—" I began.

"Thank God," she said.

"Oh, yes, thank God. But what I mean to say is, if the Communists are all finished, thank God, then who *are* they? Who are *they* who are out to get us?"

"After they destroy America, it will be England's turn," she said. "Don't you worry, it will."

"Oh, dear. Yes, yes, I see. But who are *they*? Who *are* they?"

"I'm not the only one sees things this way, not by a long shot. There's a whole lot of us get together and talk, and we all feel the same way."

"Glad to hear it. Good. But I'd really like to know who *they* are. *Who* are they?"

She thrust my postcards into a bag and handed it to me.

"I don't know who they are," she said.

On my return to the motel a few minutes later, when I went to pick up my key at the desk, the proprietor's mother said she had made a few calls on my behalf, and it was all arranged for me to get out of town that very night.

Mackinac Bridge soars into mists that in winter hide the Upper Peninsula from the mainland. Official cars run a regular service for foot passengers like me who need to cross over to St. Ignace. A bridge patrolwoman picked me up after nightfall at a gas station next door to Audie's. There was nothing to see at night, only darkness end to end, barely pierced by our headlights and the lights of the bridge. But wind strummed the running trusses overhead, and space itself squeezed the road; I could feel it contracting slightly under the wheels of our car.

"A woman drove off it last year," my driver said. "But she was more'n likely drunk."

Greyhound buses were often escorted over in the winter, she told me, and when the wind was up, empty container trucks had to wait for others their own size with full loads to shield them or "they'd flop over like turtles." Only on one day every year, Labor Day, was the bridge open for pedestrians. "It's a real parade. They come from all over to walk across it. We keep an eye open of course, in case some crazy fool takes it into his head he can fly across to St. Ignace."

BUS 15 to DULUTH

It was snowing again, with great soft determination. In the veiled darkness St. Ignace was as deserted as Mackinaw City and just as small, only it was less trim, and had a grittiness that suggested as far as tourism was concerned it was on the wrong side of the bridge. The very fact that St. Ignace possesses a bus depot is enough to make it more raffish than its counterpart across the straits. When I pushed through the door, cigarette butts and gum wrappers blew into corners. A bearded man huddling under the overhead commercial heater flashed me a filthy look. One other passenger was waiting. He sat in the only orange plastic bucket chair still attached to a frame meant for four of them; there were three broken bolts where the others had been wrenched off, and the seats themselves lay in a heap against the far wall. The seated man did not raise his head from his hands when I came in.

Painstakingly, the old man behind the ticket window wrote "Duluth" in ballpoint on the ticket in my Ameripass book, and stamped it. When I asked how long he thought I'd have to wait, and if the eight-thirty bus to Duluth was going to be on time, he gave me an unfathomable look, then very deliberately pulled the sliding panel between us, leaving me nose-to-nose with CLOSED.

"If you're going to Duluth," the standing passenger said in a sharp, sarcastic voice, "you wanna ask that fella." He nodded toward the seated man. "He's been trying to get to Duluth. And he's been waiting in this dump for twenty-seven hours."

The seated man stirred and raised his head. He was an American Indian. I guessed him to be in his early fifties; it was hard to be sure, as his face was bloated from drink. His nose was bulbous and covered in craters. When he raised the bill of his cap in polite greeting, I looked into a pair of eyes as smooth and dark as river-washed pebbles.

"Twenty-seven hours!" I cried, looking around. In one corner of the room was a pay phone with empty covers dangling where the phone books should have been. Across from it a coffee machine had OUT OF ORDER handwritten and pasted spitefully across its front. Except for the garbage strewn around, it could have been the waiting room in a forgotten outpost of Eastern Europe.

The Indian shrugged, and with a hint of amusement he said: "I'm okay." Then he dropped his head back into his hands, to sleep.

The other man was hopping mad, literally from foot to foot. He told me his truck had broken down in the snows north of St. Ignace, and his company's dispatcher had refused to pay towing charges to take it over the bridge. So there he was, waiting for the bus to Detroit that wasn't due in until four in the morning. And, boy oh boy, was he ever fed up.

"Michigan!" He spat the word. "You know what they can do with Michigan?"

"Where do you come from?"

Jumping in place under the heater, he looked out the big front window of the depot, where all that could be seen in the meager lamplight was snow, and across the street, barely visible, a big sign: FROZEN YOGURT. "Florida," he said. Behind him, the Indian raised his head for an instant, and I caught a quick gleam of laughter in his eyes.

The Floridian was a small man, about my height, and so wound up in righteous indignation he could not stand still. He paced and muttered to himself. I half sat on the ledge under the window and tried to read—*The Last of the Mohicans*, it so happens. But when the time for the arrival of the Duluth bus came, and went, I found it increasingly difficult to concentrate. My attention kept wandering to the street outside. Was that the sound of a big friendly engine at last? But it was always only the wind. Several times I crossed to the ticket window, hoping for a word with the agent. He had opened his panel again and I could see him at a desk in the back room, constantly in conversation on the telephone, or pretending to be.

"Guess our bus is late again," I said to the Indian.

"And how," he replied.

He dropped his face into his hands again before I could be sure it was a big grin I had glimpsed.

For more than an hour the single interruption of our anxious wait was when a couple of teenaged girls came in to use the telephone. Jangling coins and earrings, they made several rapid calls, trying to locate some action. "Where are you guys going? Where are you guys at? Don't you guys wanna do something?"

The Floridian watched them with a scowl.

"It's the only public telephone around," the cute one announced as they were leaving, and wrinkled her nose to show that otherwise she wouldn't be caught dead in the St. Ignace depot.

"How do you get around in weather like this?" I asked.

The plain girl looked astonished.

"We have a car," she said.

I let another forty minutes pass before I decided I had to outwait the ticket agent, or outwit him. Slipping around from the side so he couldn't see me coming, I was ready to pounce. But he slid the panel into place again, and this time I heard him lock it. I rapped hard on the CLOSED sign. Somewhere in the back room a door slammed, and simultaneously the overhead heater dropped in tone. The ticket agent had flown the coop. And first he had lowered the heat. For the Floridian, that was the final insult: he jumped up and down, trying to launch himself high enough to get at the back of the heater and punch it. The Indian woke up and watched solemnly. Finally exhausted, the Floridian fell into one of the two plastic seats remaining on a frame for four in front of where the Indian was installed.

"The bus! The stinkin' bus!" he said. "Last time I'm on a bus, this big black guy gets on, and next to me is this kid. And the big guy must've been drinking or something, 'cause he stands there in the aisle and he says to me: 'You take that kid and set him on your lap so I can sit down.' Well, first of all, it is not my kid. And second of all, even if it woulda been my kid, this kid is six, seven years old and he has as much right to a seat as anyone."

The Floridian was up again, pacing as he spoke. Then he stood in front of me and started acting out his story. He raised his shoulders to make himself look bigger, stuck out his lower lip, and put on a hoarse, deep voice.

" 'You take that kid and set him up on your lap!' The black guy says this to me. To me! Well, by this time I just about had enough. So then the guy says: 'Can you pay for that kid? You gotta pay for that kid if he sits in a seat,' and I say to him, calmlike: 'Yessir. You bet I can pay.' But I'm seein' red. And I reach into my pocket"—the Floridian reached into his pocket—"and I show him this."

The Indian gave a soft grunt. The Floridian was half crouched in front of me, a switchblade open in his hand. "And that was all I hadda do, believe me," he said. "Just hadda show it to him." He put the knife away, crouched again, brought it out again, flicked it open a few times, and put it away again. "And that black guy, he backs off fast, you bet. He's saying, 'I don't want no bother! I don't want no bother!' If I woulda had my gun, I woulda key-illed him." The Floridian straightened up, smiling a little. "I dunno. Maybe it was 'cause I was in a bad mood at the time."

For more than an hour he continued to brood and to walk back and forth, wrapped in his own arms for warmth and comfort. I finished my book, did some pacing of my own, and popped out a few times to see if there were headlights in the freezing mist of snow. Only the Indian never moved, though his head was up and his eyes on the door. My bus was by this time more than five hours late by my reckoning. Several times, in a sudden spurt of anger, the Floridian marched up to the telephone and grabbed the receiver out of its cradle, then stood perplexed. Who was there to call? Greyhound had no 800 number as far as we knew for half-frozen travelers to use when they wanted more heat. The only number either of us had for the region belonged to the very station we were in. When he dialed it the phone started ringing behind the locked ticket window.

Out of the blue came big-city inspiration: what had I been thinking of? Had my brain frozen solid to my empty stomach?

"A taxi!" I cried.

The Floridian looked at me. "A taxi?"

"A taxi!"

"A taxi! Yeah, a taxi," he said. "We can call a taxi to get us outta here."

It was close to two in the morning. There seemed little chance the Duluth bus, delayed for two days, was going to turn up before dawn. And if it did? I was cold and very hungry. For the moment, I was past caring. The number of a local cab was pinned up on the wall by the telephone. And about two miles down the road the Floridian remembered seeing a Big Boy diner, the kind of place that never closed; where it is always warm; where there is food.

Grave and detached, the Indian watched our flapping.

"You're coming, too, aren't you?" I asked, after I'd called for the cab and a driver told me he'd be there in a few minutes.

"I'm okay," said the Indian.

For the first time I noticed he wore no coat and had no luggage to speak of, only a briefcase tied with rope.

"Can I bring you something back? A coffee or a sandwich?" The Floridian was shouting to hurry up, our taxi was coming down the road.

"I am okay," the Indian said again, and there was a warning behind his carbon eyes. "I am okay. I'll wait right here." In the pocket of my Driza Bone opposite the one in which I'd stowed *The Last of the Mohicans* was a bag of sunflower seeds, bought somewhere along the line and never even opened.

"Please," I said.

He hesitated, then nodded slowly.

"Okay. Thank you," he said, and took it.

*   *   *

The Big Boy diner was empty, except for the biggest boy I had ever seen—he must have weighed half a ton and overlapped two stools at the counter. I was halfway through a bowl of watery vegetable soup; hunger made it sublime. Across from me, the Floridian picked daintily at a slab of apple pie while he told me about the guns he had left at home with his wife.

"Can she shoot?" I asked.

"Good as me, which is pretty darn good," he said. "We live in an RV park." He watched me swoop a piece of roll around the bowl for the last drops of soup. "I'm an easy person to get along with," he said, "but you know, somebody gets me on the wrong side, somebody gets himself key-illed."

At that moment, the door flew open and in rushed the taxi driver who had dropped us off. He looked around, saw me, and shouted that the bus for Duluth had arrived twenty minutes after we'd left the station. Hold on, don't panic, it was refueling at the gas station right next to the Big Boy. But I'd better get my skates on or I'd miss it.

There she was, my beautiful Greyhound, half covered in ice and every inch the brave arctic explorer. No word was ever so sweet, or imagined sound so stirring as DULUTH in big letters over the front window. The driver was already in place and about to close the door when I came tearing out of the Big Boy, trailing my Driza Bone. Inside the bus, the atmosphere was dank and overheated. I made my own way down the central aisle. Although I could not see them clearly in the dark, I knew they were there, watching me from under their half-closed lids and willing me to pass them by. I heard them coughing, saw their shapes sprawled across more than a fair share of seats. I couldn't blame them for pretending to sleep, and for guarding whatever space they had in every way they could—I would have done the same if I'd been traveling through ice and snow for ten or twelve hours since Cincinnati or Detroit and was desperate to catch a few winks. Thankfully, I threw myself into an empty double halfway down on the left and settled in for what remained of the night. I had kicked off my shoes and was blowing up my inflatable pillow when from across the aisle came a long sigh. I looked up. There was the Indian. He leaned across the space that separated our seats and he was smiling, really smiling, as he invited me to help myself out of the half-empty bag of sunflower seeds.

MINNEAPOLIS —
SEATTLE

The genius bookseller of Fargo,
North Dakota

Time after time after midnight during my months on the road, I used to sit up with a jolt to see aged passengers near me nodding off, or looking straight ahead, always upright and apparently undismayed by the nocturnal smells and noises of their fellow passengers. Not that the very same oldsters given half a chance wouldn't complain about their multimarried children and moan about the price of food and the crime rate. It's just that to sleep sitting up doesn't seem to bother those whose bones have stiffened into a final posture—some of them even prefer a chair to a bed for snoozing at home. Besides, time passes faster as we age, and a night or even two on the road is as nothing to someone who has spent twenty-five thousand nights or more in conventional ways. As for the young and youngish, they are supple as elastic. "I just curl up like a snake," said one six-footer in Montana when I asked how he had endured three days on the bus from Galveston. The ones who curse the moving dark and think it will never end are not the very young or the very old, they are we who have not quite locked into place, though we're nowhere near as loose and lubricated as we used to be. Believe you me, on any Greyhound traveling by night, the passengers suffering acutely are the middle-aged.

Whenever I was lucky enough to have two seats to myself, the best way I found to sleep was with my head on the aisle, thus removing my brains as far as possible from the heater, which on northern routes is turned up high enough to fry them. In this position, I found I could jackknife my legs against the bulkhead and occasionally walk my feet up the window to uncrick my knees. Leaving St. Ignace on the Duluth bus, I finally discovered my unorthodox strategy, and fitfully, I slept. When I knew I could sleep no more, we were on the road to Ironwood. Snow had stopped falling, and the day was already gathering strength. Before my eyes, sunrise was turning the sky from palest pink to the brilliant reds of another man's sunset. I looked over to see if the Indian was awake and sharing in the dawn, but all that showed he had ever been part of the story was a scattering of sunflower shells on the floor. He must have disembarked earlier at Iron Mountain. I felt a pang of loneliness and loss that is the perpetual price of friendship on the road.

Wisconsin passed our windows like an unfolding Christmas card. For miles we traveled without sight of a town until gradually the stately trees started to give way, first to the fast-food giants that accumulate wherever there are mouths to feed, and then to signs advertising local businesses—"Sheryl's Golden Shears," "The Pik-a-Flik Video Store," "Ernie's: Let Us Waterproof Your Hunting Clothes." On the outskirts of most towns, near steeples needle-bright against the sky, were antiabortion billboards, saying things like "Choose Life" and "Abortion stops a beating heart." Sometimes we stopped to pick up passengers and cargo, or drop them off on main streets where coffee shops or launderettes doubled as Greyhound depots. But as often, we passed straight through, and did not turn any heads or earn a second look even from the children, who pummeled one another while they waited on corners for their own buses to take them to school.

Back in deep country, the farms looked boundless and extravagant compared to the neatly parceled farms of Europe. The land itself was buoyantly young, unsculpted by tillage upon tillage since the Middle Ages. We passed road signs for Saxon and Upson. Here and there damp yellow skeletons of new houses stood waiting to be finished in fields all their own. The bus woke up; babies cried; conversations were begun or resumed.

"Everything would just drift along if it wasn't for America," the man in the front seat was saying to the driver. "I guess somebody's gotta do it."

"Yeah," the driver said, and asked: "Do what?"

"You know, shake things up. Make 'em change. America's the conscience of the world. It all emanates from America. Everything emanates from America. Without us, nothing would ever happen."

Behind me one middle-aged woman was telling another: "My doctor's got me on two aspirins a day for blood clots."

Maybe it was the way I was dressed: I felt odd in Duluth and alien in time as well as space. In Mackinaw City I had added to my wardrobe—a noteworthy event in the life of a woman traveling light—a kepi in camouflage with a knitted rim that pulled down over the back of my neck and my ears. I had come across it among implements for farming and shooting and fishing in the only serious store open for business. "Buy me," it said. I thought it gave my ensemble an arresting *je ne sais quoi* that would have passed muster in London or New York, but I was getting funny looks in the main shopping center of Duluth. I had gone there to look for a book to replace *The Last of the Mohicans*. No sooner did I take off my hat and stuff it into my bag than both my shoes gave out, parting simultaneously from their soles and leaving me to shuffle along the skywalk like a longtime inmate through the corridors of a loony bin. Clicking along in front of me at that moment were two young women, neat as pins, who had emerged from a suite of law offices. "My beau likes me to wear them," the fair girl was telling the dark one. Perhaps she meant her high-heeled shoes. "My new beau, I mean, not my old beau."

As I entered the shoe department of Minnesota Surplus, the man behind the counter was saying to a primly dressed woman of about my age: "You're lucky. This is the last pair we have in stock. We sold one hundred pairs of these in thirty minutes yesterday." And up over the counter he hoisted a pair of snowshoes. I was very impressed; it seemed tame after that to ask for a simple pair of sneakers.

*   *   *

Later, in the bookstore I bought Thomas Wolfe's *Look Home-ward, Angel*. When I was in my teens, I loved the big American romantic. But forty years on in the Duluth bus station, I discovered that the spot in my heart for him had frozen over. I was too old for his exuberance, too cold. The road to Minneapolis is not the one for recapturing grand passion.

"Remembering speechlessly we seek the great forgotten language. . . . O lost, and by the wind grieved, ghost, come back again."

BUS 16 to MINNEAPOLIS

Two richly plumed Indian boys wearing earrings and shoulder-length hair held back by beaded sweatbands got off the bus just outside Duluth, and left us to continue on a monotone journey. I had some small experience of Minneapolis, it happens. I changed planes there once between London and Los Angeles. On the main concourse was a bar I'd gone into for a quick one. The place was packed with local people who had driven out from town. At intervals a bell rang behind the counter, whereupon the bar staff formed a conga line and snaked through the crowds while singing "The Beer Barrel Polka." Our world is big, our time is short; we who want to see a lot must deduce useful truths from every shred of evidence we come across, no matter how small, and even at the risk of sometimes committing an injustice. Thus, for me, Minneapolis will always be the place where locals go to the airport for fun.

In other parts of the world, wintry cities dig underground to use the snow and ice as insulation, and at the same time, in accord with an atavistic instinct, to burrow for shelter. Central Minneapolis, however, has lifted itself off the ground onto a complex of skyways that soon had me flapping around like a bat in a maze, looking for a way out to the street that was visible below, congealing in the slush and forsaken by all but motor transport. Skyways are nothing but malls in suspension: they're for the birds.

"I hate it up here too," said the woman behind the counter of the dry cleaners where I stopped to ask directions. "St. Paul is older and more . . . " She looked me up and down: ". . . More arty than Minneapolis. You oughta stay there next time. But I don't suppose you'll ever come back. Mary Tyler Moore never did. Not that she ever lived here in the first place."

BUS 17 to FARGO

Thanksgiving decorations were up everywhere except in the cafeteria attached to the Minneapolis bus depot, where faded black and orange crepe-paper streamers for Halloween sagged overhead. Is there much in life as pathetic as the trappings of yesterday's festivities? In one corner of the room sat an enormous woman with frizzy bleached hair; her bosom rested on the tabletop. With an expression of great melancholy, she was watching her teenaged son eat a hamburger. He was blind; a white stick leaned against his chair. The only other customer was a big, broad youth with k's TOWING across the back of his jacket. The woman behind the counter was trying to charge him ten cents extra for milk and sugar in his take-out coffee.

"I just got my ticket, man," he complained. "I got no dime left. Besides, you got no right."

"This here is my place," said the woman, who was small but hugely bad-tempered, "and I gotta right to do whatever I wanna do."

"Man, that is a loada bull. Oh, man. Nobody charges extra for milk and sugar not even in Seattle they don't charge extra for milk and sugar."

"Well, I charge for milk and sugar. If you don't like it, go to Seattle and them other places for your coffee."

"Oh, man, that's what I'm doin', man. That's why I got no dime to spare. I'm goin' to Seattle."

"Well, good riddance. We don't need you in Minneapolis."

She was on tiptoe; he was crouching. He was big; she was quick. They were well matched for battle.

"Well, I got no dime."

"Then you drink your coffee as it comes."

"Here," I said, and I put a dime on the counter. "Let me treat you."

The boy muttered what sounded like an obscenity. He grabbed a handful of containers of milk substitute and several packets of sugar, and swaggered out to the waiting room.

"You shouldn't oughtta done that," the woman snapped. "You do that, they never learn. He had a dime of his own, you can bet on it. I've been working here more years than I care to say, and I've seen it all."

Frowning, she rang up my order. I carried my tray to the far side of the room. Signs on the wall said: "No Shoes, No Shirts, No Service," "No Smoking," "No Outside Food to Be Brought In," "No Change for the Machines."

"No way," said the proprietor to a woman who asked for a cup of boiling water. A nicotine-starved cough rumbled through the big blonde. Her blind son said: "Ma, you smoke way too much." The lopsided cardboard jack-o'-lantern trembled in the window.

For some time I had been hearing whispers that Greyhound planned to switch to a seat reservation system. This would be a deplorable innovation, anathema to the democratic principle of first come, first served. To arrive early at the depot and wait for an hour or two at the gate is to earn a favored seat fair and square. Only if an incoming bus originates far down the road are reboarders called first to reclaim seats they left briefly when they got out to stretch their legs, or while the bus was being cleaned. And even then, as soon as they are back in place, new boarders can choose the remaining seats according to their investment of time, and their personalities. The aged and disabled have first choice of sitting up front. Otherwise, front-seaters often turn out to be great show-offs, or people who normally drive their own cars and like the spurious control it gives them to sit up there. When they are crazy, they tend to be manic. More often than not, the front-seater is a woman cozying up to the man in charge. In Minneapolis, only K'S TOWING was in front of me in the line for Fargo and

beyond, and I knew he was bound to head straight for the back of
the bus. A quick look at the gathering behind me showed nobody
incapacitated physically, and the only passenger much older than
I was an upright man wearing a Tyrolean hat who certainly looked
spry enough to take care of himself. In other words, if I wanted
the front seat it was going to be available to me, and at last I felt
seasoned enough, strong enough, and determined enough to cope
with it.

To sit behind the big window for the first time was a revelation:
the view engulfed me, and the driver, practically at my elbow, was
more like a consort than the distant figure of authority he was to
the people farther back.

"Now, a couple of rules we at Greyhound take seriously, and
we'd like you to do so, too . . . ," he said over the microphone. I
turned in my seat to give a stern look to the folks behind us. As it
turned out, I could not have chosen a more memorable bus for my
maiden trip as a front-seater: at a little past noon, we crossed the
upper Mississippi flowing under ice not far from its source in
Bemidji, Minnesota. And hey, presto! The built-up snarls were
left behind, and our joyous Greyhound leapt into the long, open
stretches of the West.

"*On est bien en autobus, n'est-ce pas?*"

The spry old man from the depot was across from me in the
second-best seat, the one behind the driver. Why he addressed me
in French, I do not know. When I answered in kind, he switched
right back to English, which he spoke with a light, unplaceable
accent.

"I often take the bus. I am over eighty and driving has lost its
appeal."

Folds around his eyes and mouth had kept their original hue
and were darker than the rest of his face, which had faded to a
beautiful golden brown.

"Indonesia," he said when I asked where he came from. "But
forty years in Dickinson, North Dakota."

He had no good reason, or not one he could remember, or one he cared to tell me, for living in such an unlikely place. He was an engineer who had served with the armed forces of his native land. A handsome old briefcase was on the seat next to him; he rooted around in it for a photograph of himself in uniform, heavily decorated. With age, his face had dried closer to the bone, but essentially it was unchanged. Only his eyes, bright in the picture, grew dazed when he fumbled for a line of thought, but the further back his memory traveled, the more secure it became. Pretty soon he was telling me war stories. "During the war," he said, "you British"—I did not demur—"turned two Indonesian ships away from the harbor in Colombo, and sent them straight back into the hands of the Japanese. And afterwards, what do you think your British officers said? You *know* what they said, oh, yes, you *know!*" He smiled at me with big white teeth. "They said: 'Sorry!' "

Out of the briefcase he drew a bundle of sharp pencils held together with a rubber band. After selecting one carefully, he put the rest back, then took a small notebook from the inside pocket of his jacket.

"*Excusez-moi. J'ai du travail,*" he said and shrugged in the French way. After that he was too busy to say any more while he wrote in his notebook what looked like sums and long lists of figures. An hour passed, and he pulled a package of food out of his briefcase. Enviously, I watched him tuck into chunks of raw carrots and apples.

As alarming as the rumor of seat reservations was a persistent whisper that Greyhound was planning a formal link with McDonald's to make it pretty much Greyhound's exclusive purveyor of food. This would be a brutal blow to bus travel. Flavor and nutrition to one side, rest stops for long stretches afford the only glimpse passengers have of local life and temperament in the places they are crossing. Many of the stops Greyhound makes are original and fun, especially west of the Mississippi. A very good one came up on the road to Fargo in a town called Melrose,

Minnesota, pop. 2,235. Our bus pulled up in a typical main street of the flatland, its blocks laid straight as railway cars, and not a building more than two or three stories high. Del's Cafe was a shopfront down the street from the Viking Hotel, in the middle of town. Perhaps the big gal was Del herself, unless Del is a guy. She greeted our driver as an old friend, and had his "usual" going before he'd said a word. I settled for a cheese-and-tomato sandwich, with a bottle of cold grapefruit juice, which I carried into Del's back room. There, more ambitious passengers were tucking into plates of hot food that looked real and unkempt, the way meals looked back before cholesterol, when I was growing up in America.

Next door to the dining area was "Del's Meeting Room," where the ladies of Melrose were holding a rummage sale the day we were there, mostly HATS-HATS-HATS, according to the sign. Through the open door I looked in at a big room where trestle tables down the middle were heaped with old crockery, bookends, bottles of perfume and eau de toilette. All around, on hat racks and on heads, was a collection of hats, hats, hats. The ladies of Melrose were in high spirits, as women always are when they try on hats together. A handsome buxom woman wearing a rose-studded cartwheel had grabbed a shawl from a heap of second-hand clothes, wrapped herself in it, and was doing a Mae West strut around the room, while the others all laughed, fit to be tied.

"Come on and join us," she called out when she saw me watching from the doorway. No sooner had she spoken than I felt a shift within my mind, and a crack opened between what was and what could yet be. It is through just such sudden fissures in reality that urbane women have been known to leap into the arms of Neapolitan fishermen, or ride off on camels into the Sahara. Before me was a glimpse of a whole new tempting invention: Life as a Lady of Melrose, Minnesota.

"I wish I could join you," I said, and I meant it too, for as long as it took to say. "But I have to go. I'm on the bus."

"Well, you come back again," said the merry big woman. "And next time, you try on a hat."

*   *   *

It was a very local bus to North Dakota. We lost passengers along the way, and we gained them. A girl of about twenty who had been sitting behind me on the aisle left us at a small town not very far from Melrose. The moment she stepped off the bus, from a parked car nearby there poured a crowd, like clowns at the circus, who gathered her in with whoops of joy. At the same stop, an older woman boarded and took the seat diagonally across the aisle from me, behind the old man in the Tyrolean hat, who had nodded off to sleep with the pencil still upright in his hand. She was a busy woman, and orderly. First she tried to knit with wool out of her tapestry bag, but she soon had to give up against the jolting of the bus. Then she tried her Bible until reading turned out to be more difficult even than knitting. Finally, she gave in with a big sigh, and I watched her industriously try to sleep upright, her hands twitching in her lap.

Outside our windows the land was being constantly ironed out, becoming flatter and flatter, on its way to some final great flatness more remote and underpopulated than most folks ever see, except in their strangest dreams. Snow began to fall, and with little left in nature to slow the wind down, it howled around our bus. Not very far ahead a Greyhound had blown over a few weeks before; I'd seen it on the news. But the snow and the noise of the wind didn't worry me; I felt cozy and secure. The general mood of every journey is set by the skipper, and our man to Fargo was an experienced hand. All in all, it was a capital bus to be on, heading out into open country, away from the loony magnetism of huge cities. Snatches of relaxed chatter drifted forward. Some people discussed the weather; a lot of the men were talking sports; two women halfway down and across from me compared photographs, probably of grandchildren.

"The guy is eighty or maybe older," said the girl behind me on the aisle. She was a skinny carrot-top who had boarded at a village a few miles back. "Now, if he's eighty, that makes his kids forty or fifty, which makes his grandkids twenty or thirty—tell me, am I right?" I couldn't hear her seatmate's reply. But there was nothing wrong with her arithmetic. Why had the Busy Woman opened her fluttering eyes wide, looked at the girl, then too quickly looked away with a funny look on her face? "Personally," said the girl, "I think Forbes would do a better job with the magazine. At least he knows what he's working at. My apologies to the family, but I think they have been used unknowingly." Her companion had not yet managed to get in two cents. I squinted through the crack between my seat and the window to see what was happening behind me. "Actually," the girl was saying, "you have to admit all trails lead to the Kennedys, if there are any to be found." I could see her pale face leaning in; she was speaking intensely. "In the end," she said, "even the rich and powerful get no more than they deserve." At last she sat back so I could see the seat next to her. It was empty.

Out of the multitude of Greyhound's stops in my unknown America, I had chosen Fargo, North Dakota, simply because I thought it was one of the least likely places in which I could ever have found myself. For that reason, before I left London I had promised my son that I would send him a postcard of Fargo.

"And what makes you think," he said, "there *are* any postcards of Fargo, North Dakota?"

"Listen to your mother and learn," I replied. "There is no place on earth with a view, or a church, or even just a pop. of twenty-five that does not consider itself to be worthy of a postcard."

The funny thing is, from the moment I arrived in Fargo, I felt happy and at home.

"Have you ever been to Stonehenge?" asked the driver of the taxi I took from the depot.

"Why, yes, I've been there many times."

He was chubby from his sedentary profession. An air of wisdom sat on him like tweeds, and from my seat next to him up front I thought I caught a whiff of pipe smoke.

"And what do you conclude about Stonehenge?" he asked.

— · — · —

There are few innocent pleasures in life equal to holding theories above one's station, and this was just the sort of discussion I found refreshing after a long, hard stint on the bus.

"I think," said I, "what is interesting is that those massive stones are not local. They were dragged onto the plains from far away. Only religious fervor, or terror—and tell me, what is to choose between them?—could give men strength enough to do something so nearly superhuman. In other words, it is my opinion Stonehenge must be a construct of the soul, not of intellect alone."

"Ahahaha," he said, and in my mind's eye he paused to draw on a pipe. "Hmmmm-hmmm. I see you are a practical person. But let us speak 'hypothically.' For example, what do you know about the pyramids? Allow me to tell you they were not built by the heave-ho method, that is for sure. Men did not pull those blocks. Why, there weren't men enough around in those days to pull those blocks. They flooded the river, that's what they did. And they floated those blocks right into place."

He waited a moment for those floating blocks to sink in good and deep.

"Hmmmm-hmmm," I said.

"Now you should know, they have dug up shells and the skeletons of fish from around the base of the pyramids. Did you know that? And there are lines of salt—"

"Of salt?"

"Yes, ma'am, there are lines of salt inside the pyramids that show how high the water rose. The powers that be took some of the blocks of stone apart, and do you know what they found?" We had pulled up in front of the hotel he'd recommended, which was opposite a hospital. He made no move to get out. "They took those blocks of stone apart real carefully with dental tools, which is how that kind of sensitive work is done, and they found human hairs in them. Now, you tell me, how did human hairs get inside those stones?" He opened his door and was half in, half out of the car. "'Hypothically' speaking, those stones were not cut. They were poured . . . they were poured out of volcanic lava."

"Where did you learn all this?" I asked when he had walked around the car to open my door from the outside.

"Just by putting two and two together. I read a lot."

Gallantly, he carried my suitcase to the door. Before we parted there he shook my hand.

"Always a pleasure to meet an open mind," he said.

I love Fargo, North Dakota. Who can explain it? Maybe it was just luck that I hit town on a good day. I have never sneezed at luck as an element of love. Fargo is not exactly a pretty town, or quaint, no traveler's "must," but the still, unbothered feel of it appealed to me, and a sense that it was built to last through fashion and upheaval. By chance next morning as I wandered out in the snow, I came upon Duane Johnson's bookstore at the bottom of Broadway, not far from a glorified parking lot called Herald Square. "Booksellers Serving Town & Gown," said the sign that caught my eye. Inside, books were heaped everywhere. At first it seemed chaos, then gradually order emerged, shaggy, as in a garden gone a bit to seed. Handwritten labels were fixed: "Science Fiction/Fantasy: Hardcover," "Romance & Love: Softcover," "History: US & European," "Achtung! No browsing in magazines." On a business card I picked up at the high, Dickensian front desk was printed: "Buy; Sell; Barter; Browse; Haggle & Converse."

By further good fortune, Duane Johnson himself was in residence the morning I happened by, and not at one of the other bookstores he manages in the Dakotas and Minnesota. Duane is a big man and bearded, but in the bushy old-fashioned way that signifies mellow understanding. When I told him how I was traveling around America, his immediate response was not the usual one of non–bus people who asked right off what I did for food, and whether there was a toilet on board. "You must be starved for conversation," said Duane, and I nearly wept in gratitude.

"I am a skeptic," he told me when I paused for breath and to tell him what a pleasure it was to meet him, "and a pacifist, and a liberal, in the great western tradition. I believe myself to be a sane man." After I told him how much I liked Fargo and that I was surprised to feel myself so at home there, he explained that was probably because a university and several colleges were established in the area.

"You've got to remember that by and large towns in America are places being passed through. Most of America is being passed through or flown over most of the time. And that is how atrophy sets in. Local colleges keep Fargo alive." As he was speaking, a scruffy man came in and started rooting through the magazines. "If you please, sir!" Duane called out to him. "If you please, sir!" The man looked up from a centerfold. "Please, sir, no browsing in those magazines. It would affect our integrity as booksellers."

Once upon a time, Fargo had been a Northern Pacific Railway town. Although Duane was white-haired, he was not all that old, and even he could remember very well when three passenger trains a day used to pull in at the station. Nowadays it is only one train, and usually carrying just freight.

"Of course, what does not pass through towns, what sticks," he said, "is technological wizardry. You can live in the smallest town in this nation and still see bleeding gunshot victims on the streets of the big cities and be treated to the sordid details of a rape before lunch. And that's only the news. After a while, horror starts to look like normalcy. And what I call the two-percent factor sets in: two percent of the good stuff is left in the milk. And two percent of us Americans are sane."

"Now, what makes you think there *are* any postcards of Fargo?" Duane asked me when I told him I wanted to send one to my boy. "Take a look on that big rack over there," he said. "You'll find three, maybe four hundred postcards, modern and antique, and I'm willing to bet not one of them is of Fargo."

I sorted through them all, and in the end I settled for a shot of London Bridge taken in the mid-1960s.

"About the time," I wrote, leaning on Duane's desk, "your mother discovered she wasn't always right."

The rest of the day pivoted pleasantly around a five-dollar lunch. While tucking in, I thought about how someday I was going to meet an American in London, Paris, or Istanbul, and when I asked where in the States he came from, he'd reply, "Oh, you wouldn't know it. It's a place called Fargo in North Dakota." After lunch, I walked everywhere, and liked what I found, especially Doreen's Snip and Snarl Beauty Salon, and the way nobody once told me to "have a nice day" except the part-time help in the grocery store where I stocked up on trail mix for the bus. And she turned out to be a student from Detroit.

"I'm studying community health and management," she said.

"Will that earn you a bachelor of science degree?"

"Gee." She frowned. "I don't know."

Instead of going back to the hotel when night fell, I went on impulse to a performance by the Red River Theatre Company of a play called *Nuts* by Tom Topor. There were twenty or so of us present in the nicely appointed little theater-in-the-round. In the row in front of me sat a young couple with their babe-in-arms. Whenever the baby started to whimper, they took turns slipping out quietly to soothe her. A pair of middle-aged couples were over to one side; their winter coats and scarves and hats were piled up on two more seats. The rest of the audience was composed of a group of severely disabled teenagers, some of them spastic and, to judge by their erratic and confused behavior in the lobby, most of them mentally handicapped as well. They were in the charge of a sturdy young woman, a nurse or teacher. The play was going well and the acting was good. Only once occurred a moment theatergoers dread, when illusion takes a tumble and suddenly embarrassment is likely on both sides of the footlights.

"What's the matter?" one character demanded sarcastically of another. "Do you have a psychomotor retardation?"

I looked quickly toward the handicapped children in the audience. And in the dim light I saw an amazing thing: they were rapt and calm—anyone who had not seen them earlier, before the play had started, would have taken them to be a group of handsome schoolkids in good health. In spite of all my previous theatergoing, most of it very sophisticated, it was in Fargo, North Dakota, that I became a theatrical front-seater and knew for the first time the force and mystery of live drama, and why it will endure.

Afterward, in the lobby, where paper cups of mulled cider had been on offer during intermission, among the notices on the bulletin board one sprang to my eye: "Attention Ladies!!!!! The Red River Theatre is in need of one adult female in our upcoming production." Sensible reality quaked again, and the crack that had opened in Melrose, this time, before it closed, made a space nearly big enough to drive a bus through.

On the walk back to my hotel, I stopped in a liquor store for bourbon to replenish my hip flask.

"The wife and I get over to London every year we can," said the proprietor, a man more old than young, soft-spoken and gray. "We go for the theater. We love the drama. You didn't happen to see *Coriolanus* last season at the Barbican?" Outside snowflakes fell in shadowy particles under streetlights. I walked home, smiling, still propelled by the ironical impulse long before in London that had brought me to Fargo, North Dakota. Of all places.

BUS 18 to BOZEMAN, MONTANA

The bus for Bozeman was coming in from Minneapolis and I was one of only a handful of new boarders. A stout man was in front of me. As he passed down the aisle, I saw that on the back of his jacket was written VIETNAM VETERAN. When he took a seat, I saw *William* stitched in gold over his heart and an American flag embroidered on his shoulder. HONOR SERVICE PRIDE, said his cap. Behind him was a woman in an outsize sweatshirt with MINNEAP-OLIS on it. She was talking to her seatmate, who had *Festival of*

Trees written across her bosom. Opposite them on the aisle a thin, bearded man wore COWBOY VILLAGE RESORT in gold on his black jacket and *Ranger* on his cap. His seatmate had *Goofy Bear* on his cap and his jacket said: *You Mess with the Best You Die with the Rest.* I found a double for myself six rows back, bus-left across the aisle from a slender granny who had not a word written on her person. Behind her was a young man, bearded, with ZENITH on his cap and a statement too faded from washing to read across his T-shirt. Behind me sat a bareheaded, clean-shaven man. He too was without any writing I could see. But the tail end of a tattoo peeked out from under the cuff of his anorak; it looked as if it must be the classic heart, probably with a name in it done up in streamers.

At the back of the bus, the usual bunch of young people set up camp. One sleepy girl was the first black passenger I had seen on Greyhound for many a northern mile. She was a classic beauty, and her hunter's hat made a fashion statement a lot more forthright than the bleat of my own headgear. Another girl traveling on her own was several rows behind her. Before I sat down I caught a glimpse of her long, dark hair and noticed how she was staring dreamily out the window.

Several times through the window of a bus I had watched young men embrace weeping girls at the departure bay, and I had noticed how a lot of the guys then boarded and walked down the central aisle to the back of the bus, already glancing right and left to size up new talent. It is as a rule in life easier to be the lover leaving than the lover left. By the same token, although a bit of my heart stayed in Fargo, it wasn't long before I was all smiles and humming to myself. Outside, water towers could be seen from miles away rising over the plains like huge inverted vegetables, obscurely humorous against the broad sky. Snow lay thin on the ground, hardly more than a sprinkle of sugar on devil's food cake. For miles at a time, all that indicated any other human presence were the telephone poles—Duane had called them "the national tree." They are tall cousins to railway tracks, with the same air of historical residue; they seem to mark old trails no longer used. Gradually the straight road took on a cantering motion, and we could easily imagine ourselves in a stagecoach leaving Fargo.

The passengers in my vicinity had established a clubby relationship, and they picked up where they had left off.

"See how the birds are sitting all bunched up together on the wires?" said the old lady across from me on the aisle. "In North Dakota we say that means we're in for some weather."

"Like when cows sit in the field?" said the younger man with ZENITH on his hat.

"Don't know about cows," the woman replied. "Where I come from, we go by the birds."

"Folks in Montana call North Dakota a mountain reclamation area." It was the tattooed man, speaking as one who had seen it all and was seeing it all again for the umpteenth time. "People from Minnesota always poke fun at people from Michigan. And vicey-versey. I've been from one end of these United States to the other, and I have never heard anybody in any state say a kind word about the state next door."

The younger man said that he was a trucker and had been a whole lot of places too, only he didn't know that much about them because he never hung around very long. He'd had an offer once for a job in Australia, but he had decided not to take it because he was afraid he'd feel homesick. Trucking was a good life for an outdoor man. Sometimes he stopped his truck and did a little fishing, then cooked his catch on the spot for supper. He was on his way up to Washington for his vacation; he went hunting up there every year with friends.

"See any black bear up that ways?" asked the old lady.

"Sure thing, ma'am. Always remember, you see a bear, you just make a real big noise. That old bear is gonna be a lot more scared of you than you are of him."

*　　*　　*

Long shadows overtook the light. Night fell inside our traveling machine, and talk grew reminiscent.

"We used to make homemade beer when I was a girl," the old lady said. "We used to chill it in the root cellar. Only drank it on Sundays. Our nearest neighbor was fifteen miles away. A Russian family. All the folks near us were Russians in them days. Those Russian boys were big, handsome fellas. Two of my cousins married Russians. I came pretty near marrying one myself. Back then we all spoke Russian just as good as American. I can still speak it pretty good. Only there aren't many people around nowadays can speak it back."

We were quiet and thoughtful. The first Russian immigrants to the plains that were flowing around us smoothly in the night must have believed themselves miraculously transported home, so similar to this landscape were their Russian steppes. America's natural variety made it very like home to exiles from mountains, plains, deserts, and in due course, from cities too. We expatriates, for our part, transplant more than we realize. We harbor alphabets, recipes, songs, stories, memories, and other stowaways. They move in with us and set themselves up, like the tumbleweed that blows all over the flatland. A freewheeling symbol of America's great romance, it was imported accidentally along with hardy wheat from the Crimea.

"Now, you're on one of the Ameripasses is my guess," said the tattooed man. I slid over to the aisle to be gathered into the little group. "Not much I don't know about Greyhound," he said. "Been riding the buses steady for years and years now. Used to live in Baltimore until my folks died. Nothing there for me after that. So I take my disability pension that I got, and mostly I ride the buses, see the country. Idaho is one state I like a lot. I'm on my way up to have a look at 'Cor de lion' . . . is that how you say it?"

"Care de Lean," said the trucker.

"Coor de Lane," said the old lady.

"Yeah, Curdalin," said the tattooed man.

"It's really something up there," the trucker said.

"That's what I heard. That's how come I'm gonna see it. Then I'm gonna head down south—I always do about now, get away from the snow: San Diego, Phoenix, Albuquerque, Houston. Like to end up in Orlando until winter's over. Go east in the spring. That's how it is. Go when I want. Go where I want. Take that old Greyhound wherever I want. There's not much about these old buses I don't know, no sir. You mark my words, it's only a matter of time before somebody gets on and hijacks one of these here Greyhounds."

"Fat chance!" I said to myself.

Two months later I was somewhere in New Mexico and I heard on the news that a passenger had grabbed the controls of a Greyhound outside Phoenix when the driver disembarked to pick up some freight. He drove it with passengers on board to San Bernardino, California, singing "Jesus Loves Me" all the way. In San Bernardino he parked the bus undamaged with everyone intact in his own driveway, and it was there the police closed in, and shot him dead.

At a roadhouse called the Lone Steer our good old coach to Bozeman and beyond pulled straight into the parking lot, heaved a big sigh, opened its doors, and let us out. Tables were ready and waiting for us, everything so brilliantly organized we could take a choice of two hot meals, eat, pay, and be back on the road within half an hour. Over bowls of chili, the trucker and the tattooed man compared notes on the least likable Americans. The tattooed man said nobody could match the folks of Oklahoma, and especially Oklahoma City, for pure nastiness. The trucker said he didn't know about that, but the most stuck-up truck drivers were Texans.

Meanwhile, the old lady showed me photographs of her grown-up children, and her oldest granddaughter, who was in Fargo studying to be a vet: "Not small animals either, we're talking about horses and cows." The future vet was dating her high school sweetheart, who was a policeman in a town just south of the farm where the girl had grown up.

"Will she marry the policeman?" I asked.

"Well, sure," said the old lady. "They're bound to marry each other. Why not?"

Back on the bus, before we pulled out into the dark, I showed her a picture of my son taken on the street in London where we live. There was the neon sign of a local Thai restaurant behind him, and in the background a black London taxi was cruising for trade. Our driver turned off the overhead light, and just before I settled into the reverie that sometimes slipped into real sleep, the old lady leaned over and tapped my arm.

"I'd like to give you a tip my mother gave me. If you hate to iron your son's shirts like I always did, just you hang them on the line overnight to freeze. When they thaw out next day, they'll be as flat as if a steam iron went over them."

"Why, thank you," I said. "I'll remember that."

And with a smile on my face I drifted off. The only clothesline I had ever noticed in central London, where I live, belonged to the last of the Soho brothels. Until the place was closed down, it had been the view from my window. I slept better that night than I had or would again on a bus.

When I opened my eyes, the whole world had changed. For a start, I was practically alone. The old lady had disembarked and the tattooed man was gone too, having decided on impulse to break his journey at a cheap motel along the way. Before leaving he'd asked the trucker to wish me "happy trails." On our own, the young trucker and I found we had nothing much to say. Soon we slipped over to our opposing windows and studied the landscape. Out there a miracle had taken place while I slept. What had become of the flatland? Where had the mountains sprung from? They were dazzling and rosy in the early sun. On the edge of Billings we pulled in for breakfast, and the instant I stepped out of the bus, I knew why everyone who visits Montana dreams of living there.

*   *   *

"I think I'll stay forever," I told the young redhead behind the hot plate at the counter, "just to see that view every morning when I wake up, and breathe your incredible air."

"You still gotta have money to live," she said. "You think I'd be dishing out eggs to folks off the bus if there was plenty of jobs around? You'd be surprised how many folks figure they've got a good idea to bring out here to the boonies."

"We had a frozen-yogurt guy from Chicago," said the big blonde serving at the next station.

"Two glassblowers from New York," said the redhead.

"And there was that divorced gal from L.A. who was gonna make jewelry or some darn thing out of pinecones, or something like that," said the blonde.

"Real estate guys. Dog breeders. Artists. They don't last long."

While I sipped coffee, I collected adjectives to describe the view through the window beside my table. Clean. Sharp. Honed and Imperturbable were the mountains floating on air that was fresh. Crisp. Immaculate. Crystalline.

"Can I sit with you?" The dark-haired girl from the bus stood there with her tray. Up close she was very pretty, with strong cheekbones and dark blue eyes. There was trouble around her mouth, however, a slackness of early surrender. She sat down and unloaded her coffee and a plate of toast from her tray. "There's a gentleman sitting over there who has been buying me food and stuff whenever we stop. He hasn't tried anything, you know; or moved in on me on the bus or anything. But I don't want anybody to get the wrong idea. I'm pretty close to where I'm going, and my boyfriend's meeting me, you know. I've been traveling for two and a half days. I've never been on that long of a trip before. When I first knew my boyfriend, he was like the wild type, you know, didn't wanna get serious. And me neither. But it was really weird, you know. Like right off, he was jealous."

"Not too jealous, I hope."

"He just gets a streak every once in a while if somebody looks at me wrong. We've known each other four months now. He's got a job out near Missoula."

"What does he do?"

"Something," she said, as if *that* was a funny question. "Construction or something, I guess. From what he says I'm gonna love it where he is. I hear real good things about this state. He says we're gonna have mountains right outside our back door. We tried to let things cool down between us, you know. Then he called last Saturday and when my sister told him I was out, well, he just got so mad. So then I called him. And, well, you know, I just packed up what I had and hit the bus."

Her delivery was low-pitched and baleful, even when she was talking about love. Draw her words as she spoke and they would make a dead-straight line.

"I hope you'll take your time," I said. "Don't jump into anything."

"No fear. I won't do that again in a hurry. I been married once already when I was eighteen. It was a real bad marriage. He was real bad and abusive. He was on drugs. Crack. He was in the navy. You think they woulda caught him but they never did. Crack is pretty rare in the navy. Those boys, mostly they take dope and acid. But he had black friends and they used to sell him the stuff. It got to the point where he didn't eat, didn't sleep, and he stole from everyone. If I didn't give him money, he used to beat on me. Put me in the hospital twice. He's outta the navy now. He's in prison."

Outside, I noticed, the view had not lost its luster.

"Well," I said, "I hope your new guy is clean."

"I won't make that mistake again. When I was a kid, I used to smoke a little dope myself. It relieved my mind from worries."

"Did you have a lot of worries when you were a kid?"

"Plenty of them. From the age of twelve or thirteen. It was my dad mostly, you know. He drank. He smoked. He took pills. And then he used to fool around with me. You know. My mom sat down with me one night and asked me what was wrong. And I said, 'It's your so-called husband. My so-called dad.' She knew what I was talking about."

"Was he your natural father?"

"My *real* dad, you mean? Oh yeah, sure."

"Did you report him?"

"Well, I told my mom. And she right away asked him was it true. The lying son-of-a-bitch. That was when I left home. I had just turned fifteen. I was better off on my own. I hung around Louisville for a year or two. That's when I met my first husband."

A few men looked up with interest when she crossed the floor on her way to the ladies' room. She'd left her bag with me. It was a knocked-around duffel, past its prime. Torn. Soiled. Shabby. Sad.

Bozeman was a nice town. I did not meet a soul in it who was less than courteous, except a few who got hot under the collar on the subject of movie stars buying up tracts of Montana for part-time hideaways. A lot more locals, when the name of one particular movie star came up, gave the impression she was not about to win any awards in the boutiques of the main street for her impersonation of a prima donna.

BUS 19 to SEATTLE

I've seen a few sunsets in my time and the one being performed as the bus pulled out of Bozeman took the biscuit. A neon OPEN sign over the saloon all but disappeared against the blazing reds. I longed to be off the bus and outside in the open, breathing in the colors that charged the air and bounced back from every shining surface: water, snow, and glass. The sun dropped at last between sharp glowing peaks, and gradually the scene faded through the spectrum into night. In darkness we crossed the border. Everyone who knew the route said the panhandle of Idaho around Coeur d'Alene contains some of the most stunning landscape in the country. But we on the bus saw none of it, and it was still pitch dark when we were already pulling into Spokane.

*   *   *

I noticed the girl in the depot right away because of her vivacity. So many girls and young women on the buses are dragging irritable babies, or are dim and drained in the way of the abused girl from the previous bus. There are plenty of hoydens too, of course, who go straight to the back to whoop it up with the boys. But the girl in Spokane gave off the glow of privileged youth, or so it seemed when I first saw her. In spite of her bottle-bright hair and her high-heeled boots, she could have been a college girl going home early for Thanksgiving. A slim, bearded young man stood beside her, his soft brown eyes spilling over with pride. The girl looked around the depot where exhausted travelers and a few vagrants off the street slumped in corners, and she made straight to where I was sitting apart from the others on my bus. We were waiting for them to finish flushing our Greyhound out with disinfectant so we could reboard.

"You're going to Seattle, aren't you? Are you on your own? Would you mind, could I sit next to you? My husband hates for me to travel alone on the bus. Don't you, honey?" She and the dark man exchanged a deep, loving look. "Geena—two *e*'s—McCloud," she said, and put out her hand. It wasn't that I didn't like the girl—on the contrary, I took to her on sight—but I needed to overcome genuine reluctance before I returned her handshake and told her who I was when I was at home. Bus travelers hardly ever exchange names, not even when they have been steeped in each other's intimate spaces for hours through the day and night. Traveling by Greyhound is no pleasure trip, you know. Bus journeys in America are purposeful expeditions, no frills or affectations, and as long as bus passengers are on the road, it is by raw identities that they know each other.

The moment we had settled down on board, Geena on the aisle, she told me she was a dancer; there was something so classy about her I thought she must mean ballet. It's not that I'm a culture vulture, not when it comes to classical dance—I'd as soon watch a good fish tank. It was how she made even the skin-tight clothes she was wearing look functional rather than tacky, and the confident way she held her head.

"I dance in a reputable place," she said. "They bail us out whenever we get busted."

"Ah, I see."

"My professional name is Topaz. Do you like that? Topaz. I have always loved to say that word, ever since I first heard it. Topaz. It's *me*, know what I mean? I think people should all be allowed to choose whatever name they like as soon as they're old enough. What about you? What do you do?"

"I write for a living," I said.

"Why, isn't that wonderful! I'm always reading. My husband says he's never known anyone to read as much as I do. I'd rather read than watch TV. I'm studying to be a paralegal."

"I think it must be interesting to study law," I told her. And I lied: of all the things we keep and break, mostly promises and china, laws seem to me the dullest.

"Well, I want to be able to fight for a woman's right to abortion," she told me, and before I had stopped nodding my head, she added: "And her right to have implants." Geena herself was flat-chested; it was one of the reasons I'd thought she might be a ballet dancer. A little voice in my head said: "Uh-oh."

"I guess in a perfect world no woman would need an abortion or"—I paused for effect—"*think* she needed implants."

"When I was fourteen," Geena said, "I had to have an abortion, so I know how important it is. My baby was developing without a heart."

"Did your parents know?"

"My folks were never there for me. I ran away when I was thirteen and I never went back. My father was abusive. I don't even know where they're living right now. And I don't care. But don't think I don't care for other people. I wouldn't want you to think that, because I do care for other people. I had three counselors for a while, and one of them told me I was a narcissist. But no way am I a narcissist. I really care about other people. I do. You don't think I'm a narcissist?"

"Well, dancers have to be a little narcissistic, I imagine," I said cautiously.

"I really care about other people," Geena went on. "You'd be surprised the times I've cried alone in the bathroom because of how much I care about other people. I used to have a dog, half pit, half rot, and he used to lick the tears off my face. Once when I was living with this guy, the cops came to our house and my dog grabbed one of them by the seat of the pants. 'That's because he does not like the way you're handling me. Now, you just give me the cuffs. I'll put them on myself and go sit in the back of your car peacefully.' That's what I told them, and they had to let me do it. When I was fifteen, sixteen, around there, I had a serious drug problem."

"Tell me, Geena, how does it happen, getting hooked on drugs?"

"Drugs made me feel good. They stopped me hurting. And then the drugs started hurting when I couldn't get them. But I swear that is all over now. Three months ago I got married to a nice guy. You saw my husband. Don't you think he's a nice guy? You know, he won't ever come to see me dance. He hates that I dance. But I tell him his job just doesn't pay enough to keep us going. When I got married, they gave me my baby back. My little girl that I love so much. That's why my husband stayed back in Spokane, to take care of her while I have to go to Seattle."

"Is he the baby's father?"

"Not exactly." She hesitated, then said brightly, "That's who I'm going to meet in Seattle. My baby's father. He's a lot older than me. He's also the father of a good friend of mine. She's got cancer. That's how come I'm going to Seattle. I want to see her one last time." Geena yawned and stretched. "Been to Washington before?"

"Just to Seattle a few years back, and only for a couple of days."

"Washington is different from Montana," Geena said. "Washington is big and rough, like a big rough painting. Montana is . . . etched."

She curled up then and immediately fell asleep at my side, just the way my son used to do when he was little, with trust to make the heart melt.

Because the driver himself was a frustrated smoker, he pulled into an unscheduled stop off a secondary road as the sun was coming up. Icy air bit for an instant before those of us who had got out to smoke or to stretch could breathe easily under the cloudless pink sky. Fir trees were laid jaggedly against the mountains that surrounded us. At the bottom of the small field where we were standing ankle-deep in fresh snow, there was a shed without a door; bars of new sunlight were falling through cracks in its roof. "You know something funny?" Geena said, flailing at the air to keep her smoke out of my eyes. "When you're back home, years and years from now, every time you think of Washington, it will be this little spot here you'll remember. It's like you had a camera in your brain and this spot that nobody else knows will be the picture you keep out of this trip."

Almost to the word what I had been thinking.

A little while later we broke for breakfast at a truck stop. A tired woman with hair like a dandelion gone to seed slammed glasses of iced water on the counter in front of Geena and me.

"I never trust a woman who hasn't been a waitress," Geena told her. "A woman's got to have been a waitress or a mother." The woman took a cloth out of the pocket of her apron and mopped up the water she had spilled.

"Honey, you're lookin' at a waitress. And I've been a mother, too. So trust me: whatever you do, stay away from the sausages."

Perched on a stool three down from us was an old lady whose face was a mass of reverberating wrinkles.

"How many grandkids you got?" Geena asked her.

Not a tooth was to be seen in her smile when she replied: "Seventeen last count." Then, as if in explanation: "I'm an Eskimo. And my old husband? He's a Norwegian."

"Well, now, isn't that something?" Geena said. "I hope your happiness continues."

The Eskimo hooted toothlessly.

"I'm past a whole lotta kinds of happiness. I'm sixty-three."
"You're only as old as you feel," said Geena.

The men around the counter had turned to watch Geena pass on her stabbing heels. But their lock-jawed surprise faded fast and they turned away, one or two with a little shrug, as if to say: "Too rich for my blood." The girl had star quality as well as fine-boned beauty. Given the breaks, she could have been a winner, top of the heap. Why not? As I watched others responding to her, I found myself thinking that if I'd stayed at home instead of wandering, I would have had the 2.6 offspring expected of my graduating class, and the youngest of my American babies could well now be a girl of Geena's age. I'm old enough to know that I am older than I feel and past a lot of kinds of happiness. And so, alas, I knew in my heart that the charming girl beside me, at barely nineteen, was already past most happiness.

She ordered chicken-fried steak with hash browns, toast, extra jam, and a Coke instead of coffee. The waitress frowned and we exchanged a worried look when Geena pushed the plates away, barely touched. She fumbled in her squashy bag for cigarettes, then for a thick album of snapshots, which she handed to me.
"My baby," she said.
The child was barely two, delicate of feature and resembling Geena; a black child, with a mop of black curls.
"Her daddy," said Geena, "is Italian."
Seattle was barely an hour away, and I have learned the hard way that it is a bad idea on the road to start what cannot be finished by the end of the journey. So I turned the pages of the album and said nothing. Interspersed with photographs of the adorable baby were a few of Geena taken mostly from behind. In them she wore hardly any clothes as she smiled provocatively over her shoulder. The pose, the juxtaposition of promotional pictures with snaps of the baby, the "Italian" father: it all made me feel very sad and tired, and angry too, at myself, at her, and at care-lessness in general when it comes to entrusted lives.

* * *

In Seattle, Geena gripped my arm so tightly while we were waiting to disembark that I could feel the chill of her hand through the sleeve of my Driza Bone, and I sensed her terror of being alone, even for a few minutes. She asked me, please, to stay with her until the man coming to meet her turned up.

"The father of your baby?"

"Yes," she said vaguely, looking around at the people in the depot. "Sure."

We were hardly through the gate when he stepped out of the crowd. Geena did not run to him, hug him, or even smile. When he went to take the bag out of her hand, she resisted a little. Awkward for the first time, she introduced me to him, not him to me. All her vitality had vanished; blue shadows had appeared under her eyes. The stranger looked at me, not with curiosity, but with marked complicity. A handing-over ceremony was under way, but of what nature? Car keys jingled in his hand. He turned away. And with a last unfathomable look that could have been pleading or apologetic, Geena followed along behind him.

I watched them leave. He was tall, stooped, closer to my age than to hers. I had the impression he was not an American; he was too badly coordinated, too faded and pale. His skin was several tones lighter than my own. I imagined myself chasing after them, shouting: "Wait! You cannot take that child until I know who you are and what you mean to do with her!" But I never made a move, and the door closed behind them.

BUSES 20 TO 24

PORTLAND — LINCOLN

A ballet-trained traffic cop

At seven in the morning in my downtown Seattle hotel room, I turned on the TV. A rapist-torturer was describing in detail the way he'd kept women as pets, and just how he dismembered them after he'd killed them. It must have been the news. The network bleeped all the four-letter words out of his confession. Those pious bleeps really got up my nose. "Fuck," I said to the TV, and I switched it off.

Seattle got on my nerves. To be fair, it was the last stop on the great northern lap of my journey, and as I grow older north becomes an increasingly attractive, adventuresome direction. Seattle is the gateway to the Klondike and the Golden Steps and Jack London's travels on the icy fields of bonanza. Ferries to Alaska were leaving all the time from Seattle's docks and I longed to be on one of them. But until the day a bus can fly or float, Seattle had to be my U.S.A. turning-around point, and perhaps that was what put me in a bad mood and colored my impression of the place. Nevertheless, something had happened to Seattle, something bad, since my last visit there. Four or five years earlier, when I'd passed through, it had been a friendly and inviting city; this time, much of it struck me as weak and bleak and self-occupied. So I stomped around town for a couple of days feeding my extreme vexation on some of the worst food in America.

On the way back to my motel after dinner the first night, a man hunched in shadows hissed at me from a telephone booth: "Hey, lady, I forgot my glasses. Would you step over here and read this here phone number for me?"

"*Parle pas anglais*," I said, and hurried down the empty street.

"I used to walk out everywhere at any hour," said the pretty girl behind the desk in the motel, "and now even in broad daylight I make one of the guys walk with me to the parking lot." Outside, under the snazzy monorail, a strolling gang of boys were reflexively trying the doors of the parked cars.

A city does not need to be safe in order to be great; almost by definition, great cities are full of danger, vice, and scams—that's part of their very purpose. Seattle is handsome and it has an excellent public transport system, which is generally the sign of a well-intended municipality. There is so much in its favor that I feel mean to say so, but my annoyance with the place increased as I walked around it. There were signs everywhere telling tourists not to hand out small change to panhandlers because it supported "substance abuse" and increased the problem (in Seattle's opinion). Their smug tone, and the failure to mention any alternative solutions in the works, encouraged me to assert the right of sane people to give away whatever they might have to spare.

"I promise I won't spend it on liquor," the bleary, youngish chap said when I peeled off my gloves, for it was cold in Seattle, and handed him three quarters.

"I don't care what you spend it on," I snapped back. "It's your money now. What you do with it is your business."

"I hear what you're saying." His smile showed a few dark spaces. "I've had a drinking problem since Vietnam. And I'm gonna buy myself a beer."

BUS 20 to PORTLAND

Seattle's depot at 6:00 A.M.: a fat, bearded man is asleep, flat on the floor; his T-shirt says, LIFE'S TOO SHORT TO DANCE WITH UGLY WOMEN. He's snoring, and I can smell him from six feet away. On a plastic seat near the door is a blowsy blonde dressed for summer in some other city; she is cursing softly and glowering at everyone who comes in. Up and down the central aisle paces a bald black dwarf, gabbling to an invisible companion.

"Maine or Oregon?" asked the man behind the ticket window,

and my mood gave a little hop up out of gloom to think that I had actually made it one way across the country by bus.

Tacoma, our first stop, was connected to Seattle by ropes of morning traffic. A man who had been sitting behind me stood in the aisle, waiting to get off.

"Oh, God, I hate this city," he complained to his companion. "This city sucks."

Lowering clouds over Tacoma were of good old British gray and filled the air faintly with the smell of wet wool. But a few miles the other side of town, the sky cleared, and what had looked like more clouds on the horizon solidified into bright, snow-clad mountains. Our road was empty at last of traffic; it wound between impenetrable walls of dripping evergreens as old as the hills. A yellow van was parked on the shoulder. I saw the words "Explorer Search & Rescue" printed on its side, and immediately there rose up full in my heart again the exultation of an American Greyhound on the open road.

A few miles out of Olympia we pulled up in front of an Exxon station with half a dozen vending machines in front under a canopy. Four or five rows behind me at the very center of the bus was a young woman traveling alone. She was thin and birdlike, her eyes were red-rimmed, and while I was getting a coffee out of the machine I sensed her circling me warily. Next to the bus, waiting to reboard, was a Vietnamese boy who had been sitting diagonally across the aisle from me. Although I was feeling good again, and strong, and the journey to Portland wasn't very long, I was not disposed to take the brunt of another story from a troubled stranger, so I took my coffee and planted myself close to him. I have traveled alone in Japan, Thailand, and Vietnam too, and even while a war was knocking the bottom out of habitual composure in Vietnam, I never had any stranger—and many of them knew my language—address a word to me unless we were introduced first by a mutual acquaintance, or I started the conversation. The young man caught my eye and bobbed his head. I bobbed my head.

"My mom kicked me out last night in Seattle," he said. "I'm twenty-three years old and we've been in this country since I was seven, and she still treats me like a baby. Is that right? It is not the American way. Well, I've had all I can take. I hope I can find a job and a place to live in Portland. Do you think I will? Because me and my mom do not get on with each other. No way."

They were putting up the municipal Christmas tree in the main square the day I arrived in Portland. Schoolchildren, secretaries on coffee breaks, and women out shopping had gathered to watch, along with moms pushing babies in carriages and just about everyone with time to spare. Local TV was recording the event. It made me feel as if I belonged, to cheer with the crowd when the cranes raised the giant evergreen in place. I've heard tell Portland has a frenetic nightlife, but I gave up carousing a century or two ago, and I rarely go out after dark unless it's for a movie or a play. Except for a handsome gay man in my hotel bar who could not quite pluck up courage for the worldly exchange he seemed to have in mind, I saw no signs of any Bohemian trend. I didn't feel that I was missing anything special when I went to bed, as usual after a day on the bus, shortly before nine o'clock.

Mainly, I'll remember Portland as the coffee city. Movable café vans go from corner to corner downtown; there are sidewalk cafés around the main square; the checklist in my hotel room asked specifically if guests had any criticism to make of the coffee; and around the corner was a coffee center that would not have disgraced a foody city like Boston or San Francisco. Booze, on the other hand, was very hard to find. None of the people I asked in the shops or galleries had any idea where to go for bourbon to refill my hip flask. One man delivering bread to a corner supermarket pointed me vaguely in the right direction. But it was mainly by intuition that I finally came upon a liquor store tucked away on a back street. It had all the chemically disinfected charisma of a flophouse. A hatchet-headed proprietor, full of scorn, said no cards, no checks, only cash on the nose. And the whole transaction reeked of a major sin way out of my league. As I was hurrying back to the hotel, a couple of bloodshot street people sitting against a wall looked up and watched me with fellowship: they knew there was a brown bag in the pocket of my Driza Bone and they knew, oh yes, I knew they knew, what it contained.

BUS 21 to BOISE

When I was a girl, the whole of Idaho was a joke as far as we eastern schoolkids were concerned. Potatoes came from Idaho. What else was there to say about one of the last states most of us learned to place on the map? Then, when I was eight or nine, I found that the capital city of Idaho was not "Bwaz" but "Boisey," to rhyme with "Joisey," and thereafter it stuck in my mind as a place I'd like to visit someday.

The bus was bound ultimately for Salt Lake City, and the people waiting were, all in all, a mirror image of their counterparts on the other side of the continent. Like passengers on the Portland, Maine–to–Boston run, Portland, Oregon–to–Boise people were mostly well-heeled commuters carrying very little luggage. Only one woman I spotted immediately as trouble, and an example of the worst kind of front-seater. She was stout and around forty; on her left foot was a clean white cast, and, sure enough, as soon as our bus was called, she hobbled straight up to the front of the line, swinging her cane, and announcing for the world to hear that she had just had surgery. She put a little spin on the word that made it sound as if she were saying, "Sugary . . . sugary . . . sugary . . ." As soon as the driver appeared at the gate to collect our tickets, she pushed straight past him with cries of "Sugary . . . sugary . . . ," and in her eagerness to be first she nearly clobbered a frail old man whose entitlement to the front seat was certainly equal to her own. Once she had shoved her way on board and plunked herself down, she spread out so nobody could share the coveted place.

"I've had sugary three times. The doctors all say they've never seen a foot as bad as mine," she started in as soon as we were moving. "I had sugary in May. I had sugary in June. I had sugary again in September. A bad foot's no fun, let me tell you." Gripped by the urge to be universally loved, which afflicts most front-seaters and stand-up comics, she started joking with the driver, loud enough so everyone had to hear: "I had a driver once outta Portland who looked like Richard Nixon. Ha-ha-ha. I called him Richard all the way, only he was a black guy. God, it was funny. Hey, driver, driver, hit any deer lately? You know that driver they call Big John who drives this route most weekdays? Well, John hit a cow, it musta been after my first sugary in May. And when I seen him after that, it musta been after my second sugary in June, I said to him, 'I gotta question to ask you.' And he said, 'Oh, no you don't,' and I said, 'Oh, yes I do,' and he said, 'Oh, no you don't,' and I said, 'You bet I do, John, and you know what it is too.' Ha-ha-ha. 'My question is, John, where's the beef?' God, it was funny! 'Where's the beef?' Ha-ha-ha. . . ."

In the end, I was glad I hadn't murdered the poor soul. That Oregon scenery was so nearly divine its beauty was as good as music and drowned out the bad jokes and the tales of orthopedic horror from our front-seater. We were following the banks of the Hood and Columbia rivers through Lewis and Clark country. Trailing clouds hung around the tops of the tall trees and drifted between hills that had the massy, noble look of buffalo heads. The peaked formations of rocks rising out of the river were bare above the timberline and curiously wind-carved, as if they'd dropped from some other planet where nature cut according to an aesthetic plan. Logs floated downstream pulled by tugs. It must have been an hour at least before we saw so much as the big yellow M of a McDonald's mucking up the view. There was not a sign of human interference for miles at a time; you could believe the great land had been locked in a pristine dimension, and was as magnificent as ever.

"Pretty, isn't it?" said the woman across the aisle. She was about my own age and seemed very much at ease in herself, neat and untroubled.

"It's magical country," I said.

We were passing through sifted sunlight in a pine forest; there was a light covering of snow under our wheels.

"Lived here all my life. Born and bred on the river. Never felt much need to travel. I like to take the bus whenever I have to go into Portland because that way I can look around."

"I'll bet you ride a horse," I said. "This landscape was made to be seen from horseback, wasn't it?"

"I hate horses. Too high. And you never know what a horse is fixin' to do."

The land outside became practically treeless. Slabs of slaty rock tumbled like huge dominoes down to the river. Beyond them lay a rolling yellow desert.

"Living around here, you must do a lot of camping."

"My idea of camping," she said, "is a good motel with an indoor pool somewhere on the edge of the wilderness."

The Dalles, Oregon, where she disembarked, was a town with rather a grim allure. I was sorry we stopped too briefly to walk around, or even to get off the bus. Somewhere near Billings the parade of full beards had straggled to a close, and the tall man in boots and a Stetson who was leaning against the wall near the public telephone was clean shaven except for a mustache. He straightened up as soon as he saw our bus pull in, and when the local woman stepped down he gave her a husbandly hug. What is it like to be met at the station, I was wondering? Expatriates remain exotics in their adoptive lands, it doesn't matter how long they live there, and unless a traveling woman arrives as a bride in the first place, she radically decreases her chances of conventional marriage with every mile she puts between herself and home. Being met at stations is not part of my expatriate experience, and never has been. Had I stayed in my own country, the chances are I too would have a husband taking the overnight case out of my hand and leading me to our car at some station on the road. It was a fantasy to try on, like a wide-brimmed hat.

*   *   *

The local woman and her hubby walked out of view, then reappeared a moment later in a brand new pickup truck. She was turned in silence to the window at her side. She glanced at the bus as they passed it. But her heart and soul were already occupied by wifely business.

In the afternoon we entered a tundra rolling to the horizon, where faraway mountains of dull steel lay against clouds. There wasn't a tree or any grasses high enough to show that the wind was blowing, but it whistled around the bus, one sustained note of varying intensity, and sometimes it cuffed us playfully so we rocked on our wheels. Gradually, the mountains veined with ice came closer, and there in an unexpected valley was the city of Pendleton, Oregon, pop. 15,090. "World's Roundup City," said the sign beside the road. Within moments Bad Foot discovered with shrieks of delight not only that the matron who joined us there and sat across from her came from a neighboring town in Idaho, but that they were somehow distantly related. She lowered her voice at last to confide to her new fifth cousin details of her ordeal too intimate for the rest of us. And night fell early on a dignified busload of Americans, all but one or two of us busy with thoughts of home just down the road.

The bus depot is a sort of thermometer in the nether orifice of any city, and Boise's depot was downright wholesome compared to many others.

"Boise feels like a clean, safe sort of place," I said to the taxi driver taking me to a motel.

"Least little thing happens in town tonight," he said, "you're gonna read all about it in the papers tomorrow."

Walking around the next day, I passed a lot of bright new shops and restaurants, few of them serving to capacity. But the town felt poised on the edge of big things. And it was there I had my first good meal in more than a month, for in Boise I learned to head straight for the Basque restaurant in any western town fortunate enough to have one. It was only a little hole-in-the-wall, but lunch was a bowl of garlicky black bean soup, followed by real bread with real butter, and hard goat's-milk cheese tasting of wild thyme from the slopes of northern Spain.

I have a weakness for contrast, and often before an overnight bus I chose to have dinner in a restaurant with a lot of glitz and cutlery. That night I found the right sort of place within a short walk of the depot. The dining room was empty when I came in, but glittering and set for hundreds.

"I do not like Basque people," said my waitress when I mentioned having visited the local museum of their culture. "I am Fransh and for us zee Basque are a pain in zee backside." Beauty does not always spring from a radiant soul; it can have its source in accident, in sin, in pain. And the French waitress was very beautiful indeed. Her face was glamorous and had photogenic planes and hollows. When she took my order to the kitchen, I saw that she was lame.

"How do you happen to be so far from home?" I asked when she returned with my order.

"I'd razzer not sink about it," she replied in her comic-book accent. She put my plate before me and gave a little grunt of disapproval at what the chef had done to the trout. Her bitterness was bracing after a little too much New Age sweetness in the day.

"Where do you come from in France?" I asked in French.

"Parees," she replied in English; "of course" was implicit. She wore no wedding band and she was too young to be a war bride. How had such a highly colored number come to be in Boise, stranded there like fading coral at the tidemark? Was it a man who'd done it? A fast-talking mustache in a black hat who'd loved her and left her? Or had she washed up in Idaho after an unsuccessful assault on Los Angeles, which for every true Parisian is the very epitome of the New World? I wanted badly to know, among other things, if she had ever pronounced Boise as "Bwaz."

"Do you ever go home to Paris?" I asked, persisting.

"Please, please, please," she cried, "I cannot bear to sink about eet."

When it was time for me to leave, she signaled one of the young waiters and sent him over with my check.

BUS 22 to SALT LAKE CITY

The rhythm of travel with no strings attached was under my skin and I would not have minded if it were never to end, or found it any hardship to go on and on, zigzagging America for months, for years, at a steady fifty-five miles an hour. But Mother's friend in Nebraska expected me to stop by before Thanksgiving, and I needed to get a move on or I'd let her down. I planned to return to Salt Lake City later in my journey—I had always wanted to have a look at the place—but I would only be there long enough out of Boise to change buses for Cheyenne, Wyoming. When I boarded the Salt Lake City bus, the passengers were already settled down for the night. All I could see in the gray light was an unusual number of clean-shaven young men among them. We had been out in the black night for a few hours when the driver announced a break. Although I had a seat to myself, bus-left, halfway to the back, sleep had altogether eluded me. I was the only passenger to disembark, except of course for the regular kids from the back of the bus who crept into the shadows for a smoke.

It was a truck stop across from the Outsiders Motel in Snowville, Utah. And it was snowing. The cafeteria was hung with ears of corn and cardboard turkeys. I helped myself to coffee in a polystyrene cup and closed it with a plastic lid, cunningly notched for drinking on a bumpy road. There was no whole milk—what else was new?—only dire two-percent, or the powdered stuff that floats like talc then gradually sinks to color coffee without flavoring it. The place was empty at that hour except for the young cashier and a trucker. They were discussing an accident in town the day before when a scaffolding had collapsed in the main street.

"Squashed that poor fella flat," the cashier said. She snapped a bubble of gum thoughtfully.

"Yeah, I heard. Flat as a pancake, poor guy," said the trucker.

"Goes to show; a guy gets up one morning just like any other . . ."

Over the towel dispenser in the ladies' room a bus passenger had scratched into the wall: "Jean—Seattle, Washington, to Miami, Florida. Greyhound, December 1985." My heart went out to Jean. And hats off, too. Three cheers for the lady. Seattle to Miami, practically the longest nonstop crossing possible on the bus. What a girl! It was the deep, dark hour between three and four in the morning when only rough travelers, lovers, and similar lunatics are awake. I climbed back on board my bus. In the fuggy dark a few young Mormons grunted sleepily. And I settled back into my seat, perfectly at home in the state without a zip code, the great moving community that is Greyhound, U.S.A.

BUS 23 to CHEYENNE

"If you are standing in the aisle when this bus is in motion and I have to make a turn or touch the brakes, please hold on. Or I guarantee you'll be through the windshield. I, on the other hand, have a seat belt on. The lady sitting directly behind me has rode with me before, don't you-all believe a word she says. She's a born backseat driver sittin', it just so happens, in the front seat. Now, we do have nasty weather up ahead of us, I promise you that. This here road was closed last night and it was still closed early this morning over around Cheyenne. We're gonna hope it's open by the time we git there. If you got any questions come up and see me, until I git into snowstorms and around ice, at which point I prefer to be left alone. I think you can understand why: it scares the hell outta me. And there's no snorin' allowed on this coach neither, 'cause it keeps me awake. . . ."

Our driver was not the Australian, Barry, I'd heard about way back on the bus to Boston; he was a character in his own right, however.

"As I see it, my job is to warm you up for when my relief driver takes over in Cheyenne," he said, handling the microphone like a pro. "I'll put my hat back on," he told us, and he stroked his bald dome, "if the glare off my head bothers anyone."

The closer we came to Thanksgiving, the more crowded the buses were, and it was increasingly difficult to find a seat alone. I was nearer the back than usual, surrounded by kids with an average age of twenty. Two boys diagonally across from me and one row back had boarded separately, but they were soon engaged in a sporadic exchange. The taller one was a redhead with the start of a mustache like traces of tomato soup on his upper lip. His hair was shoulder-length. A dirty string around his neck disappeared into the *V* of his denim shirt; no doubt a charm or ankh was hanging from it. I wondered if his parents had been hippies. No, on second thought, they were probably grocers or doctors.

"Where you comin' from, man?" he asked his neighbor.

Baseball caps had mostly gone like beards on the recent stretch of road; both boys were bareheaded. There was a broad-brimmed black leather hat in the overhead rack that had to belong to the shorter boy. It suited him. He had pale eyes and straw-colored hair; his fine-boned face was shrewd and thin. I'd bet Billy the Kid by the time he was twelve or fourteen had such a wary, born-knowing look; I have never seen it anywhere except on southern and western American buses, and a glorified version of it in movies, usually on someone playing an outlaw or a laconic hired gun.

"Comin' from Carson City, man," he said. "I hadda do some work out there. Where you comin' from?"

"Los An-gee-leeze," the redhead replied. "Where you goin', man?"

"Home to Kentucky, man. Where you goin'?"

"Philly-del-phee-ah, man. Good ol' Philly."

"Hey, man, that's cool."

Both of them were looking forward, not at each other, and I saw the two pairs of eyes, blue and reddish brown, fill suddenly with carnal calculation: a girl was coming down the aisle our way. She couldn't have been more than nineteen or twenty; her hair was loose and her skin glowed with health. She was too well fleshed and solid to be the envy of other women, I guess, but the boys sure liked the look of her. They exchanged half winks and pained grins when she sat down next to me. Neatly, she distributed herself and her packages, then folded her hands in her lap in a way that showed what kind of grown-up woman she was bound to be someday. She was on her way to Grandmama's house, she told me, in Rawlins, Wyoming, for a family party, and she was worried about being snowed in, because three days later was her boyfriend's birthday in Salt Lake City, and she'd rather die than miss it. When she told me she was a waitress in Salt Lake, I had a vision of lonely old "regulars" turning up to order the "special" and to gawp at her abundant, oddly virginal curves.

"What are people like in Salt Lake?" I asked.

"Well, when they talk to you, they always get that look: Are you Latter-Day Saints? LDS? Are you Mormon like us, or not? And if you're not, bye-bye."

"Are they good tippers?"

"You gotta be joking. Anything they got to spare, they give their church. If it wasn't that my boyfriend's gotta good job, we'd kiss the place good-bye. We're saving up. We're gonna leave as soon as we've got enough and go back to Wyoming."

She hadn't asked, but I told her I came from England.

"Oh, yeah? My people came from someplace around there," she said.

"I live in London," I told her.

"Oh, yeah?"

"London is a lot more laid back than any big American city I've seen so far," I said, though she hadn't asked that either. "Of course, that could be plain weariness. After all, the place was bombed to hell within living memory."

She turned on me her big, blank, hazel gaze.

"Who bombed London?"

*   *   *

An icy drizzle was falling and the driver slowed his speed. We passed a big truck on its back and then, a few miles farther down the road, a car crumpled against a tree. Blue lights flashed past us, and there was a jackknifed tractor-trailer not far from another that appeared to have lost an entire segment and was rolled over on its side.

"Don't nobody look out the windows," the driver said. "I don't want no heart attacks on my bus."

"Don't you wanna do mouth-to-mouth?" the redheaded boy shouted.

"No way I'm gonna do mouth-to-mouth on you," the driver rejoined.

Next to me, the girl let out a laugh so coarse and sharp it made me jump.

"But I will accept volunteers," the driver said, playing to that shocking laugh.

"Not meheheheeeeee . . . ," she squealed.

"Now, you behave yourself," said the driver, "or I will put you out in the snow."

The screwdriver laugh came again and I could feel her quivering. But before she could think of a pert reply a woman behind us said, "A lady can always get herself a hitchhike, no matter what."

It was a voice from the mean streets, the voice of a cocky thug. And leaning over our seats was the face to match: clever eyes set wide apart under dark, curly hair—the face of an urban guerrilla who's been around a little too long and seen a little too much. "You just wait for a good-lookin' truck driver, and give him a wink," she said.

From somewhere near the back a girl shouted: "There's no such thing's a good-lookin' truck driver!"

"Have fun while you can," said Billy the Kid, his voice nasal and flat, " 'cause nothin' lasts forever."

The dangerous road flew by. Once the driver had made sure nobody objected or would take offense, he went back to his microphone and told a string of set jokes, one or two of them mildly blue. Palpable heat was coming off my neighbor. She sat up straight and screeched at every punch line. In the eyes of the boys who were watching her was awe mixed with desire; they racked their memories for a suggestive joke or comment to take her mounting excitement off the scale. But she remained at the same pitch right to the end, oblivious to everything except the thrill of being tickled by the driver. Ripe enough at the start, her body swelled to take up more than her fair share of her seat, and I wasn't sorry to see the back of her in Rawlins.

"Byeeeeee," shouted the Hippie as she swayed down the aisle, hip to hip.

"You-all be a good little girl. Hear what I'm sayin' to you?" said Billy the Kid, and won the last laugh.

Snow was falling thick and fast. I watched her disembark, saw her look around, and saw her shrink: nobody was there to meet her. As we pulled away, she turned and waved forlornly at all the fun going out of her life and down the road to Cheyenne.

There was a shift to quiet conversations on the bus. A fat girl on the aisle who had previously not said a word smiled at me.

"Going home for Thanksgiving?" I asked.

"No way," she said. "I'm going home to stay. My mama got divorced last year and dragged me out to California with her. I hate California. Too many drugs. I'm going back to Nebraska. They can have California. I'm gonna try and get my old job back at the gas station where I used to work. My boss said, when I left, he told me I could have it back whenever I wanted to. The firemen always used to come into our place to joke with the girls. There was one of them so cute."

"Did you write to him while you were in California?"

She looked surprised. "Write to him? No, I didn't. On account of I don't know his address. Only I knew he wasn't married because when I left he said he'd wait for me forever. But you know how men are."

"Especially firemen."

"I really hated California," she said.

"Anybody on board from Los Angeles," announced the driver, "don't none of you exhale. I don't wanna pollute the air on my bus."

The Urban Guerrilla behind us knelt on her seat and peeled back the sleeve of her denim jacket. She waved her arm around to show us a big, flimsy bandage on its fleshy lower part.

"Now, what I got here is a knife wound," she said. "I got it while defending my property against three muggers. They were after my camera, but they didn't get it."

"Where did that happen?" I asked.

For the first time she looked at me directly and her dark eyes filled with suspicion. Was I a cop? There was something funny about me. What kind of la-di-da accent *was* that?

"Pasadena," she said. "That's where I was living at the time."

"Well," I said, "I don't blame you for leaving."

"I'm on my way to Queens, New York, to live with my sister. You think there are more muggers in Pasadena than in Queens? Muggers didn't make me leave. Getting mugged was like a drop in the ocean. I couldn't take it no more. I used to weigh ninety-eight pounds, no kidding." She raised herself higher so everyone could see her sturdy, short-legged body. "I was bee-you-tee-ful," she said. "I used to be a model. Used to have my own business. Before I went bankrupt. I used to have a fur coat, cost forty thousand dollars. You think I'm kiddin' you? I hadda sell it for a hundred. Used to have a diamond bracelet, cost fifty thousand dollars. I hadda sell it for seventy-five hundred. Used to have a car. Waddya think, I always used to ride these crummy buses? Hadda sell my car. I hadda sell everything. I hadda sell my camera that the muggers didn't get. Them assholes . . ."

The red headed hippie and Billy the Kid exchanged a high-eyebrow look.

"Hey, don't believe me, you guys," said the Urban Guerrilla. "But it's true, all I used a have."

★　　★　　★

"Well, folks," the driver said, and he lowered his voice to a solemn note. "We're just about to pull into the depot. But before we do, I want you all to know you have been a really great bunch. I have really enjoyed myself. And I hope you folks have enjoyed yourself too."

I cheered with the others and joined in the applause.

I'd be lying if I said Cheyenne, Wyoming, was a beautiful town. Besides, about fifty miles before we arrived I had happened to look out as we were passing a snowy field in which deer and antelope were at play as the sun set. After such a stupendous eyeful anything further would have been redundant. The youngsters from the bus saw me off with wishes of good luck, all except the Urban Guerrilla, who was in an altercation with a Greyhound ticket agent and hardly noticed my departure. Swinging my case and taking deep breaths of cool night air, I started on foot toward a big, old-fashioned hotel I had spotted from the bus. Cheyenne, Wyoming. It had sung to me way back when I first heard it mentioned, and I took to the place right off. It reminded me a little of Fargo, unpretentious and genuine, only more basic in its humors. The main theatrical event of Cheyenne's calendar, for instance, is in the summer, when people come from far and wide to dress up as frontiersmen and stage mock shoot-outs in the town square.

"You oughta try to get back here for that," said the proprietor of a local jewelry store. I was admiring a secondhand ring made of buffalo horn inlaid with Mexican silver. She said it had been brought in by a cowboy: "Those cowboys are real flashy dressers," she said.

"So are those Indians, I believe." And she gave me a slow, dawning smile.

I woke early next morning in Cheyenne thanks to a dinner that lay on my gut all night like the parched sole of a cowboy's boot. The breakfast menu was scrawled on a blackboard in the dining room over the chalky shadow of liver and onions from the night before.

Big, silent men in big black hats sat in twos or threes at tables near mine. Before I'd finished my first cup of coffee, the weather had changed from sun to snow, and then to wind-driven sleet. By the time I went to check out in the vast lobby—it was uncarpeted and clanging with ghostly spurs—a brave, chilly sun was shining again. "One thing nobody in Cheyenne counts on," said the woman behind the desk, "is good weather. Then again, we don't count on it staying bad, neither."

The bus to Lincoln left late at night and I went back to the depot to check my bag so I could poke around town unencumbered. A few men were asleep in the bucket seats when I came in; they all wore their broad-brimmed hats pulled down over their noses, and their booted feet were stuck straight out in front of them, heels first. When I turned from depositing my bag in a locker up front near the ticket window, I found myself face-to-face with the Urban Guerrilla. She was emerging from the ladies' room. Damp curls were plastered against her forehead, and her eyes were red from a sleepless night; they filled with misgivings at sight of me. Barely my height, she straightened her shoulders and pulled herself together.

"They took my ticket away, the assholes," she said. "My check bounced."

"What are you going to do?"

"My sister's gonna wire me money here," she said, and made a sound between a snort and a sigh. "When I get it, I'll jump the next bus outta here."

Whether or not her story of past riches was true—I tended to think it was—I liked the way she told it. It took guts not to whine about losses, real or imagined, and to treat them with acceptance, native optimism, even: the American idea that fortunes are made to be lost and made again, again, and again.

It wasn't much of a depot; except for a few vending machines there had been no food available to her during the long night. And who could tell if she had money enough even for the machines? I wanted to ask her out for something to eat. But she did not trust me one little bit. And suspicion breeds itself in its object: if I showed generosity, I had a feeling she would play me for a sucker. She might dip my wallet, say, and consider it no more than I deserved for being not quite what I seemed.

"Let's have lunch," I said at last, and hearing how perfectly fatuous that sounded, I made matters worse by adding: "Is one o'clock okay?" I could hear her think: "Yeah. Sure. I'll pencil it in, asshole." Obstinately I went on: "I have a few things to do." And I cringed then to hear the way I said: "Downtown." But the eyes of black ice, which up to then had revealed nothing for me warmer than caution, suddenly melted, and with a sheepish smile, in a voice full of longing and nostalgia, she asked, "Are you going shopping?"

At one o'clock on the dot, in spite of mixed feelings, I returned to the bus depot, as I had promised, to take the Urban Guerrilla out for a meal. But there was no sign of her, or of the men who had been sleeping there. Only a tired young man was pushing a mop that reeked of disinfectant between the rows of plastic seats. I asked him if he'd seen a dark girl who had been marooned there between buses. He said no, he hadn't seen anyone at all.

"She was broke. I was going to buy her a meal."

"Well now," he said, leaning on his mop, "that's cool. That's a cool thing to do."

I looked again to see if he really meant it. Or did he take me for a patronizing bitch and a patsy?

It was that afternoon in Cheyenne I made contact with the beast that is sucking the life out of American towns and cities.

"Take me to the mall," I told the taxi driver, for there was no bus. But I didn't hang around Cheyenne's mall very long before I telephoned in a claustrophobic panic for another cab to get me out of there. When it came, I sat up front next to the driver. He was fifty-five, sixty, maybe more; it's hard to guess the age of a face that has been weather-beaten into the semblance of a timeless artifact of buffalo horn and leather. From the age of sixteen he had been a cowboy. His father had been a cowboy. His father's father had been a cowboy, too. And his mother and grandmother had both been Indians. "But cowboys are a thing of the past," he said in a voice that rumbled low, like a record at a speed too slow. "You got plenty of your weekend cowboys who put on their hats and their boots and go down to the local bar and chase all the girls. Those boys, they couldn't ride a barstool if it got frisky." He darted out of the mall's parking lot, narrowly cutting off an oncoming car, then switched lanes a whisker ahead of a pickup truck. "The last outfit I worked for was out in Arizona, where they've still got some big ranches. We covered a million and a half acres, twenty-six thousand head of steer. I just quit about six months ago." With two or three inches to spare he crossed in front of a van in a parallel lane, then slowed down. I looked back and saw the other driver pounding his fist on the steering wheel. "It was a good, good way of life, only it was rough on the family. The roundup wagon was out two and a half months in the spring and four and a half months in the fall. Six months out of the year you slept on the ground. And when the wagon was all done, you always had a bunch of strays in your outfit, or maybe over in another outfit. Some of us older guys who'd been around for a while knew all the brands, so we'd be sent over to cut their brand out of the other cattle that was there. These days, hell, they all ride motorcycles, or whatever you call them." He swerved into another lane; the driver behind us zoomed ahead with a hoot of rage. "There were times I got pretty disgusted, I guess. But not ever enough to think I wanted to do anything else."

"Excuse me," I hated to interrupt. "But your meter . . ."

Letting the vehicle steer itself, he reached over to pound on the meter with both hands until it began to tick.

"I got busted up quite a bit riding bucking horses, and came the time I had to retire. I didn't have to ride all them bucking horses, I guess. But you hang out your shingle one day and say, 'I can ride any horse you got,' and after that you ride 'em. No point in it really. Same reason some people climb a mountain, I guess. I did rodeos for fourteen years."

"Gosh. That must be dangerous."

A woman in a sedan swerved as we passed much too close.

"No more dangerous'n driving on a slick highway like this," he said. "Mainly what being a cowboy was about was days and days when you'd be out there all by yourself."

"I'll bet it's beautiful."

"It is. Beautiful is the word. It's the only way to go. But you got to like solitude. And you got to love nature. Otherwise, you'll never make it."

We drove a way in silence.

"Well, it's all over now," he said.

Before we arrived at the depot he asked me shyly if I liked to dance, and if I knew the Texas two-step.

"It's a shame you gotta be at the depot so early. Now, if you saw your way to take a later bus . . ."

I was a lucky girl, I was thinking, to have been rescued from the coils of the mall by such a hero. But the days when I'd miss my bus to stay in town and dance with a handsome cowboy were long gone.

"Thank you," I said, "but . . ."

"Well, it was just a thought. Watch out for yourself, ma'am. Bus depots get all the wild ones."

Behind me in the depot were a middle-aged woman and a young man. I had a glimpse of them before I sat down.

"How come you didn't get let out sooner? Those other boys all went in and got let out in no time."

"Hell, ma, it was my third time."

"I know. I gotta get used to you not being a kid anymore."

"Yeah. It's really none of your business anymore."

"I know. I don't have to do anything but cook your meals and wash your clothes when you're at home."

"I'm gonna get me a gold card with five hundred dollars' worth of credit," the boy said. "I'm gonna get me a car. I'm gonna get me some good clothes. I'm gettin' out of this cow-poke town."

BUS 24 to LINCOLN

"There is a rest room for your convenience," said the driver, a husky woman with a no-nonsense approach to the roadworthy state of the union under her jurisdiction. "But it is *only* for that purpose. . . ."

The bus had originated far down the track. Only a handful of us were boarding in Cheyenne. There was a lot of laughter in the ranks, and I figured I knew who the incoming driver must have been. I found a seat near the middle of the bus, and I hoped to be able to keep it to myself for the overnight drive into Lincoln. But Thanksgiving was only a few days off and homegoing crowds already required extra buses on many routes. Sure enough, I was barely settled and the bus pulling away from the lights of town when a skinny young man with dirty-blond hair came up from the rear of the bus and took the seat next to me, on the aisle.

"See them two girls?" he whispered in a thick southern accent. "Them two have been kissin' and huggin' all the way from Sacramento practically." All I could see over the seat backs were two curly mops, one fair and the other auburn. "They're Lisbons," he said.

A pair of young black men sauntered past us toward the front of the bus. The taller of them half sat on the armrest of the girls' seat and his slouching aide-de-camp took the same position on the opposite side of the aisle.

"The tall dude," my neighbor whispered, "he's been playin' with their minds."

The tall man leaned over the girls and spoke loud enough for us all to hear a reprise of what had clearly been an earlier theme.

"Here is what I'm saying to you. I'm sayin' if you had to have mouth-to-mouth resuscitation, be honest, who would you rather have it from? From me? Or from my brother here?"

His mate opposite smiled, showing crooked overlapping teeth.

"Or would you rather have it from your lady friend? We ain't talkin' color here. We talkin' sex."

"I don't like bossy men," said the blond mop in a whining voice.

"Hey, blackie, smile!" a man shouted from the back of the bus. "That way we can see you in the dark."

The two black men creased themselves laughing.

"Hey, whitey," shouted the tall man, "can't wait until daylight when you guys disappear. Can't see white in the light."

Everybody roared with laughter then except the driver.

"Okay, you guys," she said over the microphone. "Back to your own seats."

The tall man paused in the aisle beside me.

"I'm goin' to K.C.," he said. "Do you know what that means in American?"

Perhaps he had heard me say a few words, or my clothes gave me away. Or perhaps it was a lucky guess.

"I suppose K.C. must be Kansas City."

"Yeah. Right. Good. That's how us black bros talk. If I say to you, like, 'I'm chillin',' I mean I'm chillin' out. Like, you would probably say 'relaxed.' And if I say, 'I'm dealin' '"—he fixed the young man beside me with a significant look—"I could mean I'm dealin' drugs."

Then the pair ambled back to their seats, leaving the young man restless at my side. He started to tell me how he was going home to his mother in Nashville for Thanksgiving. Then he stopped, chewed his thumbnail for a while, and began to talk vaguely about his job in Sacramento, a girl he knew, his beat-up bike. Finally he said: "Look, I'm gonna sit back there for a while. Get to know the black dude better. I'm stuck with him all the way to K.C., right?"

The last row bus-left in a Greyhound is a three-seater that stretches from the wall of the bathroom to the window. Being as far as possible from the driver's scrutiny, and secluded, makes it

the bad boys' seat. Although it is the only space on which anyone
of average height can lie flat out, nice people do not sit back there.
The two black men were installed on the bad boys' seat. They let
interested visitors join them for brief periods, but they were not
about to share their space with anyone. For the rest of the night,
my neighbor was up and down—occasionally he sat next to me,
but as often as he was welcome he sat with them at the back of the
bus. Sometime around three in the morning a sly, unfocused lust
possessed him; he pressed his leg against mine, and his hand fell
against my shoulder. I turned in my seat, presented him with a
back old enough to be his grandmother's, and pretended to sleep
while the night drew us deep and straight across Nebraska to
Lincoln.

OMAHA —
MEMPHIS

*Thanksgiving Day on the road
in Fort Knox: soldiers calling home*

The Greyhound pulled into Lincoln an hour after icy-fingered dawn had gripped Nebraska. One more time I climbed down onto the frozen pavement of a new place with the clear conscience and all but the begging bowl of an eastern pilgrim. Mother's Nebraska friend is a splendid woman, a genuine storyteller in the salty tradition of American small-town humorists. We had arranged to meet at the Hilton for breakfast before she drove me the fifty miles or so to her home in Ulysses, Nebraska, and I was looking forward to seeing her. At the same time, however, I knew it was farewell to the light heart of the road, to anonymity, and to the fleeting demands of strangers: I was going to have to sing for my supper. It was with mixed feelings I walked the few blocks through the silent streets to the hotel.

Too hungry to wait for Mother's friend, I had already finished my third cup of coffee over a copy of the *Omaha World-Herald* someone had left on a neighboring table. A poem contributed to the readers' page by a six-year-old boy caught my interest: "Thank you, God for the turkey. Thank you, God for the food. Thank you, God for mom and dad. Thank you, God for America. Thank you, God for Nebraska. Thank you, God for us. . . ."

Suddenly, a waitress appeared and summoned me to the telephone at the front desk. It was Mother's friend, more full of regrets than she could say. In the country of the greatest technological advances on the planet, she was icebound, sealed into Ulysses like a little pea at the bottom of a deep freeze. Barring a miraculous thaw, we were not going to meet after all.

When I was young and learning to survive on the roads of Europe, Hilton was anathema to me and other wanderers of my ilk.

Hilton was the home away from home for all bourgeois American tourists; Hiltonites were becameraed and wore Bermuda shorts on the Champs-Elysées. Our parents stayed at Hilton when they arrived to check up on us. But the beats, or existentialists, or *Ur*-hippies, or whatever you call the rackety companions of my youth, had long since gone into their fathers' businesses, or married well, or died. I had done none of these things; was it such a big deal nearly forty years on to spend one lousy night, the first of my entire life, in a Hilton hotel?

"Oh, what the hell," I thought as I stood there at the desk, phone in hand. And an hour later I lay back alone in the hotel's sumptuous indoor pool, feeling the aching cramp of sleepless nights on buses wash away before I went out to make the best of Sunday in a God-fearing city of my native country. And after I had walked the streets with couples and family groups on their way home from church, between bulwarks of piled snow in the wintry sun, I did as I used to do on Sundays way back when: I went to the movies, a feature-length cartoon, it happened, where I sat happily surrounded by the youngsters of Lincoln, Nebraska.

"Bad-uh?" the girl asked at the counter when I bought a bucket of popcorn.

"Sorry?"

"Bad-uh. Bad-uh. Do you want eggs-truh bad-uh?"

My accent remains American, at least as far as the Brits are concerned, but my ears seem over the years to have acquired an English way of hearing.

"Do I want *what?*"

Besides, when I was a kid nobody needed to ask if we wanted extra butter on our popcorn. Of course we did.

That night I was too tired to look for a restaurant, and I took dinner in the hotel.

"Just one this evening?" asked the hostess, full of solicitude at my dreadful social handicap. "Leslie will be your server."

"Hi, my name is Leslie," said the bright-eyed, pretty girl. "And I will be your server."

When I finished college in 1956, I waited on tables in New York for a year to grubstake my trip to Europe. And if anyone had dared to call us "servers," with its echo of feudal privilege and serfdom, we'd have told him exactly where to get off. Server. It sounds like something to wipe your hands on and leave crumpled up in the ashtray. We waited on tables, damn it. And even though most of us would rather have been doing other jobs, we were proud of waiting well on tables. We were waitresses. And men who did our job were waiters. I toyed with the idea of letting Leslie have it with both barrels, but she was new at the job, and turned out anyhow to be a part-timer. Mostly, she was a freshman at a local college, where she was planning to go for a degree in "Human Development and the Family." From the way she described it to me, it sounded very much like the course that was in my day called "Home Economics."

"But what I enjoy most is history," said Leslie. "The history books are all wrong about Columbus, you know. He was a bad man. Native Americans were peace-loving people. They loved animals and nature. They used to store their food in the summer to eat in the winter. And that was the food Columbus and his men ate, so the Native Americans starved that year. But the history books don't tell you that."

There were no other customers, and my Caesar salad being inedible, there were no distractions from conversation.

"If the history books don't tell you, then how do you know?"

"I had to go to Native Americans in my college and ask them," she replied. "Dig a little deep and that's how you'll find out that Columbus was a bad man, and a bad Christian."

"Don't you think ideas of good and bad, even Christian ideas of right and wrong, may have changed since 1492?"

"Columbus called Native Americans savages," she said. "And they were not like that at all."

When she came back from the kitchen with my shrimp, which

had traveled too far and too slowly from the sea to taste of anything but tainted ice, I asked her what else she was studying. Could she actually have answered, "Haptics and paralanguage," or had my ears altogether lost their American edge?

"What are 'haptics'?"

"The closest I can explain is, it's, like, touching, you know? You oughtta hear our professor explain it."

"And 'paralanguage'?"

"Don't you know what that is?"

"All I know is there's never a paralinguist around when a person really needs one," I said. But not a smile cracked her earnest little face.

More customers appeared and the hostess called Leslie away from my table. A couple had come in with a little girl done up in Sunday ruffles and pink satin bows. As soon as they were seated the child burst into a falsetto rendition of "There's No Place Like Home for the Holidays." A big truck rumbled under the window next to me. I fancied it was bound for Omaha, where it would make a right to head on down to Kansas City, Nashville, Memphis. Suddenly I found myself homesick—not for London or New York, but for the road ahead.

BUS 25 to OMAHA

Two very old ladies were in the front of the line for the early bus to Omaha. Between them and me a white-haired man with crossed eyes smoked a cigarette lit from the one before, and hissed softly between his teeth.

"Last time I went on the bus," one old lady told the other, "I got spasms. I hadda go lay across those three seats at the back."

"My tooth was calcified to the bone," the other old bird was saying as I passed them on the bus. "They hadda drill a hole so the infection could run out."

Our bus had arrived from the far West, and it was very crowded. For the first time I saw people standing, and I counted myself lucky to find a seat on the aisle, at the very back. Next to me was a big girl with bleached hair; she wore a royal-blue fake-fur coat over a shocking-pink satin blouse.

"I left Reno two days ago. I'm a model," she told me. "I'm on my way to Dez Moynees—is that how you say it? My mom is getting married and I'm going to her wedding."

"I hope she'll be very happy," I said.

"She'd better be. It's her fourth time."

BUS 26 to KANSAS CITY

East was the pulling direction out of Omaha. Those of us waiting for the southbound bus were fewer and quieter than the uproarious line next to us for Chicago. Most of the passengers were single boys and girls on their way home for the holiday. Those who had come farthest slumped and squatted, or sat on their cases. New boarders were fresh and upright. A boy in an old jacket with ACES HIGH over the heart sprawled out flat on the floor, his head resting on a duffel bag. He looked up at a beautiful Asian girl standing near him.

"Hey, how do you say 'shit' in Chinese?" he asked her.

"I don't know," she said. "I'm Japanese."

My seat was on the aisle behind the driver and next to a distinguished white-haired man who told me he was bound for Dallas. His voice was uncannily like Henry Fonda's, and the fine bones of his face held vestiges of an elegant young manhood. Pinned to his shirt was a medal with writing on it. The first word was "Silver," but before I could see the rest, he turned to the window and nodded off. A thriller I'd bought in a spiffy bookstore in Lincoln had turned out to be a dud, so I passed the time pleasantly, watching the road unfurl in front of us over the hills ahead like a stripe on a flag in a gentle breeze. Every few miles we passed clusters of mailboxes at the entries to smaller roads or lanes, then soon afterward small towns appeared. As we entered each of them, I never failed to feel a quiver of homecoming, as if I were back at last from distant travels with tales to tell. The steeples and schools and white houses with porches as pretty as go-to-meeting hats are bound to say "Welcome" to any American of my generation, even a dyed-in-the-wool cosmopolitan. Through the window of our passing bus, it looked to me as if the life were being drained out of many of the towns, no doubt by malls and unemployment and restless youth. One day the dainty husks of pretty little towns, once flourishing, will be bought up whole by rich city slickers and movie stars. After all, there are only so many ranches in Montana to go around. And small towns are the apple pies of the middle states, with an American glamour all their own. Only my countrymen who have actually grown up in small towns are less taken with their charm, I've noticed, or if they do celebrate small-town life choose to do it from the safe distance of Chicago, say, or New York.

As we were pulling into Kansas City that evening, my aged neighbor woke up, muzzy and unsure of where he was. The ticket clerk told him there were long waits and many changes ahead before he arrived in Dallas. I wrote them all down for him on a page out of my notebook, and then I installed him in a seat near the departure gate for his outward bus. Whatever central confusion was at work on his mind, he looked a patrician figure as he smiled sweetly on the frazzled moms with squalling babies. When he raised his hand in a sketchy benediction of a drunk caved in against a nearby wall, his tweed coat fell open and I saw what was written on the medal he wore: "Silver Senators Club."

"Take it all down, every word of it," he said to me. "You could write a book."

The taxi driver warned me that Kansas City was crammed with "wadyacallums" in town for a convention.

"They call themselves Bible teachers," he grumbled, "but all they talk about is Socrates."

I found what was possibly the last room in town. All the rest were booked to professors and lecturers in religious studies descended for a few days on Kansas City from all over America and

THE ★ GREAT AMERICAN BUS ★ RIDE

abroad. I have been stuck before in towns where conventions were taking place, but that night in Kansas City was something special: not a funny hat to be seen, nobody ostensibly drunk, and no evidence spouses at home had any reason for concern. Groups of bearded men and sedate women discoursed as they walked; they threw their arms in the air and stopped here and there to make hot points, then regrouped in the chaste, if fervid, pursuit of higher thought. Lines of theologians waited patiently in the cold outside the only two restaurants open for dinner downtown. At last I found a saloon not far from the hotel with space and food on offer.

Four large TV screens were installed at dominant points over the bar, each of them playing full blast the video of a football game from the previous season. Men of every age with nothing in common except their color—they were all white—leaned on the bar and sat at the tables without exchanging a word, only lifting their voices together in roars of delight and thumping each other on the back at every scoring play. It was the kind of establishment you could stumble into on practically any main drag in Middle America. The last free seat was on a stool at the bar, and as luck would have it another female on her own had the neighboring stool. We sized each other up out of the corners of our eyes. She was about ten years my junior, not precisely young, not flashy, wearing a plain gold wedding band, and on her lapel a conventioneer's plastic label. A plate of french fries was on the counter in front of her. She looked down and picked at them gloomily.

A barman at the restaurant where I used to work in New York once called us waitresses together for a lecture: "Any woman you see who's alone and don't sit at a table," he warned us, "she is what you call a 'B-girl.' That means she is a girl who puts the buzz on the boys at the bar."

That was in the 1950s, and whether his dry Manhattan wisdom still holds true in the big city I do not know. But way back in Duluth I'd begun to notice that as far as the provincial bars of the

U.S.A. are concerned, a woman on her own can get away with a quiet drink as long as she sits at a table. The moment she bellies up to the bar, she is viewed first of all with lewd appraisal and then, if she is aging or unattractive, she becomes invisible. For sure, the barman in K.C. was in no hurry to notice me or to take my order for a beer and sandwich.

"Everything's out of date in Kansas City," said the woman next to me, after watching my futile attempts at obtaining service. Her name was Lynette. She was a teacher of Islamic studies at a university in my home state. She told me that since I had moved abroad and for some time now, Jersey had replaced Brooklyn as the big American hoot; all a comedian had to do to make his audience crack up was yell: "Anyone here from Jersey?"

"Growing up in Jersey City," I told her, "was sure no joke."

For the next hour, while the men around us hog-called and punched each other's shoulders, she and I talked about life in general, and about the lives we led. When the time came to part, we exchanged addresses. It was a symbolic gesture. We both knew we stood small chance of ever meeting again.

In the elevator at my hotel a serious young woman wearing a name tag pushed the button for the floor above mine.

"Are you a theologian?" she asked me.

"No. I'm just here to have a look at Kansas City."

"Jesus Christ," she said. "Why would anyone come to K.C. who didn't need to?"

A pervasive sadness hangs around Kansas City, like the effluvium of a local industry, and it is not unpleasant. On the contrary, I found it touching. Also, it was there I stumbled upon a major tool for understanding the heart and history of any American city. On an unprecedented impulse I wandered into a local pawnshop; I had never been in one before in my life. Countless musical instruments were ranged on the walls, mostly old brass, tarnished to the color of shadows.

"They used to bring 'em in on Monday morning," said the old

man in charge. "And we used to pretty well know if they didn't turn up to get 'em back by Friday night they weren't ever gonna turn up at all." He sighed. "Believe me, our books could tell you stories."

"You know something? I like Kansas City," I said.

"Well, what we got ourselves here is the ninth or tenth most violent city in the U.S.A.," he replied. "But we're still a mile behind St. Louis."

BUS 27 to ST. LOUIS

Way back in Indianapolis I'd had a bad feeling about that old St. Louis bus, and it lived up to expectations. I sat next to the window about halfway down, bus-left. The day was in a tail-end sulk; the afternoon was gray and heavy. A young woman with greasy blond hair boarded with a pale babe-in-arms and a dark-skinned toddler clinging to her jeans. The toddler whimpered halfheartedly. The seat next to me remained empty, but we were packed in like matches, and I knew it was only a matter of minutes, when a black girl boarded and gave the remaining seats a quick once-over. Everything in her demeanor showed how little she relished sitting next to me, only I happened to be the least of the evils available: the other seats free were next to the mother with the whining toddler or a thin, slack-jawed white man no woman with her wits about her would go anywhere near. The girl frowned and drew into herself as soon as she sat down. In case I cared to speak to her, she quickly enclosed her pretty, haughty, fastidious head between a pair of hissing earphones and turned her eyes away.

"What these here liberals are telling us," the potbelly in front of me told the counterpart at his side, "there is no God, and Jesus Christ is his son."

"When I get home," his neighbor said, "I'm gonna party a little, then crash."

*   *   *

In leafy summer the countryside between K.C. and St. Louis is no doubt lovely, and somewhere on earth are homesick Missourians longing to be back fishing its rivers. But on the bleak day central Missouri passed the windows of my Greyhound, it was nothing to write home about. A disconsolate silence fell on the bus; only the up-and-down sound of the engine could be heard, more clatter than roar, and as familiar to me by that time as wind on the sea to a sailor. Behind me was a monotone conversation between two young men about guns. Guns seemed to be big around there. At even the smallest stops that were barely towns, shops selling guns and ammunition were to be seen, often right next door to liquor stores.

"America is the moral leader of the world," the fat man in front of me was telling his mate. "Trouble anywhere, and who do they call right away for help? America. . . ."

Night fell early and I tried to doze—unsuccessfully, however, thanks to one of our number who as soon as it was dark turned into the Secret Farter. My money was on the social philosopher in the seat in front of me. Once or twice I nearly dropped off, but the moment my thoughts began to drift away from the Greyhound and myself into the misty province that sometimes led to sleep, that flatulent son-of-a-jackass did it again. Without hesitation I'd have shot him through the heart if I'd had a gun. Or maybe opened a switchblade into the back of his gator-skin neck. It scared me how much I hated him.

As our bus plunged through the night into the big, hard outskirts of St. Louis, my journey entered its middle age: an irritable lassitude set in. I felt the full weight of all the miles behind me, and it seemed to me nothing could ever again be as good as what had past. I have heard nice things about St. Louis from people who love the place, but I was in no mood to give it a fair shake. Besides, I was only changing buses there, and the depot was the wrong place to recover my enthusiasm. Humanity seethed thick as flies. Two men next to the seat where I'd parked myself to wait were discussing bank robberies. Every baby was crying. No couples were speaking to each other. Only one pair of youngsters in chains and leather near the gate for the bus to New Orleans were locked in an embrace that looked homicidal. On the floor by my foot lay a broadsheet someone had dropped. I picked it up: it had been issued by the St. Louis City Police Department and was headed "Ten Most Wanted Fugitives." Two of the photographs underneath had "Apprehended" stamped across them. I studied the eight remaining mug shots and surreptitiously compared them to the men leaning against the walls of the bus depot.

Contrary to logic and the evidence of a timetable I'd picked up in K.C., I had to go north, back to Indianapolis, and change buses there in order to end up due east in Louisville. "Don't wave your map at me, lady," said the ticket clerk, who was fed up to his eyeteeth with all our faceless demands. "You think it's bad here, wait'll you get to Louisville."

Every journey is metaphor for a lifetime. For two cents I'd have ended it all right there in St. Louis, Mo.

BUS 28 to INDIANAPOLIS

I think I could have guessed the ultimate destination of my bus to Indianapolis even if I had not seen it written over the front windows: NEW YORK. Once I was on board, it was apparent most of my fellow passengers were reboarders who had long ago established a rare solidarity. Punch lines to running jokes were shouted in the dark—"Where's the sick bag?" "Anybody gotta light?" I had joined a party, though one well past its peak. Already the matron in the window seat next to me was snoring softly. Our driver was taking his time; we could see him through the window of the office dawdling with the dispatchers. Suddenly a young man ran down the aisle to the driver's seat and disengaged the microphone from its cradle. There were cheers from the back of the bus. On the long road into St. Louis from whatever faraway point the journey had originated, he had obviously made himself a favorite with the crowd.

"Welcome on board this Greyhound bus to Noo Yawk Cidee," he said over the mike. "We aim to make your trip as pleasant as possible. We want you to smoke. . . ." There was a shout of approving laughter from the rear and he grew more confident. "The rest room is for your convenience, ladies and gents, and whenever you use it, it is federal law that you light up the smoking material of your choice . . . oh yeah, and you gotta inhale." He bounded on the balls of his feet and seemed determined to hit the roof with his mop of springy curls. "And hey, you guys, alcoholic beverages is what we do best. So, like, anybody found not drinking while on this bus is gonna be kicked off and maybe will have to spend, like, the rest of his life in . . . where the hell are we? Oh yeah, in St. Lou-ee." In one hand he held a can of the soft drink called Mountain Dew, and he waved it around while he was talking. Mountain Dew had not existed when I was a paid-up American, except as a euphemism for booze. But it was a favorite on the buses, especially with the boys in the back, who were often seen nursing cans of Mountain Dew for a very long time. Affecting a drunken slur, the young man said: "Who put Mountain Dew in my Mountain Dew?"

It was the best joke I'd heard on a Greyhound. The guy was a real New Yorker, all right. I had to laugh.

"Hey, ma'am," he said, turning to the sound of my laugh. "Where do you come from?"

I remembered what Lynette had told me and replied: "Jersey City."

"Hey, Joisey Cidee," he cried over the mike, and then, "Noo Joisey!" Right away laughter came from the back of the bus, and a few people applauded. But the passengers were tired, dropping off one by one. Outside, our driver was waving to the dispatchers.

"Seriously, folks," said the young man, his eye on the driver, who was heading our way, "I've flown a lot. I've trained. I've carred. I've boated. And I've bused. And bus is the worst. Except sometimes something happens on a bus. And everyone has fun. And it's magic."

BUS 29 to LOUISVILLE

A man, drunk or drugged, was in the process of sliding slowly to the floor as I disembarked from the bus in Indianapolis and prepared to wait for my outward bus to Louisville.

"Life's gettin' tough in this town," one ticket clerk was saying to another.

"Still, it's not as bad as St. Louis," the other said. I sat in the enclosure for ticketed passengers, trying to keep my eyes open against the drag of gravity. And trying to remember why I had decided to go to Louisville in the first place, except for the fact that it was on the road to Nashville and Memphis. And why not?

Sitting across from me in the waiting area and facing me was a couple who at first seemed oddly matched. He was lanky and quick. His pale blue eyes were fixed in a marksman's squint. She was wide and short-legged. Her dark hair was streaked with gray and hung down her back in the style of a healer or earth mother. He was bleached out. She was ruddy. Physically the two were as unalike as members of the same race could be. She was peeling an orange, slowly and methodically, removing the skin in little strips. Without needing to ask, she handed him a segment of orange. In the gesture and the way they sat, melting together at the edges, it was evident they had been together for a long time. I would have guessed she was ten years or more his senior. I dozed for a moment, and when I woke they were both looking at me.

"Louisville," I said.

"Nashville," he replied.

I nodded. Late at night or very early in the morning when strangers in a depot are inclined to talk, they generally begin by naming their destinations.

"Louisville ain't so bad. Our best city is Denver," he told me. "We travel all over the U.S. and we've worked in just about every state there is, ain't we, honey?" When she smiled up at him, she looked younger. He smiled back and looked older, almost paternal. "We're on our way to see some folks in Tennessee. We'll move on again after Christmas. Been workin' on a ranch in Colorado, that's how come we know about Denver. Denver and Pensacola are our two best places in the U.S. Maybe we'll go back to Denver. Or give Arizona a try. Indianapolis is a mean city. We can't say as we know St. Louis, but that there bus depot they got is about the worst."

For the first time his woman spoke, in a contralto that suited her low-slung, earthy body: "Some places, like, they don't seem all that different from each other. You take Georgia and Alabama. They don't seem all that much different."

"We hitchhike, we ride buses," said the man, "and we've rid the rails, hobo style." With immense pride he added: "Her too. She done it too."

"I've heard it's real hard to do," I said.

"Not if you stick together," he said.

"Nine years this spring," she said.

They were childless of course. Pregnant women and mothers with babes-in-arms do not leap off and on rolling stock, hobo style. But her body was so patently made for childbearing, it must have cost her dearly to deny it. Late at night on the buses, fatigue flays the soul and frees all sorts of nerve endings into the open air: a sudden intuition told me she'd had a conventional husband once, and a family. And then one day—I'd have staked my life on it—along came her traveling man, and she dumped all the rest to ride along beside him. They lifted their heads at precisely the same listening angle, and with identical alert expressions they heard the bus to Nashville being called. They took up their bags, he a sports bag and the bedroll, she a shopping bag and an overstuffed shoulder bag that sat on her hip. Side by side, they walked to the gate. A pair of great and true lovers, I do declare, in a strict formation of two. And I had spotted them in a Greyhound bus depot.

*   *   *

At first sight, Louisville had more than a fair share of pawnshops and parking lots. I was in town for barely one day, time enough to sleep in a real bed and to bathe, and to restock books, trail mix, and bourbon. I found a copy of Kerouac's *On the Road* at the central mall in a bookstore, where Mace sprays and police whistles were also on sale. As for buying liquor in Louisville, after I'd passed the correct money through an aperture in the close-meshed security grille, the proprietor sent a half bottle of Wild Turkey down a chute from his side of the counter to mine.

"Things must be bad in Louisville," I said.

"Not so bad as in Indianapolis."

It was the eve of Thanksgiving and holidays are notoriously hard on the emotions. How else account for the high incidence of heartbreak in Louisville? The girl in the health-food shop had recently been crying; her eyes were red and swollen. I grabbed my trail mix and ran before she could tell me what was wrong. The man behind the desk at the motel was pale and worried. A woman in the room next to mine shouted, "Liar! Liar! Liar!," presumably at the short, bald, barrel-shaped man I'd seen with her in the elevator. In the bar, the waitress seemed distracted—her hands shook when she wrote my order. I opened my paper fast and hid behind it. Two more customers came in and called her away before she could start to pour her heart out to me. They were men in their middle to late thirties, both broad, and on the turn into fatties. The white man sat with his back to me; I saw a bald place about the size of a fifty-cent piece on his crown. His black companion had a two-way radio someplace on his person; it squawked from time to time, and he ignored it.

"She took the house, the car," he said. "And I'm living in a dump. Man, if I hadn't a loved my kid, I'd a disappeared."

The white man replied: "It's easy for me to say I wanna be supportive. But my ex has got seven hundred and fifty dollars coming in a month, and the girls are living with us, not her. You're gonna be in that same spot, too."

"Geez, man, what can I do?"

"Well, I can tell you a way, but it will cost you. You gotta go see a psychologist, that's what you gotta do. You gotta go and get this guy into court on your side. A judge likes facts, so you get this psychologist to say the atmosphere is starting to upset your kid emotionally. That's one idea you really oughtta think about. There are psychologists out there, they charge you twenty-five dollars an hour. But if they vindicate you, it's worth it."

Suddenly the commentary from the wall-sized TV over the bar went manic and both men paused to watch a touchdown being scored. I waved to the waitress for a refill.

"Has there been any research on that psychology stuff?" the black man asked his companion.

"Write to the Bar Association and ask them. The public has a right to know."

BUS 30 to NASHVILLE

A deal was going down at the depot: a heavyset man wearing a red turtleneck and lots of gold chains and a pale youngster in jeans approached each other from far ends of the room and met in the middle. For a few seconds they whispered, head to head; still conferring, they walked outside together. Ten minutes later the older man returned, then the boy, and afterward they kept carefully out of each other's way.

Louisville slipped behind us, and I waited for the rush. Even on short, brutish laps of the journey when tempers were thin, it never let me down: soon after lift-off was always a moment of the pure delight that gulls must feel when they trust their wings to the prevailing breeze. I had become a Greyhound junkie, an addict, who couldn't bear to hang around anywhere for long without a fix, not even in Louisville, where there was, like, lots of historical stuff. My brother, a Civil War buff, could easily have spent a week or two there just looking at graveyards—an odd pastime, I've often told him, for a doctor. Small birds were sitting on the telephone lines, I noticed, and that meant rain in North Dakota. But it was a bright Thanksgiving Day in Kentucky.

In front of me, fifth row, bus-right, was a couple from somewhere in the Middle East. He was thin and wore a precise little jet-black beard. His wife was swathed in layers of western clothes; a dark headscarf was tied under her chin. Reflected in the window at her side I saw her profile, hovering like a vapory falcon over the countryside. From time to time they exchanged a few words in a guttural tongue, and then she'd rummage in a bag at her feet for an aerosol and spray the air around their heads with a highly scented deodorant. About an hour out of Louisville when we stopped for a break in a burger joint, they took all their belongings off the bus with them, right down to the furled umbrella stowed in the overhead rack. She waited at a table with their shopping bags around her, while her husband, in front of me at the counter, asked for boiling water for their thermos flask. When I passed with my coffee, they were brewing their own tea. A few minutes later, as we were jostling to reboard at the door to the bus, I stepped back and brushed against the Arab woman, grazing the back of her voluminous raincoat. I turned to apologize, and she was whirling around toward me, crying: "What! Who! Don't!" She shrank from me, her eyes full of revulsion. There was nothing a bus person could have done or said to make things right with her.

Little traffic was on the road. We passed an airport stranded in a sea of cars. Our bus was not as crowded as recent buses had been. Across the aisle from me was an ancient shriveled Japanese man accompanied by a boy of ten or twelve. The old man spoke not a word of English; his grandson, or great-grandson, spoke just enough to ascertain from me that they were on the right bus for Nashville and to make sure the compartment at the rear was indeed a toilet. He adjusted the lap rug whenever it slipped off the old man's knees, and when we hit a bumpy stretch he patted the frail hand that rested for the entire journey like a dry leaf on his sleeve. From somewhere in the back a man's voice, monotone and weak, was saying: "I left home at eighteen. I'm thirty-two. My dad don't know me as a grown man. I'm goin' home to live with him so he can get to know me."

Real Americans were at home tucking into turkey. We aliens and misfits had the road pretty much to ourselves.

The sky was turning a streaky gray. Knobbly hills knuckled into one another under a brown winter blanket. At most of the houses we passed, families had come together for a feast; six or seven cars were drawn into their drives. At Fort Knox the depot was locked for the holiday, but on an outside wall was a row of public telephones. Hunched over them were homesick soldiers crooning into the receivers to their girls and moms while their mates hung around waiting their turns. I did not feel at all left out of the festivities. I was happy where I was, and thankful.

The fields turned greener, and airborne scavengers skimmed bales of hay that were waiting for collection. The word "Dixie" started popping up on ads and hand-lettered signboards that were often misspelled or unfinished: "Denny's Last C ance Dixie Motel: Ha py T anks iving. Rooms for eniors," "Uncl Dave's Dixie Pawn Shop." Our bus passed a house half roofed in tar paper; a beaten-up old sofa sat out in the front yard. The man in back coughed long and hard. In front of me the Middle Eastern woman fumigated us again with her spray. Shortly after dark we arrived in Nashville. Tenderly the little boy from Japan helped his grandfather off the bus. While they waited for their luggage, I approached him. "For you," I said, and handed him a fragment of Idaho Picture Jasper I had been carrying in my pocket ever since Boise. I'd bought it for a dollar out of a box of similar bits, and often taken it out while we were crossing Wyoming and Nebraska to compare its striations and colors to the view outside the windows: nature, in subterranean galleries, had produced a perfect miniature of the wide, golden land above. The impulse to give the stone to the boy was so sudden and unexpected, it surprised me as much as it surprised him. Feeling lightheaded, I got out of the depot fast.

Right from the moment I stood outside my motel on Music Row and saw the sign in big letters—"Welcome to the Clogging Convention"—the whole of Nashville and all in it seemed to me to be in the grip of harmless folly. I asked the desk clerk where I could find a classic Thanksgiving dinner. He was horrified to learn I had no car; the only decent restaurant he knew that was open was "much too far to walk," and a taxi would be impossible to find on the holiday. The following day I saw the restaurant he meant, and it was merely six blocks away. But I had taken him at his word and settled for a diner across the street that was not many notches above a typical Greyhound stop, except for its waitress service (server service?). Riva was my server. She wore skin-tight jeans and very high heels. Her yellow hair had been molded into a tower that looked solid until she shifted slightly so that light from the neon strips in the windows shone through and showed it weightless as cotton candy. No sooner had she gone off with my order for "frahd shree-amp"—they were all out of turkey—than the door to the kitchen opened and three of her co-workers emerged in a line; except that two of them were brunettes, they were Riva's spitting image. Obviously what was teetering down the aisles dishing out food to those of us with no place better to go for our Thanksgiving dinners was not a uniform of the place or, as I had first thought, Riva's personal B-movie taste; it was "the Nashville look."

A surreal zaniness was in the air. At breakfast next morning, a boy of about fifteen was seated next to me. On his shirt was embroidered CLOG FLORIDA! Across from him sat a woman, the wrong age and attitude to be his mother, close to sixty and spinsterish. But she must have been in loco parentis, for when the boy said, "I'd like a great big ol' pile of eggs and grits to soak 'em up," she frowned and shook her head. "That's how I was taught to eat breakfast," he complained. My guess was that the poor kid was in training for a clog-dancing competition. His keeper shook her head again, firmly, no. "Well," the boy told our waitress, "guess I'll just settle for bagel and cream cheese."

"Don't have cream cheese," the waitress said. "Waitin' on the man to bring it."

"Well, guess I'll just have a bagel," said the boy.

"Don't have bagels," the waitress said. "I'll bring you an English muffin." She tucked the pencil into her billow of yellow hair and wiggled away to the kitchen.

A little later, looking around downtown, I bumped into a woman accompanied by a pussycat on a leash; the cat was wearing a tiny baseball hat.

"My own invention," the woman said. "I wanted to call it 'Cat Hat' but I couldn't on account of Dr. Seuss, so I call it 'Hat for a Cat.' I hadda cat once smoked cigarettes. He died of leukemia. And I have a cat wears glasses." She was a pretty woman with strange green eyes that were tip-tilted like the eyes of a you-know-what. She took a small album of photos out of her bag, and right there in the street showed me a snapshot of a cat smoking a cigarette, and another one wearing glasses.

Was there no end to genial Nashville nuttiness, I wondered? And of course there was an end to it. Before midday I had started to notice the city contained an awful lot of law firms and loan companies, both the antitheses of eccentricity. That evening I went for a drink at the motel and sat right up there with the boys at the bar. The TV suspended at the far end of the room was showing a football game with the sound turned down, while some millionaire warbler was singing on the background stereo: "Will there be any freight trains tonight ... any boxcars ... ?" Two other customers, both men, were leaning on the bar directly across from me. They had come in as strangers to each other, and I had overheard their introductions. One was a local; he wore a cowboy hat and a plaid shirt that barely buttoned over his paunch. The other was a brawny traveler from Australia, too well heeled for the buses by the look of him, probably crossing America in his own car. The bar was tended by an upswept woman on heels who finally sashayed my way, singing with the background music: "You spend an awful lot of time in Massachusetts . . . when the icy wind blows through you . . . remember me in Tennessee . . ."

I sipped my bourbon slowly. The Australian was telling the local man that he was a sharpshooter back home in New South Wales, and he asked about competitive shooting in the Nashville area.

"Well, I dunno 'bout organized competitions. But there's sections of this town, if you go, you better carry your gun with ya," the local replied. "And then y'all can shoot at some monkeys. Know what ah mean?"

In front of me at the breakfast buffet next morning was a girl of nineteen or twenty. Her angry eyes were set in a face that would have been angelic, except it was inflated like a balloon about to pop. She helped herself to three fried eggs, eight strips of bacon, grits, and biscuits, slapping the food onto her plate as if she were thinking: "Take that!" "We need more forks over here!" shouted her equally huge mother to the passing waitress. At their table was a third enormous woman, much older, and a relatively trim, oldish man in a cowboy hat who was reading a paper and paying not the slightest attention to his companions, not even when the old woman bowed her head and thanked God for what they were about to receive. "Are those grits ready yet?" the girl's mother called to the waitress. The girl ordered chocolate milk instead of coffee. Then they guzzled in silence, lifting their heads only to ask short questions: "Is it raining?" asked the girl. "Is it eight o'clock yet?" asked her mother. "Who's got the thermos?" asked the old lady. The man went on reading his paper. Nobody could be bothered to answer.

As I passed the public telephone on my way to pay my bill at the desk, a young man was purring into the receiver: "You got such pretty hair. I seen how pretty it is. Think I'll ever get to touch it and find out how soft it is?" Simultaneously, the music system was piping in a woman's voice: "I cover my ears, I close my eyes. I still hear your voice tellin' me lies. . . ."

A bouncer built like a gigantic keg used his big, hard belly to bump a drunk, thunk-thunk-thunk, past me out the door of the depot into the street. Under the chair next to mine near the Memphis gate was a pair of men's lace-up shoes, side by side. The toes were turned in slightly, and they had so patent an air of waiting that a young woman about to sit down changed her mind when she saw them, and moved along. A lonesome, bleary man in bedroom slippers shuffled by. At the end of the aisle another lonesome, shuffling man met him; together they went into the men's room, and they had not yet emerged by the time my bus was called. On the wall next to our gate were thank-you letters from Mrs. Chranach's and Mrs. Timmon's second-grade classes.

"Thank you for letting us learn about Greyhound. You maid us very happy. Did you know Greyhound is transportation?"

BUS 31 to MEMPHIS

We were riding into weather. Under a dark sky the land was the color of cedar chips and patched with dull green. Barns and houses set well back from the road were tumbledown and some of them were unfinished, as if homesteaders had run out of steam halfway and thought: "Oh, what the heck." Just before sunset we passed a ravine where four or five abandoned cars had been pushed into a heap. Beyond them in a little thicket lay a dead bus. Brushwood grew through its broken windows and there were splotches of rust on its side. I caught a whiff of the great American delta, a riverine smell of forgotten things that ran with us for a little while, and then, like the railway bridge set at a tipsy angle parallel to our road, it veered off and collapsed into the falling night.

OKLAHOMA CITY —
DENVER

The most lovable traveling companion

When I left Nashville I had half a mind to change buses in Memphis and go straight on to Bald Knob, Arkansas. But the rain was coming down in a solid sheet, and the idea of getting off the bus in a hick town in the wee hours of the morning in a downpour, then trying to find shelter for the night, daunted this intrepid lady traveler, I'm afraid. Besides, Bald Knob held no known appeal beyond its name, and the college boy next to me on the bus out of Nashville had not stopped raving about Memphis, or recommending that I stay there. The kid was a Greyhound virgin; he had taken to the bus after a quarrel with his girlfriend at her folks' house, where they'd been for the holiday. He'd stormed out and she had stayed behind with the car. Not only was he not bothered, it was clear he didn't care very much if he never saw his girl again. Memphis was lively, he told me, Memphis was fun. Memphis was sexy, or so he implied. And his girlfriend was less of all those good things than Memphis was. He kept up his rave review of Memphis until we were on the outskirts of town, where he fell suddenly into a worried silence. I knew what was troubling him. I was a woman, after all, and on my own. What if I had mistaken his enthusiasm for an invitation? Before we came to a complete halt in the depot, the kid was on his feet and running like a baby bunny.

I checked into a big chain motel near the depot. I showered and changed into my skirt, then I went downstairs for dinner. There was not a soul in the dining room. The only waiter, the one white employee I had seen in the motel, was a gaunt man in his sixties, a priestly figure somehow, whose mind seemed fixed on higher things. He led me to a two-seater next to a window in a corner. I ordered a double bourbon with water on the side. The menu was on the table and I tried to think about it. But it was raining hard in Memphis, for the first time in years I found myself craving a cigarette, and I felt a little sweetly blue. When the waiter asked what I wanted to eat, the deep-fried catfish seemed appropriate somehow.

The bag lady came into the dining room while he was putting a plate of overdressed lettuce in front of me, and a basket of soft rolls with pats of butter substitute on the side. Not that I knew her to be a bag lady, not right away. From a distance she looked stylish, even distinguished. When the waiter turned from my table and saw her, he cried out a name—it sounded like "Ellen" or "Melanie"—and went toward her with his arms outstretched, while she waited coquettishly, her head cocked to one side. But when he was close enough to hug her, I saw him hesitate and recoil slightly; he took her hand instead. They sat down together at a table by the kitchen door and talked softly. He shrugged once and threw his hands out as far as they'd go. Sometimes she laughed at things he said; it was a laugh faked to please him, not mirthful in the least.

The waiter brought the fish to my table and took away my salad plate. He waved to the bag lady as he passed into the kitchen and motioned her to stay put. But as soon as he was out of sight, she rose and made straight for me. Only when I saw the coin-sized circles of rouge on her cheeks, and she was close enough so I caught her smell of flowers left too long in unchanged water, did I know her to be a bag lady. The bag itself was a gladstone of fake leather. "Old and cracked. Just like me," she said ingratiatingly, and she put it on the table. Then she pulled out the chair across from mine and sat down. Her red woolen hat was ragged at the edges and her hair looked like unraveled knitting the color of dirty straw. There was a forced chirpiness in the way she held her head, and in her voice when she asked: "All on your own, then?" She was not looking at me, however. Her eyes had been drawn to the glass that once held bourbon and was still beside my plate. "All on your own. But you're doin' okay, right? Now me, I never done wuss. It's rainin'. And I lost my glasses this afternoon. It's rainin' and without my glasses I am 'blond.' I am 'blond' as a bat. Got nowhere to go. Gotta walk the streets this whole night, hiding in every nook and cranny." The waiter was watching us grimly from the kitchen door, not knowing what would be the best thing to do. "Memphis is no fun when it rains," she said. "No suh. Memphis is a hard, hard town in rain or shine. But wuss in the rain." She licked her lips; dark purple lipstick ran every which way in hair-thin tributaries. Was she my age? Perhaps a little older. A feeling came to me inexplicably of being in familiar territory. I held out the basket of rolls. Without a word, she took one. I passed her the butter substitute and, handle first, a knife to spread it with. As she chewed, her swollen, runny eyes were fixed on my glass; it contained no more than half an inch or so of liquid, mostly melted ice, and a twist of lemon. I held out the breadbasket again. She snapped at me: "I'm an alcoholic!" But she took the last two rolls and dropped them into her bag.

The waiter hovered behind her. I nodded to him. No sweat. Everything was cool. She wouldn't share the catfish—she made a face when I offered it. But after I'd pushed some french fries onto a side plate and put them between us, she tucked into them, using her fingers daintily enough, though they were etched with grime.

"I never thought, ever, ever thought to go so low. You know? One day you're up, okay. Flyin' high. Next night you're walkin' in the shadows. And it's rainin'. And now I have lost my glasses. Gotta scurry like a rat out there. It is fuckin' rainin'. And I have lost my fuckin' glasses!" She slammed her hand on the table clumsily, a butter pat caught on the side of it. Her eyes were streaming and suddenly there was froth at the corner of her mouth. "I am an alcoholic! Hear what I'm sayin' to you? I am a drunk!"

Immediately, the waiter was there, pulling back her chair and tugging her to her feet.

"All I need is a drink!" she cried as he hustled her away.

*   *   *

He walked back slowly to my table. Strands of wiry gray hair had been shaken loose from where he'd plastered them across his bald place; they hung down the side of his face. "I used to play piano," he said. "She used to sing. We used to work together." He was not looking at me but to the street outside and the rain that fell in slivers through the light from our window. "I coulda wrote the movie," he said.

BUS 32 to OKLAHOMA CITY

The ticket clerk at the Memphis depot was a handsome young man the color of milk chocolate. He suggested a shorter route to Wichita, back through Kansas City, but I told him emphatically, no. I had seen K.C., and I preferred to go via Little Rock and Oklahoma City, two places I had never been to before, even if it was by night and traveling in the dark.

"Ah, I see," he said. "Not travelin' fo' speed. Not travelin' to get the job done. Y'all travelin' fo' the adventure."

And his smile was like the sun coming out.

Next to where I stood waiting for the bus, so close I could have touched them without stretching, a white man with a piggy profile, wearing a good shirt and pressed jeans, passed a plastic envelope to a black man, who was thin and as strung out as a crossbow.

"Hey, man, I'll do you a favor sometime. You know me," the black man said, and then he left fast for the exit, singing "Oooooooooh! Yeah!"

Beside our line, in bucket seats, sat a rangy cowboy and his woman. He was shouting at her: "Who you sayin' don't make sense? You sayin' I don't make sense?" She sat with her head bowed, a heap of shopping bags on the floor around her feet. "It makes sense we go and get a beer with these ten bags we got? You're sayin' that makes sense? Girl, you don't make sense. Girl, you are crazy!"

* * *

A few paces ahead of me in my line was a balding, bespectacled young man reading a newspaper. His fine suede jacket was trimmed in dark fur. By the time I clambered on board, he was settled into a seat near the front. The spectacles gave him an academic air, as out of place on that bus as it could be. He caught my eye and there was a flicker of wary recognition between us. I went past him quickly and hurried to find a seat on my own.

Of the several states I had to cross by night, the one I most regret not being able to see is Arkansas. The moment we passed the loop in the bridge over the Mississippi where Arkansas begins, I had a hunch something strange and interesting was going on out there. At every little flyspeck town where we stopped I felt a great desire to get off the bus and sniff around for a day or two. Looking back, I think I ought to have done it. But there was still a bit of me clinging for all it was worth to forward planning. And I was bound for Kansas, was I not? So I let the state of Arkansas pass me by, and took from it only bare impressions of something mysterious, sighing and ticking in the Ozark night, that someday I'll go back to contemplate at leisure.

BUS 33 to WICHITA

A lime-green dawn was rising over Oklahoma City, not flattering to those of us leaving our bus after a sleepless night. As I entered the station, the man in the suede jacket and I came nose-to-nose by the gate where he was waiting for his bags.

"I usually fly," he told me, "but I was not going to pay three hundred dollars for less than one hour on a plane." His tone was asking me what *my* excuse was.

"I *like* this," I told him.

Nearby a bunch of boys were lighting up and exchanging jokes in a dialect I found incomprehensible. Sleepy children poked around the garbage bins. Some kids were crying, others were coughing and picking their noses. A mother called: "Troy, you cut that out right now, or I'll smack . . ." An old man, the worse for drink, or maybe mad, engaged the green-tinged space next to him in animated conversation. The man in the suede jacket took off his glasses and wiped them clean on a tissue before he put them back.

"You *like* this," he said.

"Yes," I said. "I *like* the bus."

"It takes all kinds, I guess," he said. He made a face and turned away.

The windows of our bus to Wichita were caked with yellowish mud. I had to strain to see what we were passing. Maybe Jack Kerouac was too citified and brain-burning for the flatlands; he thought Kansas was boring. But what I could see through the driver's windshield was the stirring landscape of the plains, and not boring at all. It was bewitching and wild. Set anything rolling out there on the flat—a barrel of beer, a wagon wheel, a new idea—and it'll be bound to travel all the way around the world and come back from behind you. The way that state is made, when a Kansas mother sees her child off into adventures, she has to stand at her front door waving good-bye until nightfall. They say when the twisters blow over Kansas, with nothing in their way to stop them, they pick their paths as daintily as geisha girls.

The flatness of the surrounding countryside exerts a malevolent spell on drivers, and the short walk from my hotel in Wichita to the post office was hair-raising for the rivers of careless traffic. Wichita was probably a really nice place to live once upon a time, before it was eviscerated by malls and became, relative to its size, as unkind to pedestrians as any city I've known, except Los Angeles and Djakarta. When I had posted my cards home, all I required was a few hours' sleep, for I was feeling every one of the miles behind me: five or six thousand weights around my ankles. And I wanted some soap powder; my underwear had been done so often in hand soap, it was like wearing a motel room next to my skin. Sleep was easy—a bed was all I needed. When I woke around noon, however, soap powder presented a problem.

*   *   *

It was sad to see what must have been a thriving main street lying bare as the spine of a critter long dead on the prairie. The sole remaining shop of human proportions I found near my motel in central Wichita was a bookstore, more a glorified newsstand: no soap. And the mall was too far to go on foot, even if I had been inclined that way. Malls are the pits. They have not evolved to suit the community's needs; they have been designed to inspire fake longings and false dependencies, not least on the automobile, which is making America at large forget what feet are for, and is starting to impose a national body shape adapted to the hollow of a driver's seat.

"Isn't there a drugstore?" I asked the proprietor of the lonely little bookstore.

"Gone to the mall," he said.

"I hate malls," I said.

He sighed and nodded: "You can say that again."

I hate malls. Malls are stagnant pools in which nothing circulates except the same old crap. There are no secrets in malls. I am told they contain sordid little vices, but only for the crass and the young; there are no temptations for the worldly, no cathedrals, no enlightenment, no windswept corners to turn and find yourself suddenly in a community of artists, or streetwalkers, or Albanian immigrants, or gay bars, or Chinese restaurants. There are no neighborhoods in malls, nobody lives over the store, the light is artificial, and mostly malls are closed when you need company. Very little as harmful as the mall has happened to the soul of my homeland since I left all those years ago.

"How true!" said the bookseller in Wichita. "How true!"

The desk clerk at my hotel sent me on a death-defying walk to a gas station and minimart where, he said, I might find soap powder. The woman there was sympathetic, and awfully sorry she didn't stock soap powder. However, she did have boiled peanuts. I bought a few to find out what they were like. They were interesting in their way. But I would have swapped them for a small box of Tide.

BUS 34 to COLORADO SPRINGS

Four A.M. in Wichita, Kansas: the downtown streets, frozen in the dark before dawn, were waiting for a good idea.

"I love the night. Time lasts longer at night," said the hotel security guard who gave me a lift to the depot. "I always choose this watch. Nobody's out but the street people and it feels like anything can happen. Even here." Inside the depot young men were forming little groups, making parties at the crossroads.

"Hey man, these here are ten-karat gold," one bruiser was telling another. His big hands were spilling over with gold chains. "I needa get 'em fixed, you know?"

"Where you goin', man?"

"Jackson."

"I know a pawnshop there, man. They'll fix 'em good for you."

Boarding behind me were two old men bound for Denver.

"I got this darn tooth trouble," one of them said.

"Well, my paralysis has subsided somewhat," the other replied. "The swelling of the ventricles in my brain has almost all gone down."

"Almost all gone down," the first man echoed wistfully. "I'm real glad to hear that."

I took my time stowing my bag on the overhead rack so the two old men could exercise their priority if they wished and take the front seat. They both passed by, however, and gratefully I slipped in behind the big clean windshield. We left Wichita and entered a space between night and day: to the south the horizon was indigo blue, to the north it was black and set with stars. Although the sky behind us bulged and blushed, the sun stayed under cover so long I began to wonder if this was to be the great day at last, the one that fails to happen. Then—a moment after we passed what was advertised on a billboard as the world's largest hand-dug well—kapowee! The mother and father of all dawns broke over Kansas. A white frame house set back from the road in a thicket glowed like a paper lantern lit from inside, and morning went into full swing.

Railroad tracks crisscrossed our road for a few miles and every time we rode over them our driver reared up in his seat like a horseman. When a husky young man came forward from the back and asked him, please, to turn down the heat, he replied: "I'll do it, pardner." He very much resembled an old friend of mine in London: he had the same upstanding hair and air of banked enthusiasms. I wondered if he too told Irish jokes and had a picaresque history with women. We had been out for an hour or so before the old man with the darn tooth came and sat on the aisle seat behind him.

"Howdy," said the old man. "I just had my teeth pulled in Wichita. They hadda use a saw."

"Musta been stuck in there real good," the driver said.

"Back in Denver," the old man went on, "they wanted forty-five dollars a tooth. Got it done in Wichita for twenty-five."

"I had mine done in Mexico," said the driver. "Twenty-one teeth, dirt cheap. But," he added with immense generosity of spirit, "they didn't need to use the saw on me."

"Yup," said the old-timer. "They hadda use the saw and every damn thing. Them dentist fellas said they'd never seen nothin' like the way them teeth of mine was stuck in there." He leaned forward, speaking man to man. "After they done it, I stayed in a motel," he said. "On that late-night TV channel they had a movie about a young girl, no more'n eighteen, falls in love with her friend's father. Goes to bed with him. She puts this camera on top of the shelf over the bed and there she is. Nekkit." He sat back. "I'm not watchin' them films anymore."

"Guess you'd better not," said the driver, who was twenty years younger, and in his prime. "Could give you a heart attack."

"Yup. You said it. It could do that," the old man said thoughtfully. "It coulda gave me a heart attack." He sat in silence for a while. "Well, nice talkin' with ya," he said, and I watched him return cautiously and slowly, gripping the backs of the seats, to where his mate with wonky ventricles was asleep.

Almost imperceptibly we started climbing and the grassland became dry brown under a thin cover of snow. Clumps of sagebrush appeared on rocks and slopes, looking for all the world like sea urchins stranded out on the central plains. In the middle of nowhere the driver recognized a demarcation invisible to the rest of us, and told us it was time to put our watches back an hour. We passed an old boxcar on top of an amber hill; it was painted canary yellow and had curtains in the windows. I'd come home to worse in my time. Then we were over the border into Colorado, and immediately everything became a little untidy. Broken-down vehicles lay abandoned not far off the road and piles of empty beer crates lay around half covered in snow. More and more cars carried plates from Arizona and New Mexico. An element of fiesta crept into the surroundings. We passed a café called The Santa Fe that advertised a happy hour, and the architecture took on an adobe look that would have been silly and affected just a few miles to the east. We were approaching the great western playgrounds of America.

"California is down the drain," a woman complained somewhere behind me.

"California *is* the drain," a man replied.

Our route was crossing fields that lay in vast striations of gold on either side of us all the way to the clear, blue horizon. The road was straight as string and showed no inclination at all to deviate from a taut line. Far, far ahead where the verges met and blended into their constant distant point, something flickered against the bright clouds, and again, and suddenly, no bigger from where we sat than a vanilla ice-cream sundae, white on white and sparkling, there was Pikes Peak, outrider of the Rocky Mountain complex.

"Gosh," I said.

"Whenever I see it I think how it must have looked to them in their wagons the first time they saw it," the driver said. "I know their life was hard and dangerous. But I'd trade."

We stopped for a late lunch outside Lamar at the Rancher Restaurant. All the other passengers were in couples, except for the boys from the back of the bus who constituted an entire college wrestling team on its way to a match in Denver. They sat down to eat en masse, hillocks of brawny American manhood that had the waitresses in fits of giggles. I sat alone near the back. As I was raising my cup for a sip, there came an almighty crash of breaking crockery from the kitchen behind me.

"Irma!" a man's voice roared.

I was halfway out of my seat and turning when a woman shouted back: "Whaddya want?"

"Bring a broom, Irma," shouted the man. "Clean up this mess!"

It's the sort of thing I imagine must happen to Janes and Marys and Tracys and Samanthas all the time. But for us Irmas it's pretty rare, and for some time afterward, even when the Rancher Restaurant was far behind us, I had the strangest feeling I had been spotted. Or was being summoned.

Our driver ended his shift in Pueblo, where a fair, youngish woman in overalls was waiting for him. I watched them drive off together in a pickup truck; she was behind the wheel. As they passed the departure bay of the depot, he turned to wave to me, and I waved back the way you do to an old friend you expect to see again someday soon. After that, it was a hop to Colorado Springs, though we all had to change to a different bus. A big girl with a knapsack snaffled the front seat and spread herself across it, glaring a challenge. When a very old woman using a cane tried to object, the girl thumped her big belly and said: "I gotta baby in there." The possibility was indisputable, and the old lady limped on down the aisle to sit across from me, eight rows back, bus-right.

The setting sun blew up behind the mountain crags in a final explosion of lurid goo. Shivering a little, I watched from the veranda of my motel. While checking in I had spotted a washing machine in a shed off the parking lot, and I wasn't wearing much more than the Driza Bone: practically every stitch I owned was being processed. Nobody knows better than a long-distance bus traveler how truly close is cleanliness to godliness. I reveled in the warm glow, so like virtue and righteousness, that accompanied the unloading of my clean, dry clothes from the tumbler. Back in my room, idly, I opened the dresser drawers. The first, the second, the third were empty, as they usually are. However, in the fourth and final drawer I found a stack of magazines: *Lusty Latins and Dusky Maids, Pictorial: A Collection of Sensuous Black Women*, and *Players Classic Black Girls*. As I was flicking through the last one, a Polaroid snapshot fell out of the back pages. Taken in that very room, or its mirror image, it showed a young white girl rocking on the lap of a black man. Her skinny pale legs in high heels streamed, one up and one down, from under a tight black sheath short enough to show bruises on her thighs. Countless times in the urban depots, especially of the Midwest, I had noticed stunned and slovenly young mothers keeping their kiddies quiet with potato chips and sweet drinks, and each time I wondered what she had been before she'd grown old too fast. And there she was. Under a fuzzy blond mop, she grinned out at me; she had the feral, triangular face of a stray kitten. The man was fully clothed too; he wore a suit of electric blue. His smile had congealed; it was going to need scraping off the pan. He must have gone hot, then cold, with embarrassment: another bad boy caught in the act. My guess was he used the pictures of fabulous black women to get himself in the mood. Then he only had to close his eyes: all cats are dark in the dark.

In the top drawer of the bedside table was the usual Bible. I tucked the Polaroid between two pages of Genesis.

The girl behind the desk recommended a restaurant and was eager to discourage me from walking to it. It was too far, she said, "especially at night." But when I arrived at the place, it turned out to be only a few blocks away. "What time do you want me to come back for you?" asked the driver of my taxi, a mountainous young man sitting in a litter of candy wrappers and Coke cans. "Oh, I wouldn't want you to do that, ma'am," he said, when I told him I'd walk back after dinner. It seems the previous night a young soldier had been beaten to death outside the pretty clock tower in the square, all for a few dollars in his wallet. "That's the situation, ma'am. Colorado Springs is a town in the icy grip of fear."

"I'm really sorry to hear that."

"Well, I come from Chicago originally," he said. "And basically, this here is a nice, clean place to live."

The next day presented itself as a bright December morning in the mountain air. Downtown on the main street I chose a pleasant little café for breakfast.

"I hear they found another girl," the woman at the cash desk was telling a blue-rinsed customer as I came in. "I hear she'd been raped too, before he strangled her."

"It's got so I do all my shopping before nightfall," the other woman said.

"Would you say this is a town in the icy grip of fear?" I asked my waitress. She was a pretty brunette who told me she had come originally from L.A.

"Down the road in Pueblo for a while back there they were averaging a murder a week," she said. "I guess it's moved here."

"Sorry you left L.A.?"

"You gotta be joking! This is a real nice place to live."

The local bus from Colorado Springs to the suburb of Old Colorado was truly the public transport of a car-addled community, loaded with rejects from the Department of Motor Vehicles. A young junkie nodded off across the back seats; a madwoman sitting behind the bored, disaffected driver declaimed in her made-up language; in front of the door was a tall woman wearing a pink and blue gas mask. Tired people up and down the aisle sat looking at the floor in front of their feet. Only the girl next to me was sparky and in good health. She told me she had recently arrived in Colorado, another émigré from Southern California, and she had not yet had time to get hold of a car.

"Are you glad you left California?" I asked.

The madwoman began keening one shrill note, and the junkie pulled himself together enough to shout, "Shut the fuck up!" before he slumped back into his seat.

"Oh, my, yes, I am," the girl said. "This is such a nice, clean place to live."

BUS 35 to DENVER

The scenery promised to be spectacular and I would have liked the front seat, but it was taken fair and square by a young woman with a beautiful baby sleeping in a cradle at her side. The dashing black driver must have had a party to attend in Denver; on the seat behind him was a suit still in the dry cleaner's bag, laid out carefully across the available space so it wouldn't crease. I settled for the second row, bus-left. There were very few people traveling to Denver and I had every reason to expect to keep both seats to myself. The driver had already closed the door when a late passenger appeared out of nowhere and pounded on it. She was one of those dramatic creatures who must be said to descend on a company, even when she has just hauled herself up the steps of a bus.

The driver gazed at her, openmouthed. She was no spring chicken, but her eyes were fringed with the best lashes money could buy, and rhinestone earrings fell nearly to her shoulders from under a hat peaked like a Tatar chieftain's cap. The black coat she wore was fitted and gaped slightly over her hips; it was trimmed with phony leopard skin, and on her hands were tight black leather gloves. She stood for a moment surveying us all, then she fixed the driver in her eyebeam.

"I heff motion sickness, dollink," she said. "If I don't sit front seat, I womit."

"Sorry, ma'am," he said, "the front seat is reserved for mothers with babies."

A blazing look at the cowering occupants of the front seat, and she said: "If there is occident, dot vot you are in with baby is called death seat." Then she turned her attention to the seat behind the driver. "I sit dot one," she said. "If I don't sit dot one, I sure going to womit."

"Look, lady," the driver said, "that seat is reserved for old people."

She drew herself up, looked at us all, who were looking at her with astonishment.

"There are no old pipple on dis bus. You see any old pipple on dis bus?"

"Well," he said, "that seat is also reserved for the handicapped."

"Aha. I see no handicapped pipple on dis bus. You see handicapped people on dis bus, dollink? And besides, handicapped pipple want that everyone should treat them like everyone else. They do not want to be treated different. You did not know dot?"

The driver shook his head, scratched it.

"I sure going to womit," she said.

A good man knows when he's beaten. Gently the driver lifted his Sunday suit in his arms. Did I mind if he draped it over the empty place next to me? Of course I did not mind. And our quietly exultant Zsa Zsa sat herself straight and queenly in the seat, now free, in front of mine.

We were passing through a land of outsize beauty. Peaks lolloped into the distance as far as the eye could follow. Some were dark red, others white with snow. Natural bastions of wild rock on summits had the same projecting angles and crenellations as their man-made counterparts in Europe. It was easy to imagine that a chivalrous history had been enacted out there once upon a time, by nations so ancient not even the Indians remembered them, except dimly, perhaps, as giants of a miraculous past.

"Are you feeling okay, lady?" asked the driver every so often. "Not gonna 'womit,' are you?"

But she held her peace and smiled out at the mountainous terrain as if it were all her own back garden.

*   *   *

My mother came to Denver from Indiana with her parents when her father was diagnosed with tuberculosis. In 1917 he died there after several years of ultimately futile treatment. In spite of the sad reason they lived in Denver, to this day my mother remembers that time as the only happy part of her childhood. The golden-domed city set among white mountains came down to me through the telling as a magic place, and her father, my grandfather, as a gentle, scholarly man who adored his little girl. A month before he died, she sat beside him one day on the lawn of the hospital where patients used to be wheeled out in their beds and settled in ranks to take the good air. He stretched out her hand, enclosed in his own, which was already frail and almost weightless; pointing toward the horizon and the snowcapped mountains, he said: "See how beautiful life is." That became mother's creed, and in due course I tried to make it mine too. See how beautiful life is. Not as simple as it sounds.

My mother's only quibble with her father's memory concerns a set of wondrous books she believed, when she was little, held all the spells and wisdom of his house. After he died they were given by my grandmother to the hospital; probably she thought they were too heavy to carry back to Indiana and not worth the trouble. Mother thinks he should have seen to it that they were left to her. Otherwise, stories concerning my Grandpa Auerbach were all good. While I was growing up he became my secret guardian, to whom I entrusted all sorts of whispered hopes: for rescue, for love and acceptance, for inherited gifts. Of course, long before middle age I knew better than to put my trust in shadows. And by the time I saw for myself the mile-high city of gold, Denver, enclosed in a greasy yellow bubble of foul air visible from afar, I could say without surprise: "So much for the castles of childhood." And so much, it went without saying, for the shining knights.

*   *   *

The next afternoon, after a little sight-seeing, I set out by taxi to look for landmarks of my family's past. The driver came from Jamaica; his accent was rich as molasses, and I think he was a little homesick, so quickly did he catch on to the nature of my quest. First, we went to the street where Mother had lived with her mother while her father was in the hospital. The driver waited in his car, smoking a cigarette and listening to the radio, while I did the street on foot, three blocks up and three blocks back. It was an area of modest houses. Tricycles were upended in front of gardens and basketball hoops were nailed high on side walls. Nobody was out, and there were few cars parked in front; bare places in the grimy snow showed where they had been driven off to work or to pick up the kids at school. Mother had not been able to recollect the number of the house she'd lived in, only that in the springtime of memory the street was green and leafy. In winter, bare branches were knitted overhead like institutional wickerwork. For once I was trying not to prepare arguments, and not to be too rational, only to let myself feel if anything was there on that street waiting for me to catch up with it: a piece of my picture, I mean, a loop of Irma's timeprint unique among the infinite, a clue, a hint, a trace of something planted in the American past for me, and me alone. At the far end, where Mother had often told me was a shining lake, there was a broad wasteland that in a rainy month could, I suppose, become a great big puddle. I stood for a moment looking down at the splotches of slush that covered it.

"Don't you despair," the driver said. "Now we'll try the hospital."

"Memory lies," I complained.

"Good memories glor-ee-fy."

The JCRS, Jewish Consumptives Relief Sanatorium, where my grandfather died, no longer exists. "Not per se," said the young woman at the synagogue I'd telephoned that morning for information. I had chosen it from the yellow pages. As soon as I told her I was in search of my Denver roots, she was hooked. In no time, while I waited on the hotel phone, she came back with the address of a shopping center that, she said, had been built on the grounds of the JCRS. She thought the original buildings were still there, however, somewhere in the neighborhood. She'd heard they had been converted from a TB sanatorium into a cancer research center.

"I guess that's progress," she said.

We had no trouble finding the shopping center. My heart sank when I saw the mass of swarming cars and people. Small chance a vestige of my grandfather's scholarly soul was to be found in that slum of shoe stores and take-out chicken chow mein.

"Keep the faith," said my driver.

We made a tour of the block and it turned out that the shops were jerry-built, about as insubstantial as a set in the back lot of a film studio. Behind them, enclosed in sunlight and calm, were the buildings of the JCRS, nearly a century old, and made to last. They bounded a rectangle of half a mile or so in length, closed at either end by halls of administration. Long ago, the two main buildings must have contained the TB wards. They stood opposing each other, attached at their far ends by two rows of smaller, irregular buildings all facing inward to the big rectangle. Cleared footpaths divided the central area neatly into big squares, each about six feet by six; no doubt they were gardens in summer. The untrammeled snow that covered them had remained fresh and white, thanks to the shelter of the surrounding buildings that also enclosed perfect silence.

I left my taxi and driver in a parking lot outside the complex. Two or three dozen cars were pulled up around us, but not a person was in evidence. I entered the first of the big white inner squares. There was no sound at all but the crunch of winter footfall. A thin layer of ice made the cleared paths treacherous, so I kept to the deep snow and crossed two more squares of white into the rectangle, leaving a line of solitary footprints. At the far end of the third square, I turned to look back at the big building that was far enough behind me so I could see it entirely. It was as if I held a glossy postcard in my hand and over a window, four up and three in from the southern corner, was an inked-in X, and scrawled beside it: I am here.

Whether my grandfather was there, or had been there, or whether I brought within myself a part of him back to the place where he had died, it was all the same. As I stood in the solemn rectangle, I felt his presence as keenly as I have ever been aware of another human being. The force of what I was feeling had nothing to do with my mother, or anyone: it was between my grandfather and me. Skeptic though I am, that one electrifying moment was all I needed, and the dead I am sure need nothing; I turned, in a hurry to leave before my dogged mind got to work and made mincemeat of what I'd felt. I had already taken a few steps back the way I'd come, when I thought: there's more.

I followed my own footprints back, then made new ones in the snow down the middle of the rectangle, resolutely not looking back again at my grandfather's window. The air was sharpening for night and already my shadow overlapped the snowy square in which I walked, and led me on toward the far end of the rectangle. A pseudo-Greek building to the left of where I stood caught my eye: "Dining Hall" was carved in the stone of the lintel, but "Library" was engraved on the brass plaque over the doorknob. Inside, it was warm; a telephone rang somewhere, then stopped. Industrious murmurs were coming from the corridor in front of me. All the doors that lined it were closed except one. The occupant of the open room was leaning back in a swivel chair, his hands locked behind his head. When he saw me through the long, narrow frame of the doorway, he looked startled. Then he smiled and said, "Hello."

He was dark, thin, and a little stooped from the lugging and reading of big books. I knew the type: an indoor man with thinning hair topside, but the lushness of beard, ear to ear, that grows on men whose body hair is plentiful. Even before he had stepped out to greet me, I saw that his eyes were rather sorrowful, though he was barely into his thirties. A traveler with clipped wings, I would have said: a hirsute, educated, romantic Jew—the type bookish Christian women find irresistible. Still smiling, he asked if he could help me, and I told him straight out that I'd come from London, mostly by bus, to visit the place where my grandfather had died.

"My grandfather had some books . . . ," I heard myself telling him.

His face fell. The JCRS library had long before been dismantled, and it was unlikely any of the old books remained. The keenness of the disappointment I felt was stupefying, though until a moment before, practically until I heard myself speak, I had barely given a thought to my grandfather's books.

"Look here," said the young man, "let's check with the librarian." I was thinking he must be a doctor. Doctors, as they approach middle age, acquire the rueful traces that were on his face; it could account for his kindness too. Librarians, on the other hand, rarely rue, or, if they do, manage to keep it quiet.

She knew her business inside and out, and she was positive not one book had been saved from the old collection. It was a *medical* library in her charge, remember, and anything worth saving in that department had been transferred to microfilm. There was no interest in keeping secular books such as those I was looking for.

"*He* kept a few volumes, didn't he?" said my companion, and he nodded toward an imposing door across the hall from the library. "*He* picked them out to decorate the shelves in *his* office. Come on," he said to me, "*he* is at a convention down in Dallas. Let's take a look. You never know."

It was a big sunny office. The windows gave out on a view I did not recognize. Behind a dignified desk, shelves reached nearly to the ceiling, and distributed on them were old books, all substantially bound. End to end, on the very top shelf was a set of volumes in dark blue, lettered in gold. My guide fetched down the first in the row and gave it to me; it fell open in my hands. Ornately scrolled and bordered in front of me was my grandfather's ex libris and a printed dedication: "This set of the Jewish Encyclopedia has been especially prepared for Morris A. Auerbach, and is hereby presented to my beloved wife Anna Kessler Auerbach, on this seventh day of March in the year nineteen hundred and seven." At the bottom it was signed, "I. K. Funk," of the American lexicographers, Funk and Wagnalls.

I do not believe in ghosts, "not per se." But if I were to believe in them, I now know they would not show themselves as gentle, whatever their nature had been in life. Their visitations would be sudden and loud, like the crash of crockery in a kitchen; they would make you jump and turn at the roaring of your name.

"Sorry. Sorry. I'm not usually this way," I said.

The camera was shaking in my hands so I could hardly focus it on the page, and the lens was blurry.

"Oh, but this is not usual. No, no, this isn't usual at all. Something extraordinary is going on here!"

A professional man, no less. And with a soft heart He was the ideal witness. I put the camera away—it collects evidence, true enough, but it's a plodder. Once again, I took the book in my hands and looked at my friend. His eyes were glowing; he'd shed years. My grandfather had entered his history too and would ever be part of him, as he was part of me. Our kinship had been established. The stranger and I had been made relatives. A match. A blessing. Mazel tov.

DINOSAUR —
SAN FRANCISCO

The best cheap meal in the West

Two TVs were playing at opposite ends of the hotel bar in Denver. One had the sound turned down, the other was blaring commentary on a football game.

"In Sheboygan," the cute cocktail waitress was saying to the barman, "all the guys had beards and flannel shirts. When I moved to Denver, I swore I'd never look at a man who had a beard or was wearing a flannel shirt."

"I know just what you mean," said the barman.

"The only time Sheboygan had a homosexual," she went on, "they wanted to give him, you know, shock treatment to his brain."

"Oh, honey," the barman said, "that's not where the trouble is."

"Believe what I'm saying to you," came a woman's voice loud and clear out of the dark room, "you'll make two thousand if you hustle."

"We still have a name," a man said, sounding a little drunk.

"If you hustle," she replied.

"Whadja mean?"

"It doesn't take a rocket scientist, dear. It isn't gonna happen by magic. You gotta hustle."

"If I misconduct myself," he said, "the bastards can cut off my balls."

The bar filled up around me and became very noisy. On the TV not showing football appeared the image of a hanging man. His hooded head was twisted to one side; his arms and ankles were tied. The body turned slowly. It must have been the news. There was no other spot of silence in the room.

* * *

"Perfection does not exist," one man was saying to another in the elevator. I'd fled the bar and was hurrying early to bed. "Never has. Not in the real world. Maybe in computer games."

BUS 36 to DINOSAUR, COLORADO

A Friday night coming up to Christmas, and the Denver depot was jumping. Buses for San Francisco, L.A., and intermediate stops were going out like shuttles, with full components of gregarious young passengers. Few passengers were going my way, toward Salt Lake City, Portland, and Seattle. Nobody else was bound for Dinosaur.

"Where *is* it?" asked the ticket clerk, and I showed her on my map that it lay practically on the Utah border.

"Well, I'll be. I haven't had anybody go *there* before. And I've been on this job pretty near eighteen months."

"Well, it has a national park," I told her. And I was pretty sure it had. The park was not why I wanted to visit Dinosaur, however. Ever since I'd passed up Bald Knob, Arkansas, in favor of Memphis, I had felt a little guilty. I was going to Dinosaur simply to make up for dereliction of a traveler's duty every so often to go somewhere for no reason but the sound of it.

In front of me in the line a bearded man flicked through a thick wedge of bus tickets and chuckled to himself: an aging hippie flashing back to laughs of yesteryear. Suddenly he turned, looked me right in the eye, and said: "You gotta be careful who you work for in this country. Do not seek top dollar. For the dollar corrupts you, and top dollar corrupts you absolutely. Do something you were designed to do."

I'd have liked to speak with him further, but our departure was called and the gate opened. When he picked up the blue laundry bag that was his luggage, it clinked cheerfully.

The Greyhound uniform sat well on our driver: his trousers didn't ride up the way they often do, and the jacket skimmed his shoulders. He looked great and he knew it too; he swaggered like a test pilot. We weren't very far out of Denver before I was grateful for his nerveless cool. No doubt by day the road through the Rockies is magnificent; at night it is very spooky. I would have liked company, but I was five rows down, bus-right, in a seat on my own. The hippie was on my left, and one up. I watched enviously how at ease he was. When he switched off his overhead light, he fell asleep straightaway, his head bumping lightly against the window. I tried to sleep too. But the road was a whip, and every time I closed my eyes, it cracked. We snapped around curves that should logically have required a Greyhound to fold in the middle, between white hills that loomed on either side like fabulous polar bears. Snow-covered firs reared up in our headlights, and ominous road signs flashed past us: they showed trucks flying, and mountains sliding into a chasm. A ramp leading off the main road was labeled: RUNAWAY VEHICLES ONLY. After one corkscrew slide the driver pulled into a stop where the hoi polloi were told not to disembark. A well-dressed collegiate boy got off alone and unloaded skis from the hold. Light streaming through the windows of a big Swiss-style chalet melted paths in the darkness. We on board shivered, not from the cold—as usual, we could have roasted chestnuts on the heaters in the bus. We clenched our teeth out of longing for a bath and a hot drink, and a soft, still bed.

Not long after three in the morning the road straightened out at last and meandered down long stretches where the snow was thin and threadbare. We passed a few scattered houses—all were dark—and a couple of motels with CLOSED where VACANCY is what a late-night winter traveler likes to see. Then, very gently, the bus pulled up to the shoulder in a pitch-black no-man's-land.

"Dinosaur," said the driver.

My impulse was to change my mind, but the old hippie was awake and watching me with interest, even respect. So I hoisted my bag and, trying to look like a true Dinosaurean coming home to roost, I trotted down the aisle and stepped off into the freezing night.

`   *   *   *

No sooner had I hit the ground than I turned back to the bus. Its doors had already closed. It was pulling away. It was gone down the narrow two-lane highway leading to the fleshpots of Salt Lake City. Gleaming phosphorescently over me in the celestial light were two nearly life-size replicas of *Tyrannosaurus rex* and brontosaurus. Otherwise, there was nothing. Only the cold moon above and blue-white stars that looked big enough to chew.

Where one Greyhound passes, another arrives in due course; that much in life is ever true, I told myself. However, a person does not flag down Greyhounds like taxis. And it is equally true that Americruisers do not stop at interim flyspecks, especially in the wee hours, unless the nearest depot alerts the driver that a passenger is waiting. And how does a passenger notify the nearest depot, possibly Denver, that she is stranded on the icy road if the only things around with the slightest resemblance to a telephone booth are a pair of evacuees from the Disney World of prehistory?

I picked up my bag, intending to start on foot the way the bus had gone, in search of civilization. And as soon as I took the first step, the old vagabond in my heart yelled: "Yippee!" Liberated at last and loose on the great highway where there was no car, no bus, no other person, not a sound but the crackling frost. To hell with the regular world, she clamored, let's keep on walking, baby, swinging down the road at night, singing, "O, how happy he, who from business free . . ." Let's cover our tracks and never come back: not for love, not for money, not to perform and repeat, until time runs out, little jobs that are of no further importance, if indeed they were ever very much to begin with. Get smart, kiddo. This is your chance to pursue forever, free as a snail, the endless trails of your inner homeland.

An open gas station and minimart appeared ahead. The crazy girl shouted and sang and danced in the black road that glistened under the moon. But I firmly said, "Adieu," and made straight for the electric lights.

It was a cozy place. Coffee percolated on a setup at the back, and a bustling woman behind the counter greeted me with a nice open smile. When I told her I had dropped off the 4:00 A.M. bus, she was flabbergasted. "Why?"

"I wanted to see Dinosaur," I said.

"You *did?*"

"It's a national park," I said. "Isn't it?"

"Well now, I'm afraid the park's quite a few miles down the road towards Vernal, Utah. All we got here is them two dummy dinosaurs you mighta seen."

What to do with me was a problem. I heard a phone ring in an office at the back, but I saw no public telephone. And who was I going to call? The very mention of a taxi made the gentle old soul behind the counter snort. And if I did manage to lure one over the border from Vernal, say, where was I planning to take it? Eventually, when the day had properly begun, I would ask to use the phone and call Greyhound in Denver to arrange for the 4:00 A.M. bus to pick me up where it had left me, a prospect entailing twenty-four hours at the minimart, topping up the cup of thick coffee I'd just poured, and eating Twinkies. And how could I be sure that the boss, who was in the back room, was going to let me hang around? Hang around, indeed: there was no place to sit. In my weary state I slouched against the wall like something dangling from a hook. Meanwhile, a flurry of customers came and went, men smelling of toothpaste and not long awake, on their way to shifts on ranches and oil rigs. Soon the woman behind the counter seemed to forget all about me.

I wandered outside and stood with my eyes closed, inhaling the clean, cold air and letting it clear the cobwebs. After a while, I opened my eyes and saw that an astonishing transformation had started taking place in front of me. Contours and depths were emerging out of the darkness. Pearly loops began to roll, one after the other, from where I stood all the way to a growing horizon, and near at hand a tumble of angular, dark red shapes, revealed by a few bold strokes, leapt out of nowhere. Everything glistened, too wet to touch. The sky itself was brightening and unwinding like a length of fine washed silk. I don't know how long I stood there before anything stirred except my own breath floating on the air. Suddenly, a flock of birds were sketched in rapidly like jokey mustaches in flight; something rustled in the underbrush beside the road; behind me in the minimart I heard women talking. Rarely in my life had I been as purely tired as I was then, and hungry, and wanting a wash. But not for a million dollars and all the comforts of home would I have missed the making of Dinosaur that morning.

The clerk had gone off duty; the manager had emerged from her office. She was in her early thirties, a beauty of the honeyed kind. Girls at school who had her classic looks were the ones who married early, often to boys they'd known from childhood, and thereafter viewed life with Mona Lisa's smile while the rest of us were breaking down all over the place and driving men crazy. A woman of the homesteader's breed like that one, if things were going smoothly, ought not to be managing an all-night gas station and minimart. By rights, at the hour just then turning, she ought to be leaving a husband asleep to tiptoe downstairs and put the muffins in the oven before she woke up the kids. If I had come as a stranger to the door of her kitchen while she was baking, to ask for a drink of water, say, or to use the telephone, she would have invited me in for breakfast. But the responsibility of an all-night business weighed heavily on her; she did not dare let herself trust a stranger off the bus. Warily, she told me that around ten o'clock a local man came to deliver papers, and maybe he would give me a lift to the park, or all the way to Vernal. I could see she thought that was awfully long to wait to get a suspicious character like me off her hands.

*　　*　　*

Another flurry of customers arrived, this time women singly or
with children on their way to school. She and her customers
engaged in exchanges of dutiful optimism: "It's no good complaining," "Life is what you make of it," "Things gotta get better
soon, can't get any worse." Then, during a lull, in walked the
best-looking man I had seen since I'd hit the road in America. He
was tall, rangy, craggy, forty-fivish, sharp-eyed: the ideal of a
far-western hombre, and not much encountered in the flesh. Anyone with half an eye to see would have known him anywhere on
earth for an American. She and he spoke together softly for a
minute. The air quivered between them. When he left, she looked
over to where I was slumping in the corner and bending first one
knee, then the other, to ease the joints.

"My husband," she said, defensively.

There are essentially two reasons for what I did then. First, I
wanted her to know I was not an escaped convict or a drug dealer.
Second, it lay in my power to give this beautiful stalwart woman
of the backwoods a surprise to make her day. Maybe there are
other reasons as well, less altruistic. Maybe I needed to prove to
myself too that I was not just moldy flotsam of the night, that I
was somebody. In front of the counter was a rack of magazines,
and in one of them, I knew, was a column that runs every month
under my name and picture. I took the magazine out, opened it,
and turned it her way. Between us lay my picture, the size of a
postage stamp: licked and used and canceled.

"That's me," I said.

And don't imagine I didn't feel silly, especially when she asked
me to autograph it. The paper first refused the ink in my pen and
then soaked it up like a blotter.

Her name was Becky Coy. Shyly, she told me she'd be pleased to
drive me to Dinosaur National Park as soon as she was off duty,
and then on into Vernal. Did I mind if her son Clinton, who was
not at school that day, came along with us? And she had recently
taken the dog to the vet in her old car. Please, she would like to

clean it out before she let me into it. "Becky," I said, "look at me. See how my Driza Bone is torn from the times I've hooked its thigh-ties on the armrests of aisle seats? My shoes, bought way back in Duluth, are already starting to let in what shoes are designed to keep out. This Minnesota hunter's hat on my head is not designed to inspire respect, or even tolerance, outside the depot. Especially when I pull the earflaps down. See? What you have in front of you, dear Becky, is a bus person. That's what I am. And a few doggy hairs on the seat ain't gonna bother one of us bus people. No way."

Of all my days on the road, and those to come, the one I spent with Becky and Clinton ranks with the very best. The weather turned out bright and cool, and nobody but us that morning decided to visit Dinosaur National Park. We three stick figures, minute in stature, were all that moved in the massive graveyard where prehistoric giants had lumbered to a halt. Clinton ran down to the edge of the Yampa River, which flows between towering walls in a bed of its own making that is not yet finished; the swift, undammed water still works its way deeper into the land. Next to me, Becky stiffened with the universal anxiety of mothers for their children near fast rivers. The digs are sheltered in galleries containing photographs and fossilized pieces that are interesting enough, but nothing to prepare the visitor for the first sight of old bonehead himself.

"It makes me feel very small," Clinton said.

He was right. Standing there on a platform, looking out at the skull of camarasaurus embedded in rock, made us relative in size to ants coming upon the remains of a long-gone mouse on the forest path. How can something so delicately contrived be so huge, or, so huge, be so frail? The sight was touching, and it was also troubling.

In Vernal, Becky and Clinton joined me for a Chinese lunch in a restaurant identical to countless others off the main streets of small towns all over the world. The dime-store Buddha over the cash register smiled down at us with his ubiquitous benevolence while Clinton, a handsome new edition of his dad, told me about hunting for treasures in the hills with his friends. At the end of our banquet, ceremoniously we opened the fortune cookies our waitress brought with a final pot of jasmine tea, and read aloud what we found.

"Your troubles will melt in the sunshine of prosperity," Becky read, and for the first time I heard her bright laugh, wholehearted.

"You will outdistance all competitors," Clinton's fortune read. What could be more encouraging for a boy on the starting line?

"Hurry up," said the message in my cookie, "or you'll miss the bus."

BUS 37 to SALT LAKE CITY

Skinless with exhaustion, I felt practically extinct. The pterodactyl in the Mesozoic sculpture garden of the museum in Vernal, where Becky and Clinton left me, gave me a sisterly wink. I dragged myself through town, killing time until it would be late enough to check into a room for the night. In the pocket of my Driza Bone was a curiously sanitized history of the Wild Bunch that I'd picked up in Denver. Vernal used to be on the outlaws' regular run, and I occupied myself looking for signs that remained of their gallops through the country. Nothing struck me until I was nosing around a pawnshop and I came upon a stack of old saddles, piled one on top of the other in a corner behind a case of outmoded power tools and box cameras. When I brushed off the dust, I could see where the leather had been worn glassy smooth from rough riding.

The woman behind the desk of the motel was concerned I would be too tired to sleep; the next thing I knew it was five in the morning, and the telephone was sounding the alarm. My bus would at any moment be pulling into the forecourt of the motel, with passengers disembarking for breakfast in a café next door, where I planned to join them. The sky was still dark and several inches of new snow lay on the ground. I was just buttering (butter-substituting?) my toast when there was the Greyhound, pulling to a stop and panting. Its door opened, and after a short pause for children to scramble into their coats and people to wake up, the passengers came trickling out into the cold, a few of them scrabbling for cigarettes as soon as they hit the ground. They all looked pale and dazed. I felt like a heel for having had a good night's sleep.

As we pulled away from Vernal, a nursery-pink dawn was breaking. Outside, acres of scrub pine were having things pretty much their own way on the high plains as far as distant peaks that encircled us shallowly, like a fashionable fruit bowl. The view was no longer painted in the golds and blue-greens of Idaho jasper; there were new colors in it: these mountains were mauve-tinged, and under snow that was already beginning to melt, the land showed terra-cotta. Not far from Starvation Lake we entered a place where brick-red boulders rose up in truncated cones, just like in the movies. Farther along, our road led into the encircling range of mountains, and it was easy to see from the bus how it had been hacked right out of rocky walls, the way children on the beach cut spirals around sandhills. How did men manage the crossing before our highway had been built? It is not hard to understand why the old Mormon fathers, having done the journey and chosen their valley, must have felt themselves safe forever from pursuit, and corruption, and criticism.

Boys started waking up noisily in the back of the bus. Apparently our driver wasn't aware of the cigarette smoke drifting forward or he didn't care; he said nothing. The road was slick with melting snow and he needed all his concentration. Abandoned on the shoulder was a broken-down car; its hood was raised and it looked as if it were yelling: Help! We entered a narrow gorge between sloping walls that seemed liquid and unstable, like ocean waves poised before they slide and slam into each other. The boys in the back went very quiet. And then, suddenly, we were in Salt Lake City.

★　　★　　★

Sunday in Salt Lake: not for the fainthearted traveler. The wide streets were empty in the morning—only me and a big black dog who had been brought to town and apparently dumped. The poor mutt crisscrossed the sidewalk, stopped to sniff at every bolted door, then trotted back to the curb and looked both ways to see if anyone he knew was coming to get him. In a state of increasing despair, he shambled across the street, catty-corner; fortunately, there was no traffic. From a considerable distance he spotted me watching him. Immediately, he loped toward me, his lop ears swinging. Strange dogs make me nervous, especially when they are heartsick and deranged with loneliness. My hotel was only a few yards away and I made for it fast. Inside, I told one of the bland and besuited young men behind the desk about the dog and asked him to telephone an animal shelter or the SPCA. He gave me the local electric grin and said surely, ma'am, he surely would. But I had barely turned away before I saw him in conversation with another clean-cut door-to-door type whose teeth and tie were interchangeable with his own. Clearly, he had forgotten about the unfortunate dog, or he just didn't care. The girl at the switchboard called me over. She had heard me talking about the dog, and she said she would make the call for me. She leaned over the desk and whispered: "They still do their polygamy, you know. Only in secret. I am not LDS myself. And I can see as how you're not. What are you?" When I told her, she said: "I met a Jewish person once. We got some of them in Salt Lake. My husband, he's met three or four of them."

Never before in my life had I heard an organ strummed. But that's what the slender girl was doing at the Tabernacle where I went to a lunchtime recital. As she strummed the Mormons' organ, the wall behind her was lit in a sequence of assorted lollipop colors. The tour I joined contained three midwestern American men, two older women from Arizona, and a perky Canadian woman. We were being led by a radiant and pure girl who introduced herself as "Sister Mumford." Other groups we passed, as she was show-ing us around Tabernacle Mount, included Japanese, French,

Russians, and Americans from all over the country. There were
no black faces, not the day I was there at least, nor had I seen any
in town. Before our group broke up, we were taken to a well-
appointed viewing room to see a short film on the birth of Christ.
It had been made in Jerusalem. Bewildered Israeli amateurs played
all the roles; even the sheep cast incredulous looks at the camera.
Afterward, elderly handmaids gently coerced us into writing down
our names and addresses. Sister Mumford then led us into the
presence of a towering statue of Christ, where we were invited to
sit on upholstered benches and "be alone with our thoughts." Just
in case our thoughts were not up to snuff, a plummy, actorish
voice sounded out of nowhere to lead us in prayer while colored
lights played around us.

"I just love this part," said Sister Mumford with trembling,
unpenetrated innocence that made me want to weep for her.

BUS 38 to WINNEMUCCA, NEVADA

A dawn of banker's gray was well suited to the masculine design
of central Salt Lake City. All praise to the traffic light for leaving
a pedestrian time enough to cross the broad main boulevard, not
that it mattered at the hour I was walking to the bus station.
There was nobody else stirring, not a person or a car to be seen.
Then, as I was starting out on the wide crossing, an unexpected
figure appeared on the other side: a nun in full habit, floating
toward me and all on her own. We met precisely midway, she in
her black flowing drapery, me in my peddler's long coat and
domed hat with earflaps down. During the moment we were side
by side in the very shadow of the walled Tabernacle, there passed
between us a look of recognition and amused complicity.

For the first time I was boarding a Greyhound bound directly for
California, though I was only going as far as Winnemucca in
Nevada. I put my bag behind two others saving places in the line,
and then found a seat where I could keep an eye on it while I
waited. Hanging around our gate was a thin, bearded man wear-

ing a braid-decorated hat that was slightly military, and a satin baseball jacket in scarlet, with nothing written on it. He was in his middle to late forties, I reckoned. He was talking to a big handsome girl who was lightly dressed in a floppy T-shirt that pulled down over khaki shorts, a Californian bound for home, no doubt. He was very animated and kept breaking off his speech to walk around in peppy little circles while she leaned against the wall with her arms folded, watching him disdainfully.

It dawned on me that the man sitting across from me was behaving peculiarly. For the past little while he had been crossing and recrossing his legs so energetically it looked as if centrifugal force would have them in a knot, and according to a strict pattern: cross, cross again, pause one two three; cross, cross, cross again, pause four five six seven; cross, cross cross, cross again, pause eight nine ten eleven twelve; then back to the beginning again. Otherwise he was impassive and the upper part of his body quite still. Obviously his condition was pathological, and I looked away discreetly. At that moment, from behind me there came dancing a shaggy old man wearing two baseball caps, one facing front, the other to the side, and two unmatched jackets over three or four dirty T-shirts. Toothless and decrepit, but light on his feet, he bobbed and weaved. "Hey! Hey! Ain't never seen anyone like that befur in my life," he shouted in a loud, cracked voice. "Never befur in my life. No siree. I ain't never seen a thing like that befur." He pointed to the leg-crosser, whose routine speeded up a little but who otherwise paid not the least attention. "No siree! Never seen a thing like that. Getta load a that! Seen a lotta things. But never seen nothin' like that befur!"

Somehow the man in the scarlet jacket managed to board the bus last, his aim, it soon transpired, to find a woman on her own to keep him company. I was not far from the front, bus-left, and his first candidate.

"Hey! Hi! Seen you in the depot with the screwballs," he said. "I like your coat."

It must have been the way I thanked him and told him I liked his coat too. Or maybe it was the look in my eye. He moved along past me. The Californian, who was across the aisle from me, turned her head away theatrically as he was going by. Near the back sat a strikingly beautiful dark-skinned girl, all alone, and the Cap'n, as I'd started to think of him, settled his scrawny self next to her. She looked at him as if a house mouse had just sat down and said, "Hi, toots!" Her surprise was tinged with disgust. And we weren't very long out of Salt Lake City before the poor guy got up fast and went to sit on his own.

"He's from Alaska," said the Californian, and she slid over her aisle seat for a gossip. "He says he lives in one of the quiet places and he hasn't seen an unattached woman in more than a year. He's on his way home—been in Detroit or somewhere with his family—and I guess he's getting desperate."

"Why is he bound for San Francisco? Shouldn't he be on the bus for Seattle?"

"This is real embarrassing," she said, "but him and me started talking way back in the Chicago depot. He asked where I was going, and as soon as I said I was on my way to San Francisco he says, 'Excuse me,' like, and I see him go over to the window. And next thing I know he comes back and says he just changed his ticket so we could ride along together. The nerd." She scowled. "He starts sayin' how he wants to marry me. Can you beat that?"

As soon as the giant cowboy made of plywood and acrylic loomed over our road, I knew Nevada was a state I could learn to love. Our front-seater, an old woman traveling alone, left us not far over the border at a crossroads where the sign said: "Devil's Gate—1 mile." Soon the snowy mountains disappeared and we entered the glamorous, barren scenery of desert romance. "Potential Truck Stop" was posted on a billboard in the midst of a bleak expanse. Practically everyone on board had fallen suddenly asleep. For all the pangs of unrequited love, the Cap'n's chin was bumping lightly on his chest. A baby who had not until then stopped yowling fell deeply silent. Death in the desert starts with a fatal snooze. And torpor sets in not just due to heat and thirst, but also thanks to the sameness of the view. Soon the California girl, the driver, and I were the only people on board fully awake. Deserts look static under the sun, but they shift unobtrusively and change their tints, and are full of landmarks as invisible as the currents of the sea or patterns of the wind. I dream of a wonderful desert sometimes, and just beyond the grasp of memory I have always had a map of one so like the ranges of Nevada that the view from the window struck me as familiar and welcoming.

A butte of extraordinary majesty soared up to starboard beside the road, and at the very instant we passed, the old wizard smashed his crystal so its shimmering colors flowed over the rock face and up into the sky itself.

"You know my dream?" the Californian said. "My dream is this: I wanna travel the whole United States on a bicycle. I think that would be a really neat thing to do."

"Oh, it would," I said. "Oh my, yes, wouldn't it?"

She was a robust girl, the kind who never feels the cold. If ever girl was born to pedal across America, she looked as if she could be the one.

"Oh, no, no," she replied. "No, I couldn't do it. Leastways, not alone. Somebody'd have to go with me. On account of my brain surgery, you see. I've got this shunt in my brain and it could pop anytime."

In Elko, the front seat was taken by a lean, dark man dressed in new jeans and a white, white shirt. He wore the kind of sunglasses people buy in airports when they figure if the plane goes down, why not have known once in their lives how it feels to wear two-hundred-dollar shades? I pegged him as a gambler, on the skids, of course: why else Greyhound? Bound for Reno, probably, or Vegas.

"Man, found a great place to stay in Elko," he told the driver. "Only forty dollars a week. You gotta share a bathroom in the hall. One thing, though: no visitors unless you're married. But for forty a week, I said, 'Okay, go for it!' It's kinda like living with Mom and Dad."

The driver was taciturn. Working hard. Staying awake. He grunted. Dead ahead was a mountain and the entrance to another tunnel; we had gone through a number of them.

"In Arkansas where this friend of mine lives each and every little heap has a name," said the new boarder. "Is this called anything special?"

"A tunnel," said the driver.

We came out the other side into a new world. From a peak with snow thick by the side of the road, we could look down and see the hills, rolling no longer, but sharp and choppy as wavelets on the swell of a rough sea, layer upon layer, racing around valleys full of mist. Narrow roads and footpaths wound round and up and over like temptation all the way to the bright horizon, but there was not a habitation to be seen. Later, I heard drivers of the western buses say that Indian passengers often ask to be let off in remote areas like the one we were crossing. They then hoist their rucksacks and saunter into the wilderness. They are thought to be the only folks who know where the trails lead. While we were in the tunnel our front-seater had moved. Now he sat very near the back of the bus, talking to himself and in a state of dangerous excitement, especially for a man on his way to stake his shirt.

Our driver was new to the route, and sunk in grim concentration. At the far end of the town of Winnemucca he pulled into a gas station, where he got out fast and drew the attendant to one side to talk to him privately. Like all men, he'd rather drive in circles forever than be seen asking directions. For a Greyhound driver the humiliation must be particularly keen, and keener still if it is the depot he can't find. Most of us had already spotted the familiar leaping Greyhound—it was over a shopfront on the next block. I had noticed a motel that looked like my kind of place a half mile back, so I said good-bye to the Californian and nodded to the

Cap'n, who was awake again and wistfully watching a few female Winnemuccans go about their business. I got out, stood back, and saw the bus on its way. There is always a pang at those country stops, when you stand all alone with your suitcase beside you and watch the Greyhound pull away like youth and implacable yesterdays.

The town of Winnemucca is neatly contained within a crown of snowy mountains. They had already begun to glow in the sunset while I was walking back from the bus. Early next morning I walked into the bright, heady air to the depot to check my departure time for the following day, and then I went on past the outskirts of town as far as the cemetery. I thought I'd look for any interesting graves to report to my history-minded brother, the ghoulish Dr. Kurtz. But the cemetery turned out to be not very old, though pleasantly moody under a thin layer of new snow. A number of Europeans were buried there: Philip Voltaire from Paris, France; Edward Bennet, born in Carlyle in 1811, buried in Winnemucca in 1890; Joseph Organ of Cornwall, dead at seventy; John Floyd, born in 1842 and simply "from England." Had they been travelers bound for the western limit of the globe? More likely, given their ages, they were expatriate settlers who had chosen to live on foreign soil and in due course to be buried in it, as I will in all likelihood be made an alien part of British dust one day, unless I'm caught on the hop. I came upon a much older cemetery, or what is left of it, in a hollow about a mile out of town up the northern slope: a small collection of old headstones surrounded by a fence and guarded by an enormous Alsatian who yanked on the end of his tether, dancing on his back legs, slavering and growling, and sent me back smartly to the land of the living.

Lunch at the Basque-American Hotel in Winnemucca: onion soup to start, then thick stew, rice, salad and hot, spicy beans. We served ourselves from big bowls and passed around the basket of bread. There were already seven at table when I wandered in looking for a meal. One other table in the room was taken by a group like ours; the rest were empty, and would not be laid until dinnertime. An old piano was set up on a stage at the far end of the room under an aquatint of a cowboy riding into a sunset not much more mawkish than plenty I had been seeing on the western roads. Across from me a leathery man complained about the rustling of his sheep: "The calves they leave alone, never had a calf taken, but they steal them sheep something terrible."

Next to me a big, grizzled uncle visiting from Spain filled my glass with chilly red wine out of an unlabeled bottle. For the first time since my journey had begun, I felt myself to be in not-quite-America, and not-quite-now. Never more than when I went to pay at the old brass register in the saloon—ancient calendars on the wall, lots of chipped ashtrays, and tables on sewing-machine legs, no TV, a short guy with a feather in his hat slumped over the far end of the oaken bar—and my bill came to five dollars.

BUS 39 to RENO, SACRAMENTO, and SAN FRANCISCO

Although I was the only boarder in Winnemucca, the little depot was very lively thanks to a couple of young men off the eastbound bus who had been left behind when it pulled away. They were yelling and carrying on, in a fury because their luggage was still on the bus. But their outrage had a histrionic quality that didn't ring quite true. After all, passengers are warned time and again that Greyhound waits for no man at a rest stop. Besides, the clerk whispered to me privately, they had been seen dashing across the street. To the casino to try the slots, she had no doubt.

"They got no leg to stand on between 'em," she said.

The complaints of the men were ringing in my ears when I boarded my bus. Two buxom women flanked the aisle at the front, both wearing pastel cotton slacks tight over the calf, and long T-shirts. Facing each other, they sprawled on hip and elbow across the front seats like favorites in a harem. The one behind the driver wore her red hair in an upsweep of curls. From where I sat four rows behind her I couldn't see much more than a ketchup-colored froth over the back of her seat. The other had frizzed blond hair. A big pink orchid undulated over her breasts. She spoke with a nasal twang. They were complaining about the bus, how filthy it was, how uncomfortable it was, what dirty people used it, and how they were never going to travel by bus again.

"The reason I'm taking this trip to the coast is it's gonna do my relationship a whole lotta good," said Blondie. "My husband's back in St. Louis, and he's gonna see he can't do without me. That man doesn't know how to boil an egg. That man could never clean a house. He's gonna have to sleep on the sofa, 'cause he hates to sleep alone in the bed."

"I loved my husband," said Red, "but, damn, he was a pain in the ass."

I had a seat to myself. Across the aisle from me was a skinny, quick-moving kid all in black.

"I'm goin' to California to see my dad," he told me. "My dad used to be an alcoholic—that's how come I left him two years ago and dropped out on my own. I been living with my half brother out in Wyoming. I like Wyoming real good. But I had a fight with his wife. I can be a stubborn son-of-a-bitch."

He took off his black cowboy hat and a lick of fair hair fell into his eyes. I remembered the corn-silk touch of my son's hair when he was a little boy. There's more than one kind of love at first sight.

"How old are you?"

"Seventeen, ma'am," he said.

Halfway to Reno the driver announced a rest stop.

"I'm so hungry," whined Blondie, and she asked Red: "You like grits?"

"Yech," Red replied. "You like chili?"

"No way! You like chicken-fried steak?"

"Now, I'll join you there," said Red.

I don't know if they crammed a meal into a ten-minute rest stop. I settled for a turkey sandwich out of the machine. It tasted of nothing at all and had a very unpleasant, slippery consistency. After one bite, I dropped it into a bin. When I turned, I saw the kid from the bus, watching me. I lowered my eyes. His fingers were nicotine stained; his hand trembled. I realized he had no money for cigarettes or food. Before I could think what to do, our driver called us on board. We had lost a couple who'd been necking on the three-seater in back, and the kid hurried back there to stretch out and sleep. I thought about him off and on for the rest of the journey. There was nothing I could have done to help him. Nothing he would have wanted me to do. But I wish to this day I'd eaten the damned sandwich.

A man sitting on the aisle opposite and three rows up had his eye on me. Even now when I try to conjure him from memory, only his perfect similarity to countless other beefy middle-aged men on the buses makes him striking. He wore a baseball cap, his zippered jacket was open over his paunch, and when he stood up I saw GODWIN: HEAVY DUTY FILTER PEOPLE written on his back.

"May I join you, ma'am?" he asked, at the same time flicking a sly glance at my ring finger. "I'm divorced," he said, settling into the seat at my side. He left a little pause.

Anything for an easy life: "Me too," I said.

"Well, there's a coincidence for you."

He was from Virginia, he said, and semiretired. He didn't say from what: possibly from Godwin Filters. He was crossing the country by bus, taking his time and stopping wherever he pleased, for as long as the fancy took him.

"I'm goin' to Reno for a few days," he said, and archly: "Ever been there? I hear Reno is a real fun town. You oughtta have a look at it. We could spend a couple a days, like, I mean . . ."

"Well, " I said, "you know. I mean. How it is. I have family waiting for me in California."

Now, wasn't that something? He was bound for California eventually too, to see his daughter and her family for Christmas.

What part of California was I aiming for? No kidding. There's one for the books: he was going to be twenty, thirty miles down the coast.

"They got these real good dances down where I'll be at. Most Saturday nights they got these singles dances. Real dancing, I mean. Not this jumping around the kids do nowadays. Dancing for our age group," he said. "You like dancing?"

"Nope," I said truthfully. "I hate it."

Conversation flagged after that. Pretty soon, he dozed off. I turned to the window just in time to see a herd of longhorn cattle. They were good-looking creatures, but nowhere near as mystical or divinely cuddly as the bison we had passed back in Wyoming. Rust-colored bungalows started to appear among the jagged rocks, only a few at first, then more, and Reno accumulated bit by bit out of the desert, looking as showy and well preserved and high spirited as a second- or third-time divorcée.

My admirer checked his suitcase in a locker and gave me a rather timid wave as he passed by. That was his system in a new town, he'd told me, to check his suitcase and then go out to find a decent motel room before he came back and got it. In the cafeteria attached to the depot, I chose a salad plate of tomatoes, lettuce, and highly colored egg salad, knowing in advance it was bound to taste of nothing but bottled mayonnaise. As usual, I found a table by the window and looked out just in time to see my erstwhile swain come out of the motel across the street, which was apparently not to his taste, and walk out of sight looking for another one. When I turned back a woman was standing by my table; her suitcase was looped by its handles over her right forearm, and she carried her tray awkwardly. She asked if I minded, could she sit with me? Women of her age, which was around my own, are not all that often to be seen alone on long-distance hauls; usually they travel with a husband or a friend. I had noticed her earlier sitting near the middle of my bus.

"I've never been on a trip like this before," she said. "I was on a bus trip with my first husband. But I've never been on my own."

She was entering the time of life when friends, and enemies, start to say what a fine-looking woman she used to be. Her eyes were the kind that take on the strongest color near them: this time it was the forest green of her dress, which was frilly for bus travel and looked wilted.

"Where are you coming from?"

"Tennessee. I'm on my way to see my boy. Him and his wife live outside Sacramento. They say they want me to come live there too. But you wanna know something? I feel like I wanna let my boy wait at the depot and just not turn up. I feel like surprising people. I feel like I wanna cut loose."

"Well, why not?"

"It's not like I can't afford it," she said. "I'm selling my house back in Tennessee on installments. I could live off of them easy and just sort of travel around where my wishes took me."

"What's stopping you?"

"My first husband left me the house and a little more. My second husband is a no-good. He drinks. He smokes. He's expecting me in Sacramento, too. He's not exactly my husband, if you know what I mean." She looked at me keenly. "You married?"

"Nope," I said.

"You got, like, a regular man?"

"Not in years. And he wasn't all that regular in the end."

"How do you manage? What do you do without a man? I mean to say, what do you *do?* You know."

"If you mean what I think you mean, it's like sugar in your coffee. Once you know it is doing you more harm than good, you learn to live without it."

She shook her head and sighed.

"I don't believe I could do without a man. I wish I could. But I need to be needed. I don't believe I could manage all on my own. I got my bag right here with me off the bus because I was thinking, why not stay in Reno?" We both turned to the big glass window. "I wonder if the motels fill up their swimming pools in wintertime," she said. "It looks like a real fun town. But I just could not do it on my own. No, I could not, and that's that."

At that moment, my old flirt came striding down the street toward the depot to collect his bag. I waved. He waved. I gestured for him to come over to our table. I said: "Mr. . . . uh, is staying here in Reno. Right? Yes. And he likes to dance."

"Why, I love to dance too," she cried, "but not like kids do nowadays."

As I ran for the departure gate, he was pulling out the seat I'd vacated, and he was saying: "I'm divorced, ma'am. . . ."

The barren hills slowly drew upon themselves a blanket of snow and thick firs. A sign warned: "Truckers: Steep downgrade ahead. Check your brakes." A car with the license plate GINRIC took its last chance to pass us before the road fell away on my side of the bus onto acres of steep wooded slopes. Far, far below, toy cars and a tiny replica of a Greyhound just like ours followed the eastbound route. At the back of the bus someone whistled sharply between his teeth. A child's voice called out: "California!" And the Donner Pass, like an echoing roll of drums, led us down into the Sacramento Valley.

BUSES 40 TO 41

LOS ANGELES — OCEANSIDE

Southern California — where else do you get a psychic taco?

Our incoming bus lost most of its original passengers in Oakland and the new boarders all were speaking Spanish. Spanish speakers in California and Texas, where they are always in the majority, take to the buses without any grumbling, and of all bus people make themselves most easily at home on board. They were the first passengers since the Russian and Israeli grannies I saw tucking into picnics on the road. Their rapid exchanges flew like freshly milled pepper, and spiced the air for our entry into San Francisco.

I like San Francisco. One of my lesser theories is that the everyday bread served up by locals is a barometer of many attitudes: crack your teeth on a hunk of Russian rye, for example, and know you are in a poor land-loving nation far from the pretensions of Viennese sweet rolls, say, or the righteously white and packaged sliced bread of breakfast in Salt Lake City. I like San Francisco's bread—it has texture and real flavor. In America, San Francisco is my Paris. This is not to say I find it European. There is no city, at least in Western Europe, currently so disaster prone, and no European city anywhere with its eclectic jumble. My first night there, I was served Pacific bay prawns in an Italian restaurant by a Chinese waitress, next to a heavily decorated Christmas tree that was topped off by a great big Star of David. The first time I saw San Francisco was back in the early 1970s, before impulsive sexual coupling carried a government health warning. I was flying to New York and London from New Zealand, and with a week to spare I decided to stop over in San Francisco. I had never been to California before, or west of Chicago, come to that. By her thirties, any woman who is a traveler and an expat has probably begun to lead her sex life, if she is free, in a traditionally mannish way, port by port. And in San Francisco I enjoyed one of numerous inconsequential flings. He was a Canadian doctor I picked up on the Qantas flight; his name was a color, I cannot remember which. But I remember his crackling eyes, and that at a restaurant in Chinatown he ordered our dinner in fluent Cantonese.

After he and I had first met, when we'd disembarked together from our flight, we shared a taxi into the city. We were already interested in each other, and had agreed to have dinner together that night. But we'd only been acquainted for a few hours, and when we arrived at the hotel our driver had recommended, we asked for two single rooms. The desk clerk was a lanky, aging boy with a bad complexion. He looked up lazily from a crossword puzzle and half stifled a yawn. "Why don't you folks take a double?" he said. "It'll save you a lot of money, and you both know you're gonna end up in the same room anyways."

People who say San Francisco is European actually mean it is the least American of all the cities in the nation.

BUS 40 to LOS ANGELES

Although my brother's town was not home for me, the idea of loving company, and fresh clothes, and homemade grub, filled me with an ache very like homesickness. At the same time, however, the footloose hobo of my heart I thought I'd kissed good-bye on the road to Dinosaur was back and whimpering in my ear, "Don't stop! Don't stop!" like a sex-crazed virgin on her first night of love. How a body can contain two powerful opposing impulses I cannot explain. But I am here to tell you that as much as I wanted to rest for a while, just as much I wanted to ride the old night bus right on past my family and spend Christmas on the road, and Christmas, and Christmas.

I arrived very early at the depot in San Francisco and was right up there in the front seat as the bus was filling. A boy of around my son's age boarded behind me; he was being seen off by a stout woman wearing slacks that fit like plastic wrap. She jingled car keys to show the world she did not travel by bus, and she climbed right on board with her boy to settle him into a seat two down from me, across the aisle.

"Now, you call me as soon as you get to L.A., hear?"

"Okay, Mom," he said, and as she stood there waiting, blocking the way of bona fide passengers trying to edge past her, he said, "Love you" in precisely the tone of dutiful afterthought I hear from my own boy. Only then did she push her way off the bus and post herself to one side, watching, until we had started rolling. No sooner had she turned at last to drive back home, there to wait for her son's call, than up he gets from the seat where she's left him and heads straight to the rear of the bus, where the usual gang have already started roaring and bragging and passing around cans of Mountain Dew.

In San Jose our half-empty bus filled up with predominantly Latin and Asian passengers. A healthy reek of garlic rose from the row behind me, where a Mexican family had broken into their provisions, and the Chinese girl next to me nibbled on something dark and shriveled that had a pleasant fishy smell. Leaving San Jose, we passed the main square, where effigies of Santa and his elves gazed wide-eyed at the sun, and the cardboard reindeer attached to Santa's sleigh lifted their hooves nervously out of fake snow. Soon after San Jose was behind us, the bus made its downhill turn toward Los Angeles, and immediately there fell upon us a fog so thick it was as if the Greyhound had plunged into a whole new element that was more solid than gaseous. We continued that way, sightless and unseen, for more than four hours, until we were about eighty miles from Los Angeles. Then the fog lifted and released us into the light at last. Naked brown hills were rolling and swelling around us; fifty miles or so outside the city their curves were dressed in scrub and sagebrush. The slopes grew angular, and dainty trees with lemon-yellow leaves filled the paths of dry streambeds. With an hour yet to go, the highway proliferated to a dozen lanes of busy traffic that filled the air with a poisonous haze and lay waste the beauty of America's final great descent to the Pacific.

BUS 41 to OCEANSIDE

Los Angeles is not my favorite city. I prefer Calcutta. Or even Jersey City. I don't believe Los Angeles is a real city at all. The last of the opportunists out of the great land of opportunity were in such a tearing hurry to stake their claims that they threw the place together any which way, and it lacks all fidelity to venerable urban design. It is a chunk of climate on a short lease, humorless and self-important. I have been to parties in L.A. where cloaks of invisibility were handed out at the door, just the way maître d's keep a stock of ties, for those of us who did not look pretty enough, rich enough, or able enough to do big favors. Among Europeans the main group to think L.A. is the cat's pajamas and come back raving about the place are Parisians, who also maintain a label-based society.

Los Angeles, relative to its size, provides probably the worst public transport system of any American metropolis. Thus, citizens who are disqualified from owning and driving their own cars for whatever reasons make a particularly frustrated and loony lot of bus people. I only had an hour between buses; all I wanted to do was stay inside the depot, keep my head down, and avoid trouble. America had at last run out of west, but thousands of travelers were heading from Los Angeles to points east, north, and south. Christmas was a week away and the waiting room was wall-to-wall people.

In the ladies' room I found an oasis of freakish calm, like one of those silences that fall out of the blue over a noisy party. I was alone before the big mirror, doing what I could with the few cosmetics I carried. Suddenly, behind me in the glass arose a towering black woman. I turned to face her. "I need five dollars,"

she said. "I'm five dollars short for my ticket to Jackson, Mississippi. I just got out of the penitentiary."

"How long were you in for?"

"Seven years," she told me.

I handed her a five-dollar bill.

"My God! How did that happen to you?"

Her hair was gray over her ears, but her face was quite unlined
and youthful. She tucked the five-dollar bill into a plastic wallet
out of her shopping bag. She sighed.

"Well, ma'am," she said, "guess you'd just have to call me a
victim of circumstance."

As soon as the chance came, I grabbed a seat near my departure
gate. It had been vacated by a Rastafarian when he woke suddenly
and made a dash for the departing bus to San Bernardino and
Phoenix. On my right was a big Mexican family; we were squeezed
in so close I could smell the heavy scent of night-blooming flowers around the women, and the dark-tobacco smoke of the men.
On my left sat an elderly woman, neatly dressed in an old-
fashioned way, traveling on her own for Christmas with children
and grandchildren down the coast, I figured, and too timid to
drive alone. Then she turned and I saw her wild eyes.

"I don't know what I'm gonna do about her," she said. "I told
her and told her he was no good. But did she listen? I gotta get her
off that stuff she's on."

"Is it cocaine?" I asked.

"No, it ain't. Not cocaine. He manipulates her all the time. And
her baby's due in three weeks. I just been lookin' at a cocaine
baby, and it works its way out all right."

"I thought you said she wasn't—"

"Our neighbor has one of them cocaine babies. He had a wife
and kids for years. Then he starts livin' with Melanie. And his
wife, she starts livin' with that young guy Dave. And he starts
dating blondes. And Bill says he's the cooker of the damn stuff in
the back, that's what Bill says. And he got a settlement and a court
order. And Melanie's got a free lawyer. But she just bawled me out

last night. So I'm goin' down to see this guy in Santa Ana who can help me out. He's Basque French. I was married to a Polish man once. My daughter ain't like she used to be. She took stuff last January, February, March. He says he's fifty-five but he knows damn well he's older than fifty-five."

"Who's 'he'?"

"This guy I met through the Christian Singles. No way he's fifty-five."

"Hell no," I said. "He's sixty if he's a day."

"Believe it. And he's tall. And he's been a widower for three years. And he sells real estate. I haven't met him yet, though. I was supposed to get married to this guy in Vegas. He came to see me. I went to see him. I live on about one hundred dollars a month and a hundred dollars stamps. My daughter gets about nine hundred, and three hundred more from the store. So she sold the whole thing for fifty thousand. She gave it away. Sold it at cost. They had her in a corner. I'm goin' down there, and if I have to, I'll put her in a goddamn home. I gotta get her outta that environment. She'll never make it on her own. The guy she's living with is named Len Lurgey, and then there's her manager, who's named Ted Bratley. And his sister is Wendy May Bellita. See, she cannot leave that speed alone. She thought she could. She told the sheriff that she'd been off it for a year, but she'd been off and on it. Wendy May is forty. And we gotta break that lease. See. I gotta lotta problems. I shoulda put her into a goddamn home down in Birmingham. It shoulda been done two years ago. She's gotta do that herself now, or I'm the one's gotta do it. And the lawyer will be three, four thousand dollars. Now, if I can get the kid back from Washington."

"Whose kid?"

"Hers, from before. He turned fourteen the other day. I sent him five dollars in a card. Saw on TV the other night, this guy, football player or something, trying for three years to get off that stuff. Just can't get off it. He broke down and cried. Does he need a kick? Or a pat on the back? What does he need? I hate to be hard-hearted, but I gotta. Last night she just bawled the hell outta me, you know. And her lips are broken out. And I cannot read her eyes anymore. She'd deny it. She'd deny it. She'd deny it. She'd stand there with her hand on the Bible and she'd deny it. And this poor girl of mine, she is nearly thirty years old. This guy he has got her under his thumb. He can take the kid from her too. You see, there is this no-fault divorce. Remember old Reagan and Jane Wyman back in the 1960s? No-fault divorce. No-fault insurance. That means no morals. Nothing. Joan drinks like a fish. Ed drinks like a fish. Why don't they just get back together again? 'Cept he married somebody else. Well, it's sink or swim with my poor child. The neighbors and a lotta people will come as witnesses. That stuff will ruin her brain. Back in July she got hit by a mud bike. And her four months pregnant at the time. I think they wanted to kill her. For the store, see? I'd rather see her in a home or something where at least she's safe until she gets better. If she ever does. Barry Simpkins last year, you know how he crashed his car and the sheriff hadda come let his dogs out of where they were locked up? That's booze did that. I don't know why people take drugs. I don't know why they get a buzz from booze. Now, Dora Nash, her daughter's hooked on cocaine. And one of her kids is in a wheelchair because their motorcycle went outta control and they were taking acid. Both brothers. I don't know what they put in speed. Could be anything. But she don't like cocaine. Least-ways, she says she don't like cocaine. Last January she got some bad stuff, couldn't even hardly keep any food down. I dunno what they put in that stuff. We don't have heroin up there. I don't think. I seen hashish once. I was about ready to throw it out. And she hit me over the head once. She hit me just the right way, so the blood ran all over the place. I shoulda called the cops on her then. I'm gonna get hard-hearted and ask this guy down Santa Ana what we can afford. All this trouble. . . ." They called my bus and I stood. She looked up at me and said: "What did I do to deserve all this trouble? I don't understand any of it."

We pulled out of Los Angeles. The Mexican woman next to me peeled an orange and offered me a segment. An ancient black couple behind us, dressed in starched Sunday threads and as tender with each other as new lovers, were bound for Mission San Juan Capistrano, where they had been invited by a local radio station.

"We're going to the studio to sing for the Lord," the woman said when I smiled at them.

California was a black space outside our windows, sprinkled with lights, yellow below and white where they became stars. Only a few hours down the road, past the crepe-paper chic of Disneyland and beyond Laguna Beach, Mother was waiting for me with a good stiff shot of bourbon, and my brother, in his English-style "den," would regale me with recondite tales of medical practices at Andersonville in 1847. We passed the Hair's to You Beauty Salon in the Mission Mall. I was bound for home. Nearly. When my son was a baby and I watched him in his sleep I used to feel the same ache that begins in the throat and flows so rapidly to the pit of the stomach. I had to lean my head against the window of the bus and gasp from the pain and sweetness.

LOS ANGELES —
LAS CRUCES

*One of my great collection of hair
salons, in a California flyspeck
desert town*

Mother used to call my younger brother and me opposite sides of the coin, and suitably enough the kid and I have ended up on opposite sides of the globe. The funny thing is Michael is an Anglophile who loves London, and I have always wanted to live next to a great ocean. Although he and I do not meet or communicate for years at a time, the fine bonds attaching us grow stronger as the world grows smaller and time goes faster. Sometimes, when I'm walking down an old London street or browsing in the bookshops of Cecil Court, I find myself thinking: "Hi, Mook. How's things?" And he, I like to imagine, greets me similarly in his mind when he's jogging on the sand by the Pacific. Since we have both had children, these occasions of closeness in spite of distance occur more frequently.

The day before my departure from Michael's town on the Pacific was New Year's Day. He was on call at the hospital, and practically everyone else was hung over, so I spent it alone whale-watching off the Oceanside coast with a lot of other tourists. On my previous visit a few years back, our boat had come so close to a migrating gray whale we could have reached out to touch the crust of barnacles on his back, and when he sounded, his upended fluke filled our frame of vision with its quintessential symmetry. That great whale's somersault will always be a one-two beat in memory, and I was hoping to experience it again. But the whales have learned to be cagey about us, and the only one we spotted when we had gone out to our limit was so far away he looked like hardly more than a minnow.

We braced ourselves on deck when the captain came about for home. At that very moment, just as the coast hove into sight dead ahead, the ocean exploded, and a school of what must have been two or three hundred porpoises were suddenly all around us in a sparkling froth, tiptoeing on their tails, slapping the water in belly flops, and diving gracefully under our hull, back and forth, trying to tickle us into the dance. In an exultation of life, baby and adult porpoises leapt as high as our eyes. We didn't know where to look first. Children on board were wild to jump in and swim with the troupe. So was I. People with cameras clicked away frantically, and gave up. There is no evidence that the emotional range of animals other than ourselves is more than basic, and when it comes to moral judgments, the lucky critters haven't a clue. But never before in nature or in art had I seen joy so purely embodied as it was in that company of porpoises, and the silver spray of droplets in the air was indistinguishable from laughter. It was more than happiness we were being invited to share: it was innocence too. And none of us who were on board the tour boat out of Oceanside that New Year's Day would ever be quite the self-important, avaricious, opinionated, road-hogging sons-of-guns we'd been before.

BUS 42 to LOS ANGELES

On a streaky pink morning I left on the last lap of my journey. It was cool enough so I decided after all to take my Michigan hunter's hat, which, according to my brother, made me look like a botched lobotomy. The thick black tights had been replaced by a thin pair. Otherwise, all was as it had been, except I was rested after ten days with family, I had regained a few pounds of weight lost on the incoming journey, and I'd had my hair cut at a salon in Carlsbad called Kinks. My sister-in-law is Mexican and shares her nation's strong tradition of familial courtesies; she was puzzled when I turned down her kind offer to drive me to the depot. The fact is, I hate to be seen off when traveling. The bus to Los Angeles turned out to be forty minutes late, and what could be worse or make a shakier start than to shift around a departure lounge with nothing left to say but good-byes to restless relatives who are, to be honest, a little scared of bus people, and who cannot help but hope deep down that you'll hurry up and leave so they can get on with their life?

It was practically a suburban route to L.A., and very crowded. With an hour left to go, there were more standees on board than I had ever seen until then. My seat was halfway down on the aisle. Next to me sat a girl of about eighteen. On her lap she carried a big box; according to the blurb on the side it contained a "Three-Color Rotating Musical Shell Lamp." An older woman standing in front of us in the aisle managed with difficulty to take off first one high-heeled pump, then the other, without losing her balance. I watched her open a white box she had stowed on the overhead rack and take out a pair of slippers designed like two fluffy puppies, and obviously never worn, which she put on while we were moving. Sharing the front seat with her mother was a little girl who was waving around a brand-new doll done up like a Hollywood prostitute in vinyl and boots and a brittle blond nylon wig. Close to the back of the bus sounded a wristwatch alarm not yet mastered. And thus, as weighed down with thoughts that count as the ghost of Christmas past, we entered Los Angeles.

BUS 43 to LAS VEGAS

"My name is Jimmy. I'll be your driver today. . . . Some of you are gettin' off in Barstow, transferrin' to the bus for Flagstaff and Albuquerque. . . . Some of you are transferrin' in Vegas to the Denver bus. . . . The rest of you, I presume, are all gamblers. So goo-ooo-ooood luck!"

"Everyone going Vegas!" cried a Chinese man across the aisle from me, as he clapped his hands: "Have fun!"

I was in the second row, bus-right. In front of me, the front-seater was a blind woman in her middle thirties accompanied by a stern older woman I assumed was her paid companion. The blind woman was big and happy, and so pleased to be Vegas bound she slapped her companion on the back and shoulder every so often, and said: "Yippee! We're gonna win us some money!" Unless they had cards and slot machines in braille, sourpuss was going to be the eyes of the pair. I wondered how long her righteousness was going to last after the first time she saw aces. It's not awfully easy to be high principled when you're drawing for an inside straight.

My brother had loaned me a book about Devil's Island. In some ways the penal colony resembled the worst of the urban bus depots, and I was enjoying it very much. I heard a little girl of about ten in the seat behind mine ask her grandmother, who was traveling with her, how come I was able to read on a bus. When she tried to do it, she said, it made her feel sick. The old lady had been in back of me at the L.A. depot and she must have overheard me asking about buses for Vegas. "Well, honey," she said, "I believe that lady is English."

"Do you come from England?" the little girl asked, standing on her seat to loom over me.

"Yes, I come from England," I said, truthfully enough. "Where do you come from?"

"I come from Las Vegas."

"Funny. I never think about children growing up in Las Vegas."

"Oh, yes. There's quite a number of us," she replied, and then she asked: "Do you English people still call us the Thirteen Colonies: Rhode Island, Massachusetts, Denver . . . ?"

"Let the lady read, Vanna honey," said her grandmother, and tugged her back into her seat.

"Is England a democracy?" I heard the girl ask.

"Oh, yes, honey," said her granny. "It's not Communist."

A few minutes of silence passed while I read about the sweltering punishment blocks where men died mad, and the expense of lives to build roads that led nowhere. Suddenly my inquisitor was back, poking my shoulder with her finger.

"Do you have religious freedom in England?"

"Why, yes, it happens we do."

"Well, well, well," she said. "Things certainly have changed over there."

Behind me Vanna inveigled Granny into a game of gin rummy. Apparently the old lady did not live in Vegas or go there often. As they played, the little girl was describing all the great casinos: the one with the white tigers and a volcano, the one with Roman columns, the one like a riverboat. She was as familiar with Vegas gimmickry as my son at her age had been with the ins and outs of London parks, or I myself once upon a time with the movie houses of Jersey City. I put my book away. Outside was a highly original composition of reds, beiges, and deep purples. For a few miles we drove through a pygmy forest of blackish-green cactus; every hour or so the driver pulled into an inland California town, dusty and embattled against the forces of nature.

"You'll have to buy me a soda out of the machine, Vanna honey," Granny said at one of our stops. "You won all my small change."

In due course we crossed the state line and rode smack into a fantasia of Ferris wheels and peppermint sticks that rise like a loopy springtime out of the desert. These are last-chance casinos that tease a final contribution out of Californians driving home from Vegas. My brother, who goes to gamble cautiously for a few days every year, once stopped at Whiskey Pete's for the ninety-five-cent breakfast, and on his way out flung his last four quarters into one of the machines. On the spot it coughed out five hundred smackeroos. My brother scooped up the windfall with both hands and bundled my sister-in-law into the car, and they raced hell-for-leather the few yards over the border, as if every racketeer west of Atlantic City had a gunsel on their tail. This is the only case I can document of the house failing to win back a percentage of the prize before the lucky bettor splits. It was a whole year before Michael returned to pay the devil his due, with interest.

★　　★　　★

On some level a gambler has to be potty about dollars and cents, even if only as his symbol for a whole lot of other things. Like those seers who read the entrails of strangled hens, the gambler sees portent and terror where there is actually not much more than chickenshit. But I believe myself to have a wholesome attitude toward money, which, as I see it, is a dirty by-product of civilization, and I have never been tempted either to hang on to it or to play with it. Thus, in my opinion, gambling had always been a squalid little vice; I thought I was immune. But of course I had never before been to Vegas, where advanced technology combined with an American kind of exuberant laziness has done away with any element whatsoever of skill in the game, or intelligence. All you gotta do is push the button and wham-bam! No sweat. No strain. No dithering of conscience. Gambling in Vegas was as easy to fall into as a coma, and as hard to get out of.

At first it made me laugh, to roll out of a Greyhound bus straight into a great big den of iniquity. But it wasn't long before an essential gloom about gambling in general wormed its way out from under the razzmatazz. By the time I'd walked around downtown and hailed a taxi to the Strip, where the flash casinos are, I was already starting to feel an aversion to the scene, intensified I guess by being all alone in a town full of people out for a good time. It makes a body feel downright depraved to perch alone at a slot machine pumping in coins with nobody to remind you that it is all really a huge joke. And it doesn't ease the sickly sensation either to lift your eyes for a moment from jacks or better, and see looking back at you the moronically stupefied face of someone you know, who turns out to be yourself in a mirror on the opposite wall.

I stayed in Vegas for a day and a half, and the only relief I found from a faint nausea was when four aces came up for me on a machine in one of the fancy casinos. I'd bet merely a lousy quarter, wouldn't you know? But it felt so darn good, and the clatter of my winnings so like music, I just had to keep on trying for it to happen again. And I tripled my little old stake, to triple the good feeling, right? Then, a few hours later, when I was down about twenty dollars, I noticed across the room a fat man wearing a crown and a golden cloak who was deep in play at a machine.

"Who's the guy in the crown?" I asked the waitress bringing free drinks, and to whom in a parody of savoir faire I'd just slipped a dollar bill, as if I were a woman of the night at chemin de fer, and not just another daytime sucker in the nickel-and-dime factory of America.

"Oh, that's a big winner," she said. She nodded toward the far side of the cavernous, clattering room, and there I saw a dollar slot machine that was decked out in a crown and a cloak that matched what the winner was wearing. "That's the machine he won on," she said.

The winning human was mindlessly pouring money into another slot; the machine he had emptied earlier was in retirement for the day. Otherwise, there wasn't much to choose between them. For the first time I noticed that my fingertips were tarnished and reeked of hot quarters: at last I understood why other middle-aged women I saw everywhere in serious communion with one-armed bandits all wore surgical gloves. I'd had it. Enough was enough. Granted, Vegas is more like a day at the zoo than a safari into the darkest heart of vice, but it gave me a glimpse of the gamblers' jungle, and I'd taken the point. Thereafter in Vegas I ate pretty good cheap food, drank cheap watered booze, and walked the Strip, digging the special effects and resisting a nagging urge to shower money around.

BUS 44 to KINGMAN, ARIZONA

The slot machines on the ground floor of my hotel were going full blast at barely 8:00 A.M. In the coffee shop were people at the ragged end of a long night, mostly red-eyed men, and five'll get you ten not a winner in the bunch. It isn't easy killing time in downtown Vegas before your bus leaves, not if you keep your hands in your pockets. I poked around the local pawnshops, where

I saw tray after tray of class rings, wristwatches of every make, and lots of jewelry specially designed to say "I love you" to Gloria, Maria, Swee'pea, Odile, Tracey, and countless others spelled out in sparklers when times were flush.

In the depot I wondered how many of the dozy people waiting in bucket seats had arrived in Vegas in their own cars, or come by plane and cashed in their tickets. The proprietor of a pawnshop at the wrong end of the Strip had told me that several times a week desperate customers came in to hock anything from watches to wedding bands, and oh yes, he'd been offered a baby's silver teething ring once, by someone who needed to buy gasoline for the trip home. All passions, I was thinking, are subsumed by the passion for a quick buck. And at that moment I became aware of a woman's voice behind me; we were sitting back-to-back.

"It doesn't make any difference about this relationship you told me about. Last month it was something else," she said. "It's always something. I wish you'd chill it down, man. This is upsetting me. For you to understand . . . I don't know how to put it in words for you to understand. Usually I'm good at words, but now I can't find the words to tell you. Rather than make this big of a mistake, I'd take my kid and go back to my husband."

Her companion did not reply.

"There's nobody in my life I appreciate more than you," the despairing woman continued. "But you gotta understand I have made it to my own understanding, and my kid's understanding. I know my marriage is over. If yours is over too, that's up to you. But you don't tell me. Tell me why. Tell me. Tell me why. . . ."

The bus to Los Angeles was called. There was motion behind me.

"Tell me why. Tell me. Why, why? Don't you see, if there's a doubt in your mind for one minute, guess what? It puts a doubt in my mind too."

I wondered how all the others, waiting slack-jawed and tuckered out, could be so apparently deaf to her grief. "Tell me, please. Tell me why. . . ."

I turned around to see what was going on. A short, dumpy woman carrying a smart bag was racing for the departure gate. Barely turning, she waved a quick good-bye over her shoulder to an equally stubby woman who was standing behind me. Tears were streaming down her sad, plain face.

"There's no doubt about me," she was saying, though the other was already through the gate, and far out of earshot. "I'm sure about me."

The afternoon was overcast, and outside Las Vegas hills rose out of a sea of dull mercury. We passed lots of things begun and left: what looked to be a half-built racetrack, a car tipped on its side, a mobile home dewheeled and up on cinder blocks, an oil rig out for the count. The desert was like lead except for a ground plant growing in irregular patches of blazing scarlet. Then dark fell as swiftly as an ax. Branching succulents that by day had been leafless travesties of shade trees were suddenly blacker than the night, and like the encircling hills they appeared to have been hacked out of space itself. To walk out there, I was thinking, would be to cut a path of my own shape deep into the field of stars.

"When he had that last heart attack, he just couldn't breathe to save his life," said a woman's voice somewhere on board.

"Yeah. You gotta watch out for potassium deprivation," another woman replied.

Out of nowhere a searchlight rose up and swept the sky. A little farther on we passed a towering neon sign that said: "Four 7's Pays Triple." "Folks," said the driver, "we'll be pulling into Laughlin pretty soon, where we have a real short stop. So don't you folks go getting lost on me."

"Why not?" shouted a wag from the back.

And that's what I'd been thinking, too.

BUS 45 to ALBUQUERQUE

The station in Kingman was not much more than a truck stop and without a conventional dispatching system, so we passengers had to look sharp not to be left behind. A bunch of us off my incoming bus and earlier buses from other parts of California gathered in good time around the door of our bus, which was headed due east to Albuquerque.

"I just got outta the hospital with pneumonia and my veins," a middle-aged woman in front of me complained to her friend.

Behind me a young man with soft brown eyes was talking to an older man who had something odd about him, something I couldn't put my finger on; a detached curiosity, almost haughty, that seemed not quite right for Greyhound.

"We're talking about her, over there," the young man said when he saw me looking at them, and he nodded toward a brunette in her early forties, well dressed, well coiffed, and well preserved. She was standing on her own just at the edge of the light that was streaming through the windows of the building behind us. "I think she's very sad," he said. "I think she could use spiritual help." To me, she belonged in the passenger seat of a silver-gray Mercedes or at the wheel of her own little runabout, and my guess was she had taken the bus in a spiteful temper after her husband or boyfriend had complained because she was spending too much money in Vegas. "I work for the Salvation Army," said the young man. A rheumy old man was leaning against the side of the bus and singing "My Darling Clementine." I would have thought him to be more up the young fellow's street, or even the three boys who were smoking and passing around cans of Mountain Dew. But his gaze was fixed adoringly on the New Mexican Princess, and as the people behind surged forward to board, he managed to push in right behind her.

"Wotcha," said the older man, the odd one. "Isn't this supposed to be a queue?"

"Why, I'll be," I shouted as we were being funneled willy-nilly onto the bus. "You're English!"

He was a merchant seaman from London with time to kill before he shipped out of Seattle, and he had chosen Greyhound as the best way to get around. He was only going down the road to see the Grand Canyon. Had I ever seen it? he wanted to know. No, to my shame, I had never seen the Grand Canyon. Or Yellow-stone Park. Or Hoover Dam. Or Vicksburg. Or Graceland. Or even Mount Rushmore, which I considered the ultimate in American graffiti; it was the only national monument I had ever really cared to see. Soon, we were rapturously exchanging place-names that sounded like a poetic reading of the London Underground system: Notting Hill Gate, Chalk Farm, Elephant and Castle, Aldgate East, Covent Garden. We tapered off after a while, trying to remember London, as unreal in memory as a fairy tale told at bedtime about an enchanted land where the next day's sun was already rising. A few minutes went by in silence before we began comparing notes about the best way to brew a decent cup of tea, and that's where our conversation ended, when he left the bus in Flagstaff.

Just before midnight on the far side of Flagstaff we ran into a fog that made all other fogs look thin. It was as dangerous a stretch of road as I had ever seen anywhere. Conversations and running commentary from the back died out. The only sound was the engine, which had long since become elemental and no longer counted as a man-made noise. Our driver was a tall, laconic black man, and brilliant: not only was he cool as a cucumber, his knowl-edge of the road seemed to be clairvoyant, and he kept up a smooth, steady pace, even when the fog, impossibly, grew deeper still. Road signs bobbed up beside us out of a milky sea. An oncoming truck loomed out of literally nowhere at all, and dis-appeared, hooting, into nowhere again. We passengers all sat forward and added every ounce of concentration to that of the driver.

"I'm scared!" a woman's voice cried out from behind me.

I turned in my seat, scandalized, to see who dared to imagine it mattered, or we cared, that she was scared. It was, of course, herself, the Princess, half out of her seat. "Would you please pull over right away!" she said.

Nobody knew where to look or what to say. The driver stiff-ened, but he was too busy to bother to respond.

"I told you to pull over. Pull over right now. I'm scared!"

Finally, she fell back into her seat. But I sensed her tense and upright behind me long, long after we had left the fog behind.

We arrived with the morning in Albuquerque. The driver hopped out of the bus first; they always do, so they can wait at the bottom of the steps to help anyone who needs it, and to refer ongoing travelers to connections. Ahead of me the passengers, one by one, were congratulating and thanking him: not protocol by a long shot or even the "done" thing on Greyhound. It was because of the Princess of New Mexico; we were atoning for her earlier faux pas. The rheumy old man clasped our driver's hand in his and said: "God bless you!" The young man from the Salvation Army thanked him too, and hurried away without a backward look.

"You are the best driver I've come across in more than two months on these buses," I told him, and I hung around to see what Her Royal Highness was going to do. She swept right past him without a word and straight into Albuquerque's relatively genteel depot. A young woman who bore her a striking resemblance, and was also beautifully turned out, ran to meet her. She was squealing: "The bus! You on a bus! You took the bus! I cannot believe it! I just cannot believe it!"

I was beside them when they fell into each other's arms and I saw the Principessa's look of ecstatic relief at having taken a Greyhound and got out of it alive.

For the first time since the ice storm prevented me from meeting Mother's chum in Nebraska, I had plans to see some people on the road, and chief of them all was my New Mexican friend, my Lady of the Greyhound, Josephine Coates. It was on the very first Greyhound I'd ever taken, when I'd gone from Ocala to New Orleans the previous year, that I'd had the great good fortune to meet Josephine. Ocala had provided a lalapalooza of a bus depot with possibly more varieties of pathology in the cafeteria alone than my brother had seen in all his years of medical school. To make things worse, the bus arrived very late from

Miami on its way to Tallahassee, and it was packed with foul-tempered passengers. If I hadn't bumped into Josephine at the gate, I think I might have thrown in the sponge. She took one look at me, smiled, and said: "Stick with me, dear, you'll be just fine." Thanks entirely to her savvy I found a seat; it was on the aisle, but in the respectable front half of the bus. And a few hours later she got me through the tricky business of changing buses after midnight in Tallahassee, where we were both proceeding west. Then, in the morning, somewhere outside Biloxi, while the Gulf of Mexico beamed at us, she and I got to know each other. She turned out to be exactly my mother's age—1910 was a bumper year for people!—and what's more, she was born in my mother's home state of Indiana, and both women worked for the social services. Josephine lives now in a community of artistically inclined old chums in a remote part of New Mexico. She is a Quaker and active in her faith. Like the Amish and the Salvation Army, Quakers are a thrifty sect, and I frequently met quite high-up members of these groups traveling by bus. There turned out to be not much to do with Greyhounds Josephine didn't know: she taught me about front-seating, she warned me about back-seaters, she told me always to double-check departure times. It is she who recommended that I travel with hand luggage only, for greater freedom. Why, before I met Josephine I hadn't even known enough to take a pillow on long hauls. When we said good-bye in New Orleans, Josephine gave me her old Greyhound route map; I used it until it fell apart and I had to buy a new one, but I kept the pieces and I guess I always will.

The moment I'd checked into my hotel room in Albuquerque I called to let Josephine know I was going to be in Las Cruces the next night. The following day, she said, she'd drive in to pick me up and take me out to her homestead in the Gila Wilderness. After we had spoken, the high point of my day off in Albuquerque was a visit to the Rattlesnake Museum in the pleasant Old Town. The two handsome herpetologists who run the museum have an affection for their poisonous charges that is downright heroic.

"Every time someone kills a baby rattler," one of the snake men said, "I'd like to go out and club a baby seal to death."

"Snakes' lives'd be a lot easier and they'd be a lot more popular," said the other crossly, "if only they had eyelashes."

BUS 46 to LAS CRUCES

"Folks, there is no smoking on this coach. And that includes magic cigarettes in the rest room. You know about them magic cigarettes, don't ya? You go back there and take one puff, and magically you turn into a hitchhiker."

Our bus to Las Cruces had come down from the snowy mountain pueblos onto the plains, where scrub and tumbleweed take on spines and seem gradually to metamorphose into cacti.

"We're from Minneapolis," said the old lady on the aisle across from me. She was prettily dressed all in pink. A Bible was on top of the pink plastic bag at her feet.

"Are you on vacation?"

"Not exactly. He"—she nodded toward the old man seated at her side—"he went and bought some land down here. He has this bright idea he wants to move to New Mexico."

He turned from gazing out at the view and gave me a bright smile.

"How do," he said.

Outside were rolling dunes of white sand, a perfect beach, the beach of dreams, high and dry in the hollow of purple mountains.

"It really is a magnificent state," I said.

"So's Minnesota," replied the old woman tartly. "And all my folks are there."

"One way to stay young," the old man said, "is move, move, move. Keep moving and you stay young."

His wife sighed and tapped her forehead. In a little while she fell asleep, sitting bolt upright. But her husband continued to gaze out at the dark hills that were folding themselves around innu-

merable secrets; it could be that even the secret of eternal life was
out there in one of those sealed valleys.

As soon as I checked into my motel in Las Cruces, I rang Josephine, who said she would be with me by noon the following day,
as it was a long drive from the Gila Wilderness into town. I went
to bed early and woke up very early with a cough and sore throat.
To be caught by even a minor illness on the road is a chastening
surprise. As the old man on the bus had said, moving is supposed
to keep us young, and travel is one way a person fools himself that
bad, bad things can be left at home. Apparently there was a bug at
work in New Mexico: at breakfast in the motel, a white-haired
woman with her husband at the table next to me had a hacking
cough just like mine. We wheezed in concert. Our eyes met.

"I see you've caught this cold too," I said.

"No," she replied. "Cancer."

I hoped it was a macabre joke. But her husband nodded sadly.
I heard myself babbling about success rates and wasn't modern
medicine wonderful?

"I have other tumors too," she said cheerfully. "I guess if they
can cure one, they can cure them all."

When I said I lived in London, she told me that her husband
had flown B-17's out of England during World War II. "But he
never talks about it. He went to a reunion of his old squadron and
it depressed him something awful. Isn't that true, dear? It depressed you something awful."

"Well, some of them seemed to be real enthusiastic," the man
said. "Some of them remember it like they had a real good time.
But not me. I was scared."

His wife was stirring her coffee. She coughed again, but her
head was turned away so she didn't see him looking at her with his
blue eyes open very wide: the eyes of a scared boy.

When we were on the bus going into New Orleans, Josephine
told me that a long time ago, in her early teens, she had been
sitting on the porch one evening in summer, watching the people

pass back and forth and hobnob under the trees, and one of her neighbors stopped for a chat.

"It has gotta be said, Josephine," he told her, "you are not one of the pretty girls. But your time will come, and you will be a beauty."

When Josephine stood in the doorway of the motel looking around for me and I saw her keen, bright, strong-boned face, I thought: "Well, that time has come, sure enough!"

How beautiful she was. My Lady of the Greyhounds.

SAN ANTONIO —
HOUSTON

Everything the Anglo tourist could want, except the spelling

I was not to see the Gila Wilderness. Even Josephine's indomitable spirit was not enough to fix the weather, and by the time she picked me up in Las Cruces, dark clouds weighted down with snow were hanging low in the western sky. Mother Nature was at it again, showing us whiz kids who's boss. But Josephine has a far-flung network of Quaker Friends, and nonsecular friends too, whom she visits pretty much as the fancy takes her, always sure of a welcome. For my Lady of the Greyhounds, the whole continental United States is just one big neighborhood. So instead of returning to her place, she took me in her chocolate-brown jalopy to visit some Quaker Friends who live in a splendid house on a hill overlooking Las Cruces and the distant mountains, which are accordion pleated, dusky rose, and very, very chic. After a late coffee in that lovely place, we went to a restaurant she knew that was full of indoor vines and birds in cages as big as rooms, where we lifted the roofs of our mouths with a wonderful Mexican lunch. When I said I'd better hurry for the bus, on the spot she decided to give me a lift all the way to El Paso, where, she said, we could spend the night with a good friend of hers.

"But Josephine, what if you find yourself snowed out of your home in Gila Wilderness for who knows how long?"

"Aw, hell," said my Greyhound heroine, "I have a toothbrush in my bag." And then with a mischievous sidelong look, she said: "Oh, shit! Let's go for it!"

I know most folks would rather octogenarians set a nice example and go properly into the long night. But spunky little old ladies like Josephine and my mother, who also throws around four-letter words, mean to proceed with a geriatric swagger. And if you don't like it? Well, you know what you can go and do.

BUS 47 to SAN ANTONIO

Josephine's friend in El Paso was a widow of more or less her own age, who lives in a small house in the barrio where we were immediately made welcome. Churlishly, my cold blew itself up during the night, and when I stumbled out of bed next morning, I was bursting with it. Josephine managed to drag me up to see the view of El Paso from the surrounding mountains. I found the mountains a lot more impressive than the town, but I was largely occupied all day waiting to sneeze, or sneezing, or scrabbling for Kleenex. After lunch at home, I lay on a sofa dozing feverishly; Josephine slept on another sofa across the room; and her friend fell asleep in the easy chair. I woke once and reckoned the combined sleeping years in the room to be somewhere around two hundred and fifteen; the resident dog, flaked out in a corner, yipped in a dream, and I tacked on twelve years more. I half woke once again to hear the women laughing in the kitchen, and then again to see both Josephine and her friend watching me intently: I thought they were speaking to me in unison, but before I could make out what they had to say, I was dragged back into sleep. When I finally woke up an hour before my bus was due to leave, I felt nearly as good as new.

A dozen Mexican boys lounged around the doors to the depot in El Paso. Josephine and I embraced under their estranged, incurious gaze. In the cafeteria, a Cro-Magnon clone lurched between the tables; I caught his bleak, ditch-water eye and he growled low in his throat: was he hungry? Out in the waiting area, only an islet of the Amish was calm in a sea of movement and high-pitched noise that made the air feel volatile and likely to blow up. A young man was pounding on the door to one of the departure bays. I figured him for a passenger left behind— poor guy, nobody seemed the least bit concerned. "Have you missed the bus?" I asked him, speaking slowly in case he spoke little English.

"Missed it? Hell no!" he cried. His eyes were spinning like little

Catherine wheels. "Can't you see? The damn thing's been taken over by enemy agents."

It was a long way to San Antonio. I remembered Texas from my last bus trip: it was big. I had taken the state in one enormous gulp, and except for waking up once to see Dallas at midnight decked out in colored lights—"Cocktails" was all it needed in pink neon overhead to complete the picture—the crossing had been uneventful. I dozed a lot in the heat, and whenever I woke I saw tumbleweed turning in the breeze. But it was in Texas on that first crossing by bus I gave in to the special charm of Greyhound. It was the dark side of morning, and we had stopped at some nowhere place on the road to Abilene. Our forty or fifty passengers raced out to stuff their faces fast in a burger joint. I brought my breakfast outside and sat alone on a curb. Behind me the plastic fast-food joint still flashed nighttime neon. Nearby our bus was at rest with its door open to the cool air. In front of me the sky was just turning pigeon-gray over an empty Texas main street: a movie house, a feed store, a shoe store, a bail-bonding office—was there a town in Texas without one? And there was I, sitting in the early dawn chomping on a ham 'n' egg muffin that had been prepacked and microwaved. And suddenly my heart burst into song. I was hooked. That was the moment I had known for sure I was going to come back to see my native country coast to coast to coast, and there was only one way to do it: by Greyhound bus.

Night aboard the bus to San Antonio passed between sleep and wakefulness. I sensed the others around me suspended in the same limbo of an all-nighter on the road. Then morning rolled in at last on waves of pink and deposited us in San Antonio. The city's graceful charm woke me up. It was more like Old Spain than anywhere I had been, including Old Spain. Until San Antonio I had always thought of Texas as a big space containing big ranches, big oil wells, big high-rising cities to accommodate big business, big men with big bellies and big hats, and big beautiful nouveau-riches girls who sometimes married British pop stars or politicians. That was how I thought of Texas, when I thought of Texas. I hardly ever thought of Texas.

BUS 48 to LAREDO

Crossing the border from America into Mexico is getting away from it all for a good time. Crossing the other way, however, entails a serious change of status, almost spiritual, a bit like getting into heaven: not all are chosen, and the trip is worth unbelievable risks. The only traffic sign I know to break the heart is one seen at intervals beside the road in California near the Mexican border. It shows a man in silhouette; he is running, and a few paces behind him is a running woman who is dragging a child by the wrist so forcefully the little one's feet are practically off the ground. It is there to warn American motorists that they must watch out for Mexican families making dashes into the land of dreams and promise. Never before having encountered thundering freeways, they do not comprehend the speed of oncoming vehicles or understand that it is deadlier than the rattletrap traffic of home.

I had decided to bus through southern Texas in order to see more of the frontier that hangs like a badly stitched hem between San Diego and Brownsville in Texas. I suspect it is the most heavily policed and the best-defined border remaining in the western world, as forbidding as borders in Europe used to be when I first went to live there.

"You can see them coming to work in Laredo, crossing the Rio Grande every morning on blown-up inner tubes the way other folks take the bus," said a fat young Texan I started talking to while we waited for our bus to Laredo. "They wanna save the seventy-five cents it costs to cross the bridge. And also there's the risk of getting sent back by Immigration."

Strictly speaking, on the level of bus travel, Texas is hardly America at all. Our line for Laredo was alien, nervous, withdrawn, and altogether unlike the noisy, easygoing bunch next to us going to

Los Angeles. From what I could tell, all but three of us waiting for the bus to Laredo hardly spoke English at all, certainly not as a mother tongue. Apart from me and the fat young Texan, there was a tall, iron-haired woman who was so successfully haughty it required the merest flick of her sideways glance to discourage women laden with babies and plastic bags from taking the seat next to her on the bus. The dark men in straw hats did not even hesitate as they passed her. Although the bus was crowded, she remained alone all the way to Laredo.

A pretty young dark woman in a navy-and-white suit and very high heels sat down next to me, smiled, and said: *"Buenos días."* As soon as she was seated, she took a package wrapped in wax paper out of her navy-blue leatherette handbag. Carefully, she folded the paper back, and there lay six plump green chili peppers. With another smile, she offered them to me so I could help myself, and she smiled yet again when I said, *gracias*, but no. She chose a chili for herself and munched it as contentedly as her northern counterpart would chew gum. We were entering a state, or a state of mind, where the usual American prerogatives, such as saving time and making money, no longer prevailed. The bus made a detour of nearly twenty minutes to an unmarked crossroads where we dropped off a passenger who had missed his earlier connection. More than ten thousand American bus miles lay behind me at that point; I thought I'd seen it all. Not until the road to Laredo had I known mighty Greyhound to come to heel like a tame hick taxi.

Cars and trucks passing in the opposite direction had started to look like kiln-baked objects, and pretty soon we rode out of lush green into a vast expanse of red mud and slopping ditches full of dark red water. Around noon we stopped for lunch at a fly-bitten café that doubled as a small town's local depot. My pretty neighbor had fallen sound asleep an hour earlier. As we were pulling in, she roused herself: this was her destination. Neatly she repacked the chili peppers and returned them to her handbag, from which she drew a small mirror and a plastic bag of makeup. Lipstick:

check. Eyeliner: check. Dab a moistened forefinger across each
eyebrow. Check this side view; check the other. She patted the
oiled hair over her temples and straightened the red-and-white
polka-dot scarf that tied her ponytail in place. Again she flashed
me her winning smile. A navy-blue leatherette overnight case and
three neatly tied plastic bags were stowed on the overhead rack
and I helped her fetch them down. Flip-flopping behind her over
the puddles of slippery unbaked clay outside, I was thinking how
different life would be had I learned to move as seductively as she
was doing on three-inch heels. Before we were halfway to the
café, the door flew open and a short, dark man came toward her
calling out in Spanish. Quickly choosing a high, dry spot, she put
her bags down, then hurled herself sobbing into his arms. She
screamed and tore at her hair. As I passed, she was pummeling his
back and calling on God to witness their meeting after so much
time. Could this shrieking maenad be the same sweet girl who had
nibbled green fire and dozed beside me on the bus? Comparable
scenes take place regularly at landings for boats that ply the isles
of Greece like waterborne buses, and arrivals in Arab countries
are often attended by a ritualistic frenzy that gives an added dimension to the concept of "public transport." But never before
on an American Greyhound had I seen anything to touch the
emotion of that reunion on the edge of a sodden South Texas
town where little wooden houses were bobbing on a sea of rusty
mud.

By rationalizing the previous night on the bus and those that lay
ahead into massive savings, I talked myself into a night of uncom-
mon luxury at the Posada Hotel in Laredo. It was the right decision, I knew, as soon as I walked into the lobby and heard
somewhere the splash of fountains. In an excess of high spirits I
put through a call to my son in London. The American interna-
tional operator who was dealing with the call thanked me effu-
sively for using MCI and: "Thank you for staying at . . ." She
hesitated. "The Placebo Hotel," she said.

*   *   *

Days earlier, coming into Las Cruces, I had crossed the Rio Grande, where it sweeps up into North America and loses itself in the pueblos of New Mexico. But on foot over the bridge between Laredo and Nuevo Laredo in Mexico I stopped midway to look down and for the first time I saw its swirling gray-green waters in irritable flood, a symbolic frontier as well as one in fact. Somehow the town of Laredo manages to straddle the Rio Grande and is like a tiny nation all its own that is almost entirely borderland, not one thing or the other, but a little of each. Laredo is rich in history and turned out, with her hand-painted signs and traces of lacy Iberian style, to be much more interesting than I had ever dreamed. In fact, I want to go back there someday and sit with drink in hand beside the great river to watch the sun go down: I don't give two cents, either, from which bank I see it.

That night on my way in to dinner at the hotel, I saw the Iron Lady from the incoming bus. She was standing ramrod straight at the front desk; the clerk had to crane his neck to speak to her. When I'd seen her last, she had been wearing a Burberry. Now she was in a gray cashmere twin-set gone nubby at the elbows and a tweed skirt; her gray hair was swept up into a puffy bun. Thanks to cheekbones like tiny suspension bridges, she had some resemblance to Katharine Hepburn. She was speaking bread-and-butter Spanish in precisely the same sort of superenunciated tone the old British retirees use when they speak the local language in their retirement communities of the Dordogne and Marbella. But when she lapsed into English, her accent was pure Boston, Mass. I fiddled with some brochures on the desk and listened to her asking the clerk to check the following day's schedules of buses down to Monterrey in Mexico and find out which ones arrived quickest. She glanced at me. I looked away and hurried to the dining room.

The waiter brought my bourbon and a menu. I was thinking about the Iron Lady. I thought I had her number: she was an expat too, only not like me. Expats to hot, cheap countries are a breed unto themselves. Some of them go for the drink or drugs, or the pretty boys and girls who do it uncritically for money; she was most certainly not one of those. Others go south because they imagine they will find their elusive muse there. But I did not think she was an artist, or an artist's moll. I figured her for one of the type trapped south of the border by a diminishing fixed income. I would have bet she was on her way back to her husband at their home in Monterrey that had once seemed such a good idea, after a visit to San Antonio to consult a branch of her American bank, or a doctor she could trust.

Suddenly she was there in the doorway looking around. Even before the publicity about skin cancer, her kind of expat never went out uncovered in the sun, and she was very pale. She was looking my way; her chilly gray eyes met mine and registered a glimmer of curiosity. I felt a twinge of guilt and dropped my gaze to my book: *The Plumed Serpent*, it so happened. The waiter led her to a table diagonally in my line of vision. Good. I would be able to continue watching her surreptitiously and speculating on her life. If my waitress instincts served me yet, for example, she would not order shellfish. She was slim for a woman in her sixties: tummy never got used to Mexican food. She was not robust enough for the steak or lamb stew; she was bound to order chicken. At that very moment, she stopped cold and glanced at me once, twice, still registering nothing much. But she told the waiter she would prefer another seat, and she pointed to one in the corner directly behind me.

For the next hour while we ate I felt her watching me. Furthermore, she was able to see me in a mirror directly across from my table, and I could not do the same because my own reflection blocked hers from view. In short, I had been outfoxed. Of such drama and ordeal is a lone middle-aged woman traveler's life composed. At least I saw the waiter bring her a big bottle of mineral water, unopened. Clearly she knew the ropes and had ordered it for a hot, thirsty journey to Monterrey on a bus full of noisy babies, smokers, chickens, possibly even goats. I looked down quickly to my book so she couldn't see on my face how much I envied her.

BUS 49 to McALLEN

Dentistry is big business in Nuevo Laredo. It was probably there the bus driver to Colorado Springs left twenty-one of his pearly whites and had replacements made. According to the society notes in my copy of the *Laredo Morning Times*, Leyla Maria Garza, queen of the local Stockmen's Ball, was studying to be a dentist someday. A guide in the Laredo museum had warned me that Brownsville, where I was bound, was pretty awful, and that its Mexican counterpart, Matamoros, had none of Nuevo Laredo's charm.

"What about dentists?"

"No dentists," she said. "College boys go down there a lot to get drunk and things. Maybe sometimes they knock each other's teeth out."

Every passenger on the bus to McAllen was Hispanic except me, and so was the driver. Any lingering impression of being in America soon disappeared. The border between California and Mexico is man-made and abrupt, the way European borders were in the old days when with a single step across an invisible demarcation everything changed: language, religious observance, cuisine, even the smell of tobacco. In Texas, however, the river makes a natural border from Laredo down to Brownsville, yet Mexico is clearly the dominant culture for quite a distance north of it. If the Rio Grande had cut in and meandered down to the sea just south of Corpus Christi, common sense would be better served and Texas more honestly proportioned.

The windows of our bus were so thickly coated with mud we could have been riding inside a badly made clay pot. All I could make out through the chinks was a flat red alien rain-soaked land, broken here and there by patches of grass and cacti, and planted with an early crop I could not identify. We passed a wooden shack with screens in the windows. It stood in a puddle that covered most of a field: "Mendoza's Dance Studio," read the hand-lettered sign out in front of the porch. Farther along were Chacho's Auto Salvage, Garcia's Pill Box, Carlo's Ice House, Club Los Amigos— only in La Joya was there a campaign sign for the utterly non-Hispanic Boggus Ford McAllen, who was running for judge. And in Mission, down the road from the Ramirez Food Market, was the perfectly Anglo Head Hunters Beauty Salon. Whatever the tough cops might say who stopped the bus here and there to board and check out faces and papers, it was I with my American passport who felt myself to be an intruder in South Texas.

Outside Mission, a handsome woman flagged the bus down for one of its off-beat stops. She was dressed up as if for Sunday, right down to her strappy sandals with rhinestone buckles. In the driver's rearview mirror I could see a grin spread slowly under his suave mustache when she took the seat behind him. Until that point he had been a morose son-of-a-gun, but soon he and the pretty woman were chatting in Spanish, and it wasn't long before all the passengers started to wake up. Two ancient women in black across the aisle from me started to giggle; food was unwrapped and pungent odors filled the air; children squealed, and backseat baritones began their running jokes. It was noon before the whole bus came alive—it was my guess that neither South Texans nor Mexicans were by nature morning people. Meanwhile, our proud Greyhound was being converted steadily into a local pussycat: we stopped every ten or fifteen minutes to take on passengers or let them off. A till materialized beside the driver so short-hop people could pay their way in coins, as they would on any dinky tram. And what ought to have been a hop to McAllen turned into a five-hour trek.

BUS 50 to BROWNSVILLE

I spent the short time between McAllen and Harlingen, where we turned right for Brownsville, in the unique uncertainty of a rough traveler who does not speak or perfectly understand the local language. It was additionally unsettling to find myself confused in what was, after all, my homeland. Although the Spanish-speaking dispatcher tried to assure me I was on the right bus for my destination, I had grave doubts. And to make matters even more disconcerting, it was not a genuine Greyhound to Brownsville but a run-down vehicle belonging to a local affiliate, Valley Transportation. The seats were not upholstered, and the pint-size windows were covered with filth. In spite of the best attempts of an old man in a straw hat to kick in the door to the bathroom, it remained locked for the entire journey. Our driver cared about nothing except the awful sounds coming from his personal stereo and leaking out to the rest of us.

We had entered the third world of public transport, where buses run according to rules of their own, and comfort as well as punctuality count as frivolity in the greater aim of getting there eventually, dead or alive. Naturally, the bus was very crowded. For the first time I sat in the back row. I was alone in my seat—none of the young men with gold incisors who headed straight for the rear of the bus cared to sit next to me. Graffiti were scratched into the metal back of the seat in front of me: "Lalo was here on December 12," "Fuck ya, Lalo"; "H Street Rules," "Fuck ya, H Street." At the rate we were going, and stopping, and going, it looked as if I would have only a few hours to spend in Brownsville and Matamoros before I caught the night bus to Houston. And I was glad.

Brownsville is well placed, like the drain at the bottom of a sink. Perhaps it holds lovely secrets, but what I saw of the place was one-hundred-percent charmless. Soon, I hailed a taxi for the short, grim ride across the border to Matamoros, and was charged twenty dollars for the pleasure. A heavy gray rain started falling before we reached the market, so I slopped around in the mud, feeling bad about refusing the importunate traders, who had probably not seen another customer all day.

To be honest, I was not having a great time. Then suddenly everything brightened, as it will when you're on the road and moving fast from sun to shadow, and back to sun again. Declining another expensive ride back over the border to Brownsville, I opted instead for a form of transport known locally as a "Maxi Taxi," a small metal van with two fixed benches that picks up and deposits passengers between relatively stable points—in this case, the market and the customs shed. A version of the Maxi Taxi exists in every land where life is cheap; they cost pennies to ride, are generally packed to the gills, and are said to have high accident rates.

School was out in Matamoros, and I found myself surrounded by small brown-eyed children with inky fingers from their day's work. Accustomed though they were to seeing North Americans around the market, finding one on board a Maxi Taxi was a surprise. At first they darted me quick looks and whispered about me behind their hands. But in a short time, we were babbling to each other in "Espanglish." They told me about their brothers and sisters at home, I told them about my big boy in England. They asked me if I liked jalapeños and fell about laughing at my imitation of spontaneous human combustion. All I had to share with them was trail mix doled out from the pocket of my Driza Bone; they hated it, but were too polite to say so, and even managed to get some of it down. One little girl, after consultation with her best friend, gave me a stick of luminous green chewing gum. Most of the children stayed on board, until the driver careered around a corner on virtually two side wheels and screeched to a halt at the end of the line.

Ten or twelve of the children walked with me to the border station. There, one by one, they shook my hand. A rainbow had appeared in the direction of the Gulf of Mexico and there was a faint tang of salt in the air. I waved good-bye and watched them turn for home before I crossed the bridge back into my own country.

BUS 51 to HARLINGEN

The Brownsville depot was no bigger than a neighborhood store and filling up fast. I grabbed a space on the end of a narrow wooden bench and settled down to wait for a northbound bus. The same down-and-outer I had glimpsed on my arrival a few hours earlier was in place by the door. Six inches of thin, dark legs covered in sores was all that showed between the tops of black shoes without laces and the ragged cuffs of trousers. Otherwise, it could have been a pile of rags huddling on the mean little plastic chair. Whenever the door opened to let someone in or out, a tremor took place deep inside the layers of cloth. Once I saw glittering brown eyes watching me through a gap between the buttons of the huge old overcoat; immediately, out shot a bony dark hand to hold the coat closed up as high as it would go: a brown bagful of human being.

A departure was announced in Spanish, made totally unintelligible by the booming loudspeaker. But I had arrived at a philosophical stance imposed by travel in a poor unknown country: Harlingen, or Houston, or neither, I did not give a damn where the bus was going, as long as it got me out of where I was. I rose and hurried to the gate.

BUS 52 to HOUSTON

The journey to Harlingen and my Houston connection was eventful only at the start. Right after tickets were collected at the gate, a skinny man stepped out of the shadow of an empty bus and infiltrated our line of boarding passengers. He wore a gray-and-maroon tracksuit with the hood pulled up to hide his face. Big as you please, he marched straight up onto the bus with the rest of us and, wouldn't you know, headed right for the backseat, where he appeared to fall instantly into a deep sleep. It was his bad luck the driver did a head count before we left and, of course, spotted him right away as an interloper. He stood over the hooded figure, now fully awake, and chewed him out in crackling Spanish.

"Wajoo min? Wajoo min?" the hooded man tried to object. "I gave joo my teeket!" But it was a last-ditch try, and he didn't sound very hopeful. The driver said something threatening, and the hooded man finally rose and started back down the aisle to the exit.

"Gee-zeus Christ! Gee-zeus Christ!" he kept saying as we all watched him go. "Gee-zeus Christ!" Playing the affronted gringo right to the end.

The bus for Houston was waiting in Harlingen, a big, beautiful Greyhound with upholstered seats. Before we forty-odd passengers could climb aboard, a pair of patrolmen checked it out, had a good look in the hold, and studied us, too, as we filed by them. Although I had gone through several similar checkpoints near the border, the Harlingen once-over chilled me. I hated the submissive silence that descended on the Mexican passengers, who a moment before had been the most cheerful travelers on the road. I wished a race of tall, fair-haired people lived south of the border, or that we were all dark-skinned together, so if official scrutiny must exist for any good reason, it would have been extended equally to me. But the border patrolmen let me pass without a second glance.

Barely outside Harlingen the bumpy road becomes a smooth six-lane highway back into the heart of the United States. For a while, I made desultory conversation across the aisle with a young Brazilian of German origin—"My family moved to Rio," he told me twice, "between the wars. *Between* the wars. . . ." He was a medical student in Mexico City, and he said he loved the Mexican people for the warmth of the welcome they had given him. He was on his way to visit his brother in Boston. It wasn't long before our exchange petered out into the usual muzzy half sleep of a night on the Big Dog. He stretched out as best he could across his two seats, and I leaned my forehead against the window for a while, nibbling trail mix and looking out at the dark shades. Our road ran straight, black, and shiny, past silhouettes of trees and unlit houses reflected in the tarry residue of recent floods. Lightning flashed on the horizon of a heavy sky, sagging with unspilled rain. Heaven and earth were giving a good display of bad temper, and as if in sympathy our bus started to lurch and grumble, too. For the rest of the night that irascible Greyhound gave us all just enough smooth time to close our eyes before it shook us up again. At one point, I was awakened to an amazing sight: beside the road, a fleet of fairyland ships were outlined in lights, their gauzy pennants fluttering against the evil sky. It took a moment before I realized the tall masts were actually oil refineries, and the rippling gauze was smoke out of their chimneys.

As we were entering Houston, the pale predawn gave a semblance of beauty to central Texas, but not much. The bus slipped into its bay in the depot, and I flexed my strengths like an athlete before another race. Mood? Not too bad considering the Greyhound's juddering transmission. Stamina? Pretty fair. Sense of humor? Functioning well enough to wonder why the girl behind the ticket window, when I asked about buses to Louisiana, was so dead set on keeping me from leaving Texas, when she so obviously despised me. Determination? Never better. Yes, I was feeling up to another stint on the road. As soon as I persuaded the stubborn shrew to fill in my ticket, I was gonna git mah li'l ol' self on the next bus for Lafayette, Louisiana, and put the peevish Lone Star State behind me.

BUSES
53 TO 57

LAFAYETTE —
ATLANTA

Pre-computer business center of Houma,
Louisiana

In 1976, an English newspaper sent me to Louisiana to interview a Grand Gizmo of the Ku Klux Klan. Under such circumstances, I ought to have formed nothing but negative impressions of the place. However, as I shlepped along behind His Wizardship to a cabin in the bayou from which he and his gang disseminated racist propaganda, rustlings in the moist night air and the thumping of big bullfrogs made a primordial music I knew was bound to outstay bigotry and local politics. In my mind, Louisiana's low-lying marshlands have a special, spectral, eerie allure. Shifting between weighty elements, neither land nor water, they form a limbo where strange creatures breed, not all of them vile by any means; some are of spectacular beauty. Men who settled such places had to retreat from everywhere else and learn extraordinary skills, or how could they survive? The French patois preserved in the Cajun backwaters increases their fascination for me. Like most young Americans of my generation, I was attracted first of all to Paris and began my travels as a Francophile.

BUS 53 to LAFAYETTE

The young Brazilian and I were the only new boarders in Houston for the eastbound bus. There were an awful lot of reboarders, however, continuing on to New Orleans and beyond. For the first time in days the predominant language was English, and there were as many blacks as whites among the passengers. I only hoped there were going to be seats to spare for us after the incoming mob was back in place.

"Don't you worry none," said a voice out of the blue. "I been traveling this bus since California with an empty seat beside me. I'll save it for you. Y'all just look for me about halfway down on the right."

She was buxom and dusky and gorgeous, like a North African belly dancer, or the descendant of an English sailor shipwrecked on a South Pacific island.

"Bat'n Rouge," she told me.

"Lafayette," I replied.

I'd almost forgotten how good a good bus could be. I sat on the aisle next to the big friendly girl from the depot. Behind us the last remaining seat on board had been taken by the Brazilian medical student. On the other side of the aisle from me was a stunning black woman of about forty. She wore her hair in a million tiny braids, like a princess of ancient Egypt. We three women chatted about breast enlargement, it so happened, and the danger of silicone implants. The black woman was a nurse and knew more about the topic than either of us.

"Anyone asks, I just say to them, 'Honey, they gonna pump you up like two party balloons."

She was divorced; the handsome teenaged boy glued to his headset beside her was the younger of her two sons, and all new men who came on to his beautiful mama had to be vetted by him.

"He is better than a Geiger counter. He says to me, 'Mama, don't you even *talk* to that one!' Never been wrong yet." She smiled over at him. He was drumming his fingers on his knee, staring out the window. "We have been living in Phoenix. But Phoenix is not much good. Where we lived, sometimes I'd come out and find eggs frying on my windshield. I don't know whether you can rightly call that racial prejudice. We were the only black family on our street. And nobody else had eggs frying on their windshield. Anyhows, I've had enough of Arizona. I'm gonna give Alabama a try."

"Do you think things will be better in Alabama?" I asked.

"They'll be different," she said. "Now, my older boy, he is twenty-one next month. This here one is my baby." The boy's eyes were closed; he was making rhythmic popping noises with his mouth. "I bought my older boy a bus ticket in Phoenix. It's good for three months. I told him he could use it and come on to

Alabama with us. Or he could cash it in and after that he is on his own."

A redheaded man with tattoos buried in the hair of his forearm leaned forward from his seat on the aisle behind the nurse and said: "Orlando." The Brazilian, who had been reading, closed his book and said: "Boston." "Mobile," said the nurse, and nodding to her son, who was swaying in his seat and snapping his fingers softly: "Him too." The girl next to me said, "Bat'n Rouge," and I said, "Lafayette."

"I'm going to Orlando because work in California's all dried up," the redheaded man said, "and I hear tell Disney World is expanding, so there's bound to be something to do. Disney World is the McDonald's of the entertainment industry. They always got a job if you don't mind dirty work."

A short, dark man hidden by the bulk of the redhead suddenly popped up in his seat, looked us all over, and said: "New York." He sat back once he had our attention. "I'm goin' home to New York," he said. "New York's my kinda place. New York's got it all. Disease. Street crime. Corruption. Lotsa corruption."

"Hey, hey," I said, "don't forget cockroaches. Potholes. What about Lithuanian taxi drivers who don't speak a word of English."

"Oh, gawd," he cried. "You too? Ain't Noo Yawk the greatest?'"

"Inhuman noise," I said. "Manhole covers that won't stay put . . ."

The old stab of bittersweet pain made me stop and catch my breath. For the first time, I realized I was actually homeward bound, almost.

No sooner were we into Louisiana than every advertisement by the side of the road was for food or a place to eat. My neighbor started to plan dreamily the meals she'd have as soon as she was home in Baton Rouge.

"I been in San Diego for a year, and when it comes to good

eatin', those Southern Californians don't know shee-it. Pardon my French." She would be staying with her sister in Baton Rouge, she told me, and her sister was a fabulous cook, with beignets to make you weep for joy. She showed me a picture of her sister, a fair woman with an oddly quizzical look on her pretty face. "She's so lucky, my sister. She got the blue eyes in the family. I always wanted blue eyes like hers." She sighed and shrugged, and added by the way: "She's a deaf-mute."

Our rest stop was a cafeteria not far from Lafayette where our little group shuffled together past the self-service counter. Ahead of me, the handsome teenager, still attached to his headset, executed a few tricky little dance steps and let his mother choose his food. My neighbor from the bus was behind me in the line. While she told us how she had to take pills for her arthritis and for nerves, she studied the shelves of gooey cakes and pastries. This was to be her first down-home food in a year, and she wanted to make the right choice.

"And just before I went on this trip," she said, "my doctor told me I had diabetes."

"Why, I've just been reading about diabetes," said the Brazilian medical student, who was behind her in our line.

"Is it serious?" she asked.

The nurse turned to her and said: "Why, sure it's serious, honey. You gotta take regular medication. Your doctor never shoulda let you travel."

"Not until you'd had more tests," the Brazilian said, "and he'd explained the situation to you."

The girl said, oh yes, in fact her doctor had called her in for an appointment, only she'd left early for her vacation and hadn't bothered to keep it. A six-inch-high quivering slab of chocolate pie was her considered choice; she reached it down, put it on her tray.

"Uh-uh, honey," the nurse said, and, leaving no room for argument, she put the plate right back on its shelf. "That is a no-no. No more of that. No way you gonna eat that. You wanna kill yourself?"

"I'm afraid sugar is, well, a problem for diabetics," I said.

"Sugar is out," said the Brazilian.

The big girl's eyes filled with tears and her mouth trembled. Wasn't it just her rotten luck to find herself bound for home on a Greyhound with a nurse across the aisle, a budding doctor behind her, and in the next seat a know-it-all like me?

I had chosen Lafayette as a jumping-off place for Houma. And I had chosen Houma because I was curious about life in a small town of the delta. And I liked the sound of it. Houma away from Houma. Houma's where I hang my hat. There's no place like Houma.

After the best meal I'd had in America, I went early to bed at my motel in Lafayette and slept the deep, dreamless sleep of the exhausted traveler by bus. The next day was bright and smelled of cinnamon. With hours to kill before the afternoon bus to Houma, I took a leisurely stroll around town. Quiet, empty Lafayette streets were full of the same presentiment I remembered from my very first trip to the Deep South, of a swirling entity not far beyond the city limits. At last, I'd come to understand that the lush immanence everywhere, the very southernness of it all, came out of the Mississippi, and *is* the river, not simply as she flows now, but as she has flowed throughout history, depositing her cargo in the muddy depths of America. I wasn't long in the thick air of Lafayette before a lethargy—I remembered that too as an attribute of the southland—had me looking for a place to rest, and I slouched into a gift shop run by a huge, highly scented blonde.

"I have been on retreat," she said to me the moment I walked in off the street. "We were addressed by a German woman from Germany. Come all that way to address us. And she had the odor of sanctity on her robes. Oh, yes. I stood near her. And I could smell sanctity like roses. I just knew I was gonna meet someone else interestin' today. Sometimes I know things like that before they occur. And you are that person. I saw you," she said, "takin' pictures out there in the street, and I thought, 'She looks interestin'.' "

I sank into the chair across from hers, the counter was between us. True enough, I had taken a few snaps of a dilapidated shop nearby because I liked its weathered look, and the fact that it offered "discounts to senior citizens," which, as it was a saddler's, struck me as funny.

"I knew you the minute you walked in the door," she said. "By your coat."

"It comes from Australia."

"Aha. You see? I said you were an interestin' person!"

Even if I'd had a mind to buy a set of cake forks with thistle handles, a picture frame edged in tiny china roses, or tea towels printed with the state flower, her stream of chat would have given me no chance. My hearing slowed to the speed of a drawl as she talked to me, mostly, about the importance of her church in her life. Phrases like "dawning of the glory day" and "wondrous spirit" stuck, the rest washed over me, and I felt my eyes wanting to close. I fancied she had been waiting donkey's years to open her heart to the stranger in the long brown coat.

"Are you a Christian?" she asked at last, face beaming and gray eyes lambent.

"Early," I said. "Very early."

Before I dragged myself away, she took my hand in both of hers; they were soft-skinned, with hardly any grip at all.

"Jesus loves you," she said.

She looked purely happy. And I noticed she was not wearing a wedding band.

BUS 54 to HOUMA

Three of us were waiting in Lafayette's poky depot. Across from me was a man in a red baseball cap who was sleeping with his mouth open. He had buck teeth, sandy hair, and long, curling eyelashes. His legs were stuck out into the space between the facing rows of plastic bucket-seats. A duffel bag under his chair was printed with a logo: all I could make out was the word "off-shore." To my left was a very old black woman. Her lower lip closed up high over a toothless space. A plastic bag chock-full and bound with string was on the floor between her feet; her skinny legs were splayed either side of it, like slats in a shaky picket fence. She was very neatly dressed, and when she looked at me her eyes were quick and canny.

"It sure is hot in here," she said.

"Yes," I said. "It is, a little."

"Is you goin' to N'Awlins or to Houma?"

"Houma," I said. "And you?"

"Oh, sure. Bin waitin' here since moanin'."

It was just past three in the afternoon.

"That's quite a time."

"Sure is," she said, then nothing for a time until, casual as a smoker asking for a light, she said: "Got a quarter?"

"Sorry?" I said, taken aback and English.

"I needs a quarter for that there machine."

I fumbled in my bag, found a quarter, and gave it to her. But the vending machine resisted her, and when I went to help, I saw that the bag of cookies she wanted cost fifty-five cents. So I gave her thirty cents more and showed her what buttons to push. The offshore rigger, no doubt bound for New Orleans, was awake and watching, sleek as a sea lion under his long lashes. I wondered if he had pretended to be asleep to save himself fifty-five cents.

A sprinkling of sleepy passengers was on the bus to Houma. One gray-haired man with Nordic blue eyes sat about halfway to the front, and I felt his gaze on me as I slid into the seat behind the driver; we were the only two white folks on board. The old lady settled into the front seat, the door closed with its familiar hermetic whoosh, and off we went for Houma, sweet Houma. The old lady and the driver, who was black too and no youngster, immediately began the exchange of melancholy complaints that typically occurs when oldsters meet on buses.

"Ain't nobody ridin' these buses today," she said. "People flyin' and they got they own cars. That ol' quarter-to-nine bus, used to be so many folks on that one. 'Member? Now what you got on it? Ain't got no more'n three or four mos' days. What's everybody in such a hurry for? Where I git off, I gotta cross that big ol' highway, cars comin' this way and that. Buses not good enough for folks these days. They generally have took off the buses. Men used to go to work on 'em. People used to flag 'em. 'Member? Things have changed. Peoples have changed. And chillun, they's changed. Everybody out for the dollar now. Lord have mercy."

"Ain't these schoolchillun gettin' to be somethin'?" said the driver. "One of 'em killed a principal down in Bat'n Rouge. Buried him yesterday."

"We live in turrible times," said the old lady.

"No discipline. When they took the discipline out of the schools, that's when everything went bad."

On the approaches to small towns we passed grand white houses set back from the road; their porches and porticoes were trimmed in beaded railings, and they looked like gigantic wedding cakes. The driver pulled up for a red light on a small main street. No other vehicles were to be seen coming or going, no people out on the streets. Le Jeune's Bakery still had a Christmas nativity scene in the window.

"In N'Awlins," the old lady said when we were back in motion, "they shoot their teachers every day. We live in turrible times."

Just outside Houma a vast expanse of pea-green liquid lapped at the sides of our road, and a little farther on, the driver pulled up in front of a row of ramshackle houses so the old lady could disembark.

"You tries to raise your chillun good," she said, "and the other chillun calls 'em chicken."

The old lady hoisted herself up, then took the steps down to the road in a gingerly way, pulling the plastic bag behind her. "Lord have mercy," she said and sighed for all the sorrows of our times and the stiffness in her knees.

Alligators, having done their bit for tourism in Louisiana, were resting for the winter. Most of the swamp tours were resting too. The clerk at my motel finally found one for me that was still functioning, and early the next morning I turned up to join it. We assembled in a wooden building in the Cajun style, high over the water and low under trees, with a dock running its length. Inside were glass cases containing shed skins of snakes, alligators' jaw-bones, and other zoological curios out of the swamp. A potbellied stove held out against the morning chill. I thought it would be very pleasant to live there for a while, beside the bayou. Two middle-aged couples from Texas were going out, too, that morning, and a pair of Oklahomans similarly festooned with expensive cameras. The women wanted to know all about London, as soon as they heard that was where my funny accent came from. Their husbands drew back, however, and the more animated became our woman-talk, the more I sensed their suspicion grow. "How do you wash the smell off?" the bigger-bellied of the two Texans asked, when I said I was on the buses.

Our young guide helped us board the ungainly Hovercraft, then stood by at the helm. Moments before we cast off, we were joined by a breathless young couple who turned out to be from Lyons in France. She had won a trip for two to America in an office lottery, and her boyfriend had come along.

"You won a trip to Houma?" I asked, incredulous. The French take their Louisiana connection very seriously, I knew. On my last visit to New Orleans the place had been swarming with Parisian schoolchildren on a history tour. Houma, however, seemed a little *little* for a first prize, and it turned out the young woman had two weeks in New Orleans with a rented car. It was a peculiar vision of America they would be taking home: spicy food and funny French; herons flying low ahead of us, white wings spanning the corridor between groves of cypress; turtles laid out fussily in order of size on a fallen oak; snowy owls turning their clockwork heads all the way around to follow the noise of our engine. A fine few hours flew by in bayous that were cold and creaking in winter sleep.

"How is that one there called in French?" asked the young man. He and his girlfriend spoke barely a word of English, and the boatman, being of the younger generation of Cajuns, knew very little French; I was the adequate, if uninspired, interpreter. The young Frenchman was pointing to a raccoon. The bold little creature knew the guide always brought stale jelly doughnuts, and she had been waiting for us at the water's edge. She jumped on board as soon as we were close enough. Her young one watched us cautiously from the shore, crafty little bandit, waiting to see if Mama was chopped for the pot before he was fool enough to follow her. "Yes, how is that one called in French?"

"Oh that creature there," I said, "is called Mathilde, and the little one behind? He's called Jean-Pierre."

Our boatman said that when he was a boy he used to go out alone and camp overnight on high ground under the loose-barked trees. I envied him his courage. I'm not sure I'd have the nerve to close my eyes in such a strange and watery place. A place, by the by, that happens also to be vanishing, thanks to the oil lust and general intemperate greed of the greatest predator on the planet.

End to end, Houma wasn't all that much to see. But I liked the way the main street backed onto water, though it was hardly more than the width of a stream. There was a sleepiness to the place and a total absence of hustle that could get under the skin after a while. In the cemetery the tombs were built up high, the way they are in New Orleans, to keep old bones dry in flood. Across the street I came upon a vast and barnlike store that sold a dusty accumulation of every goshdarn thing, and could have come down entire from another century when countryfolk used to ride into town once a year or so for calico and pitchforks and seed and canned peaches. In the back, at the far end of the sagging floorboards, was a small office of spectacular untidiness. Receipts and bills were staked everywhere on spindles, in defiance of the computer age. It was hardly any surprise to learn that this was the oldest store in Houma. The manager, now in his seventies, had come to town back in 1944 from Boston. Boston could be a candidate for Houma's direct opposite in the federation, about as far away as a body could go and still be in the United States. What on earth had brought such a man to Houma? He'd come for love, he told me. He'd been married for a good deal more than forty years, too, and never regretted a day of it.

Because I wanted to send my son a tape of Cajun music, and nobody sold such things anymore in Houma, I took a taxi out to a big mall that had replaced who-knows-how-many main streets of who-knows-how-many delta towns. A tall, nice-looking boy in the music shop tried to help me, but it was soon clear he knew less about Cajun music even than I.

"Where do you come from?" I asked.

"Buffalo, New York," he said.

"What brings you to the delta?" I asked, and jokingly added: "Love?"

"Yes," he said. "My girlfriend comes from around here and she doesn't wanna leave."

"And you're going to get married and live happily ever after."

"No way," he said. "She can stay if she wants to. But as soon as I raise the cash, I'm outta this dump."

BUS 55 to NEW ORLEANS

Where were the black people of Houma? I had seen none in the café where I had lunch, or in the knitting shop I'd popped into, which was the only shop doing much business. I had seen very few black people on the streets. In fact, I could not remember having seen many black faces in Lafayette either. Do there exist shadow towns where they lead a parallel life, going to their own cafés, and the women chitchatting in knitting shops of their own? When I was a kid and we used to drive down to Florida for winter holidays, the world divided suddenly into light and shade just south of the Mason-Dixon line. I remember how delighted I was when I saw the drinking fountains on the ferry over Chesapeake Bay that were labeled "White" and "Colored." My little brother and I rushed to drink out of the "Colored" fountain, until a fat white lady saw us and indignantly made us stop. We figured the water must be flavored: what else could "colored" water be? Lemon, orange, lime, and red wild cherry.

One English friend of mine recollects that when she took a Greyhound bus across central Texas in the late 1970s, black passengers were afraid to get off at the rest stops. True, I had noticed no such thing when crossing Texas; but my trip was a lot of years later, and by that time the rest stops were mostly all burger chains. Whatever crime the chain food places perpetrate against taste and nutrition, they do not discriminate among their customers. On the contrary, ethnic minorities are often in the majority at Burger King and McDonald's. The Greyhound bus and its depots are also somewhere the races mix in America, though sometimes uneasily.

A low and sullen mood prevailed in the Houma bus depot. Everyone sat staring at the floor except for a dark old man in ragged clothes and sneakers without socks, who was removing the tops of the ashtrays in search of a sizable butt. A lean, twitching boy puffed cigarette after cigarette, lighting one from the stub of another he'd just put out. Over his head a sign said, "No Smoking." Behind me a pair of young black men were talking softly about a friend in jail.

"He nevah gonna get out, man. He gonna do it hard."

A sudden yowl of rage made everybody jump. The old scavenger dropped the lid of an ashtray; the smoker coughed. A thin black man who had been dozing on a seat in the corner leapt to his feet, pointing at a big pockmarked white man next to him, he shouted: "You called me a black . . . Y'all said I was . . ." The pockmarked man jumped up, towering, his eyes blazing and his mouth turned down belligerently.

"Go fuck yo'sef, y' black . . ."

Fast, either side of the thin man stepped the two young men who had been discussing their friend in jail. Each took an arm.

"I'm gonna let yah live this time," the thin man shouted as they pulled him firmly toward the exit. "Y'white bastard. But don't you never say nothin' like that again." The pockmarked man sat back muttering in his chair, and in no time at all ugly somnolence closed over us again.

"Don't you even think about going to visit the cemetery in N'Aw-lins," the friendly matron in the aisle seat warned me. "Every tourist goes to N'Awlins wants to see the cemetery, but don't you go in there."

"I'm not staying in New Orleans," I said. "I've been there before."

"They kill people in that cemetery these days. Murder 'em, I mean. For money to buy their crack co-cay-een. So you watch your step."

"Thank you. But I'm not stopping in New Orleans. I plan to go right on through."

"It's all your life is worth these days to visit that cemetery, hear? You stay outta there."

"In fact, I plan to go straight through to Biloxi. I'm only chang-ing buses."

Whatever New Orleans had been once upon a time, my general impression was of a honeymoon town, a claptrap town, a danger-ous town. Through the windows of the bus I saw the big city all lit up for the cocktail hour. No, I was not sorry to go right on through New Orleans and straight to Biloxi.

"Now you be sure and hang on tight to your pocketbook when you walk around the French Quarter," said the woman next to me. "Hear what I'm sayin' to you."

BUS 56 to BILOXI

The loading bays in New Orleans were outside, and I was in plenty of time to stand in the warm, damp evening air and watch my fellow passengers assemble. They were mostly men, black and white, young and youngish. Off to one side, supervising the stowing of a big, expensive bag, stood a fair-haired man in his early thirties. Greyhound travelers are not as a rule bursting with vitamins and bronzed good health, or glowing with confidence. When his bag was placed to his satisfaction, he turned and gave me an appraisal similar to the one I'd just given him. He said he was a stockbroker from New Orleans, and an amateur yachtsman, on his way to a regatta in Key West. His boat had been delivered to Florida earlier and he would have driven down to meet it, but he was planning to sail home, and as there was nobody he trusted to drive his car back for him, he had decided to take the bus.

"Tell you what," he said, looking not at me but at the others around us. "You seem to be an interesting person. Why don't we sit together on the bus so we can talk?"

Being "an interesting person," I broke with bus protocol, and when we were installed on board, where somehow he had snared the window seat, I told him my first name. When he told me his, I said: "Oh, that's my brother's name, too."

For a moment he looked at me searchingly under the bright overhead light.

"Well, yes, it's a popular name . . . ," he began, and I saw a sudden flash of recognition in his eyes just before the driver turned off the light; out of the dark he said, ". . . among Gentiles."

New Orleans began to slide away. In spite of everything two interesting people like us were supposed to have to talk about, he sprawled next to me, dense and pampered, and pretending to sleep while the bus hurtled through the night on a road so bad it was hard to keep myself from being thrown out into the aisle. Fortunately, the trip to Biloxi was not long. When we pulled into the station, he stirred and sat up.

"Fair winds," I told him as I was leaving. "And break a leg." I realize it is what should be said to an actor, not to a yachtsman. But it perfectly summed up my feelings.

*　　*　　*

The burghers of Biloxi divide their homes from the bay with a thundering big highway that swoops in at places on stumpy pillars over the water. Walking on the beach entails ducking under busy lanes of traffic that are suspended less than a child's height over the soft, gray sands. Had they put the highway inland, they would have one of America's most attractive coastlines and Biloxi, would be as pretty a city as anyone could hope to see. There is a quiet and dignified old city underneath modern Biloxi, trying to make itself known. At the Mardi Gras Museum in the Vieux Quartier two couples from the Midwest and I shuffled past the sequinned regalia of past carnival kings and queens, though the antebellum building itself was more beautiful and refined than anything it housed. I would have felt easier in my mind if the Mardi Gras units were not called "Krewes": whenever a *C* is cutely replaced by a *K* south of the Mason-Dixon line, justly or not, my memory skips to Klaverns of the Ku Klux Klan. But the woman in charge of the museum was an elegant dowager who, to my astonishment, told me she had taken a Greyhound once, through Florida and Tennessee, and loved every minute of it.

"Why, we practically went through people's backyards. Chickens were flying as we passed. Going through one town, I saw a barber reading a paper in his barber's chair, and we passed so close I could practically make out the headline. My golly, if you're nosy, it's just about the best way to see America."

I had dinner by myself at the window of a restaurant looking out onto the bay. An iridescent sunset lay over the sky in scales, like the skin of a freshly caught fish.

"I recommend the flounder stuffed with crab," said the waitress. Her French accent was thick as good mayonnaise. She told me she had come to Biloxi as a GI bride when she was barely eighteen.

"You certainly have kept your accent."

"What else have I left?"

"Was it hard to settle down here?"

"Pah," she said. "I had to teach my husband to stop eating shoe leather. They call it steak. Well, we only live once," she said, watching the sunset beyond us. "What can you do? You make the best of it."

Although her face was well painted and her hair was bright, when she walked away to the kitchen I saw she had the varicosed legs of a lifetime waitress.

In 1969, Biloxi was hit by the killer hurricane Camille, an event recollected almost obsessively by the guide on my tram tour of the city. He pointed out to us holes in the landscape that prior to the onslaught of "that lady called Camille" had been shops and local businesses, and two or three of them the homes of his own widespread family. Ton after ton of Gulf water had churned through the streets of the city. He would never forget how the deluge roared out to the cemetery, where it toppled mausoleums and uncorked the graves. "I seen the dead with my own eyes hanging outta the trees. Not the new dead, I mean the dead dead outta the graveyard. If a blow like that ever comes this way again, I'm leavin' this town for good."

A pair of middle-aged midwesterners on the tram exchanged a look of distaste; they found the bit about dead bodies in trees pretty gross.

"You have an accent," the woman said when we happened to meet later at a café after the tour. "Where do you come from?" When I told her, she asked how I was getting around the States. "Why so are we!" they cried in unison on learning I was going by bus. You could have knocked me over with a feather. "Greyhound?" I cried, looking at their permanent pleats and white collars and polished shoes. They laughed uproariously. I could bet my bottom dollar they did not travel by common bus. They had their very own bus. Believe it. They had bought a bus, gutted it, and converted it to contain a kitchenette, a fitted bathroom, and a queen-sized bed. For nearly ten years they had been touring America in their house-bus and towing a Lincoln Continental behind like a dinghy. When they started out, they told me, only about three hundred people were doing the same thing. Now, six thousand bus owners, and maybe more, were expected at their annual jamboree down in Naples, Florida. They invited me out to their house-bus, which was parked on the edge of town. But the hour was drawing on, and I barely had time for a drink at the hotel bar before I had to leave Biloxi. Besides, the idea of a bus with organdy curtains at the window and fluffy nylon berets on the toilet seats made me feel sad.

Across the bar from me sat a heavily made-up woman. Next to her was a beefy man I would have bet was a local sheriff in civvies: he had an air of convinced authority.

"She was layin' on top of a car and exposin' you-know," the woman said. "Now, she may call that posin', but I call it you-know."

"Polaroid," said the man. "It hadda be Polaroid."

BUS 57 to ATLANTA

"What's gonna happen in a few years, they're gonna replace the dollar with another currency," the big man was saying to his short companion. These two had just struck up a conversation in the waiting area of the depot and the short guy seemed wary, as though not quite convinced the big guy was sane. "I come from Oregon," the big man said, "and I tell you, all the sawmills in Oregon have closed down. Greed and laziness. They'd rather ship their logs right over to Japan."

A young black man mopping the floor between the rows of plastic seats paused and leaned on the handle of his mop.

"Them Japanese are buying up our national parks," he said. "I can't recall which parks it is, but I heard about it."

On the opposite side of the waiting area sat a young Asian man, impassive as a tree. He was not Japanese, he was Vietnamese, probably from one of the local shrimperies that are owned and staffed almost exclusively by his countrymen.

"It's not the passengers make my life hard," said the black man, when I lifted my bag so he could mop the floor around my chair. "It's the winos. This here depot is a mecca for every wino in Biloxi. When Amtrak gets its show together, Greyhound's gonna be right down the tubes."

Six rows of seats lay one behind the other. In front of me sat two young women. One of them had come in on the bus from Memphis and was waiting for a friend who was due any minute to pick her up. I'd noticed her trying the telephone without success; no doubt her friend was already en route. A suitcase was beside her on the floor. The other girl had already checked her luggage and was shipping out any minute on her way to Jacksonville.

"A bus only broke down once I was ever on," she was saying. "The only time a bus ever broke down I was on, I had this big fat person next to me. I sure wish those seats had armrests in between. That was the only time I was ever on a bus that broke down. And they hadda send out another bus. And on this other bus, you know what? I got the front seat all to myself. And you know what I think? That's how come that first bus hadda break down, see? So as I could get the front seat all to myself."

"Those seats are hardly big enough for two people," the other girl grumbled.

"Yeah, that's true," said the first girl. "But, man, I just love the journey. Don't you love the journey? Oh, how I love that old journey, every time."

A few seats to the left in my row sat a stocky bearded man in his midfifties, wearing tweeds and a smart, unnautical yachting cap. For some time he had been fidgeting, and suddenly he jumped to his feet and strode to the ticket window.

"Isn't that St. Louis bus in *yet?* Do you have any idea how long we've been waiting in this . . . this *depot?*"

A white-haired woman was sitting quietly next to the seat he had vacated. Her hands were colorless and attenuated against the navy blue of her coat, her fingers like melting icicles. When she turned my way her face wavered in the overhead light.

"That bus is two hours late from St. Louis," she said in a tone as thin as vapor. "My brother"—she nodded at the big man who was stomping back and forth in front of the ticket window—"he drove all the way down from the state of Washington. We're waiting for our sister. She's on the bus from St. Louis. I come from Illinois originally. I moved down here with my husband more than thirty years ago. This is where all my friends are now. To see people I know when I go out to the store, that's real important to me. I'm a widow. My husband died six years ago. He's back in Illinois." She looked down at her hands, seemed surprised they had not vanished, and held them out for a moment like a woman admiring her nail polish. They were practically translucent and the veins stood out, as blue as routes on the Greyhound map. "When the time comes," she said, "that's where I'm going too. Back to Illinois."

How cold those silvery hands would be if I reached out, as I felt a great urge to do, and held them in my own. Her brother's squawks and fulminations were in vain; the timetable that enraged him was not in the province of any bus line.

The St. Louis Greyhound pulled in at last. Arriving passengers emerged, stunned and blinking like creatures yanked out of another element. They claimed their luggage and drifted away. Soon nobody was left except a dozen or so of us waiting for the outgoing Atlanta bus, which had also been delayed, and the girl with luggage, still expecting her friend. She moved herself and her suitcase to the seat next to me.

"What I figure is this," she said: "my friend telephoned Greyhound, and when they told her my bus was three hours late, well, she probably figured if that's what they said, it would be even later, so she stopped to eat or something. That's what I figure." She sounded confident, but she cast troubled looks at the telephone on the wall, and I had seen her try it twice more since the first time, always without any luck. "I've been visiting my sister in Montana," she said. "Been on the road for nearly forty-eight hours and I gotta work tomorrow morning at six. I'm a nurse. My friend who's coming to get me? She's a nurse too. She just broke up with her boyfriend. So she's been staying in my apartment, like, feeding my cat and all. I let her use my car and things, and my place."

"How come your bus was so late in?"

"There was an accident on the road about ten miles outside Biloxi. It was bad. There was an ambulance. The car was a write-off, a white car . . ."

She had been glancing beyond me to the door, and I saw her face register first delight, then surprise, then something like horror. A tall young man in an air force uniform was coming toward us, his hands outstretched, not in welcome but as if to say: "Calm down!"

"What are you doing here?" the girl asked shrilly.

"I have some bad news. . . ."

"Oh, God! Oh, God! No! It wasn't my car! Say it wasn't my car!"

"It's gonna be all right . . . ," he began.

"Oh, God! I've got no insurance. Don't you understand? I'm gonna be arrested. Oh, God! I'm gonna go to jail!"

He took her bag and steered her toward the door, saying over and over again it was going to be all right. But she pulled at her hair and cried that she had no insurance and she was going to jail. I felt sorry for her. And even though it was none of my business, I would have given a lot to know what had happened to her best friend behind the wheel of the white car. A person gets up one morning just like any other. And by the end of the day? Nothing will ever be the same.

Outside Fairfield, Alabama, the overhead lights were switched on suddenly and we all woke, complaining. A couple of armed hulks in uniform patrolled the central aisle, looking right and left. They didn't find what they wanted and disembarked with a cheerful "Sorry, folks."

"A woman killed her husband down in Mobile," the old lady behind me said to her companion. "They figure she's on a bus."

"Shee-it!" a girl shouted in the dark when we were under way again.

"What's the matter back there?" the driver asked.

"I lost a contact lens!" she yelled back at him.

I could feel it in the air: familiar territory lay ahead in Atlanta, where people joined health clubs and checked their diaries a month ahead to see if they were free for lunch. How well I knew the locale: the Big City—Contact Lensville.

Southern-fried chicken, Key West style

Atlanta was hard to get a hold on. My general impression was of a city in flux. But whether it was on its way up or on its way down was impossible to say.

Because the lights at the little tables in the hotel bar were dim and shaded, I was sitting right up at the bar where I could read: I was in the middle of Peter Matthiessen's *Killing Mister Watson*, not a book to put down, even for the sake of propriety. Besides, I was the barman's only customer, and there was nobody in the dining room either, where he doubled as the waiter. A young black man came into the bar. I glanced up at the mirror and saw how he hesitated at the door before he chose the stool right next to me, even though there were a dozen others free. I glanced at his profile, saw an ear as neat as a chocolate-covered pretzel, and then looked back at my book. But my concentration was shattered; he was too close, and I could feel him staring at me. The bartender was a tough man around fifty with a lot of tattoos showing. Of course, he'd had his doubts about me. He knew for sure a woman on her own sat up at the bar for one reason and only one: reading Peter Matthiessen was not it. Contempt came off him in waves when the black man started trying to pick me up.

"Where d'you come from? On your own? Readin' will ruin your eyesight. Whyntcha have some fun with me?"

"Look here," I said, "let me save you a lot of bother. If the light were better in here, you'd see for yourself that I'm a lot more over fifty than you are over twenty."

"Hey, baby," he said, "age is not the issue. I been upstairs in my room for five days without once coming out. I gotta lotta good things up there. You'd like what I got up there."

With exaggerated care the barman put a beer down in front of the young man, and in a tone of vitriol asked me: "Another?"

The stools were fixed, but that didn't stop the youngster from getting so deep into my space I could feel his heat. His after-shave was a cry for help.

"I've been incarcerated eight months out of the last twelve," he whispered.

"Why?"

"For bein' in the wrong place at the wrong time," he said, and tucked into a plate of nachos the bartender had brought him. He first attacked the food like a man dying to eat, then, before he'd finished half of it, pushed the plate away and turned again to me. That was when I knew he was out of his skull. I saw no sense of self, or limits to hunger, in the red-rimmed yellow eyes so close to mine the quick flinching of my head was reflected in them. He was mad, or on a drug I had never before encountered face-to-face. "I didn't do it," he'd say when they came to get him. And he'd be right: he was not all there.

"I'll have my dinner now," I said in my most imperious English English to the bartender, who had been slowly drying glasses while keeping a hard eye on me in the mirror. I slid off the barstool, and with feet firmly planted, I held out my hand to the youngster. A handshake is the most disarming and least suggestive gesture in the human repertoire. His hand was rough and hot; it felt surprised. "Good luck," I told him. "Good-bye."

The bartender in his role of waiter pulled out the chair for me at my table. And for the rest of the night he treated me with such extreme courtesy it was as if I were dressed in green velvet, and the carriage waited outside to take me back to Tara.

BUS 58 to OCALA

The only friend remaining to me from childhood lives in Ocala. Since he moved to central Florida, I'd seen him very rarely.

Thanks to his fierce and critical nature, and the abiding frustration from my teenage years when I'd been simple enough to fall in love with him, long periods passed when we did not speak or communicate. Seven years of silence had recently ended, and I was looking forward to a few days with him.

Atlanta is a gateway depot for traffic going every which way, and it was frantically busy. On my way for coffee before my bus I collided with a big solid girl wearing knee-length khaki shorts and slightly stooped under a towering rucksack.

"Excuse me," I said. "Are you okay?"

"Yiss," she replied.

"Why, you're from . . ."

"Australia," she said, and: "I like your coat."

Her companion was not what I'd expect to find with a brawny bus traveler from Oz, and she was at instant pains to let me know he was a passing acquaintance of the road. His yellow hair was cunningly swept up and over an embroidered tarboosh; the rest of his outfit was black leather. There were traces of blusher on his cheekbones, and his mouth was a trifle fuller, his eyebrows more arched, his demeanor more quivering with vitality than nature had intended. I thought he must be the bravest man in the world, to waltz around a Greyhound bus depot looking as he did.

"Hi," he said, and put out a manicured hand. "My name is . . . call me Rick. I just changed my name. From here on, I'm Rick. Like in *Casablanca*, you know? It's better if you don't know my real name. I'm on the lam to Walla Walla, Washington." If he was trying not to attract attention, he'd chosen the wrong ensemble. Two passing children craned their necks, nearly stumbled, ended up walking backward.

"Every word is true," Rick said as we three walked together to the cafeteria. "Cross my heart. Last night my friend tried to knife me. I had no idea, no idea, not the slightest i-dee-uh he was heavily into cocaine. Not until I was abducted by Colombian drug dealers in Fort Lauderdale. How I got away from them is something you do not want to know. And now I'm on the run," he said cheerfully. "I'm going home to Walla Walla. All I want is the quiet life and time to find myself. Florida's crazy. Too crazy. Too cuh-ray-zee for a little boy from Walla Walla."

The poor Australian looked pained. She was on her way to Denver to meet up with her fellow backpackers who had gone ahead while she spent a few days at Disney World. The way the bus schedules ran, chances were Rick would be with her all the way.

"I gotta get rid of this weight," he said pinching an incipient double chin under his jawbone. A layer of new fat was draped over him uncomfortably, I noticed, like a borrowed coat that didn't quite fit or match his wardrobe. He made a big show of pushing away the sugar bowl on our table. "When I get rid of this weight, I'll go back to acting. Just do modeling and stuff on the side."

Later, as I was boarding my bus to Ocala, I saw Rick talking intensely on the telephone with his hand cupped over the receiver. Curious behavior for a man severing all links so he could go underground. I hoped it didn't mean he'd spotted his pursuer closing in on him.

It was not a noble Greyhound to Ocala, but a bright yellow number with slippery plastic seats and skimpy windows. Behind me two middle-aged men in baseball caps passed the time of day.

"I'm an alcoholic," said the man on the aisle.

"Oh, yeah? Me too. I fell down drunk in a swamp last year, and when I woke up I was bit on my foot by a cottonmouth snake. 'Don't go gettin' your blood pressure up,' I says to myself. I gets into my car and drives three miles to the hospital. Right after that, my wife left me."

"These women these days," said the man on the aisle. "I blame liberation. They know all about the bedroom but not a damn thing about the kitchen."

"Well, that alcohol's real bad. After the snake bit me I spent three months in a drying-out hospital."

"When I was a boy," said the man on the aisle, "I plowed. I picked cotton. I like as broke my back. Then my daddy says,

'We're movin' to town.' I was pretty near all over m'self to live in Atlanta. They still had streetcars back then. That was when I started on the drink for real."

"Well, you know how it is," said the other man. "I didn't want for my mom and dad, or my kids, to see me in that place."

After an age of bleak gray landscape we pulled into Ocala. I saw my oldest friend, a little older, leaning on his car, scowling at the bus people. When I stepped down he saw me and came my way, languidly. We shook hands.

The next three days passed in a haze of bourbon, home cooking, and nostalgia. We went out only once for more food and drink. The rest of the time we talked, the way we used to do when we were both at Columbia University in the 1950s, and we listened to the same music, except on compact discs instead of 78s and 45s. The house was sumptuously furnished. I remembered many of the pieces from his former apartments in New York, Cambridge, and London. I'd been with him when he acquired some of the first editions, the Jean Cocteau drawing, and several pieces of his collection of Greek and Roman antiquities. There were some Indian miniatures I hadn't seen before; I don't think he liked them very much, and I would have asked him to leave them to me in his will, but I hadn't the nerve. Besides, he has every intention of outliving me.

A couple of weeks later, when I was back in New Jersey, I called my son in London for the news. He told me that two days after I'd taken the Greyhound out of Ocala, my oldest friend called and asked him to tell me that his house had burned to the ground. Fortunately, he was not in it at the time.

BUS 59 to TAMPA

It must have been all the good food my oldest friend prepared for me, and the drink: I slept solidly for two hours out of Ocala, and woke at midnight to change buses in the Tampa depot. A young woman in cowboy boots sat near the gate for Chicago. She held a giant stuffed panda on her knees; no doubt it had seemed a good idea at the time. An Amish man in a brown shirt and dark blue trousers paced back and forth in front of the gate for northbound buses. He was hatless and coatless—he must have left his things on board when he got off to stretch his legs. It is so rare to see one of his sect without others around; perhaps the befuddlement on his face and of his movements was what a bird would feel, separated briefly from the migrating flock. Native Floridians were easy to pick out in the depot: they all wore knitted hats pulled down over their ears, though the night felt balmy to me, and downy soft.

BUS 60 to NAPLES

Bus sleep being what it is, I woke regularly enough on the trip to Naples to notice that the silhouettes outside were changing. Tall royal palms rose with increasing frequency out of the flat, and sometimes I could see water, black as obsidian and so still it was hard to imagine fishes swam in it. Night drew on and the air grew chilly, perversely biting deeper than the clear bright cold of Montana or Michigan's Upper Peninsula. Towns we drove through were neat, and showed the high polish only professional cleaners can give. The usual highway chains were there, but even McDonald's toned down its act to blend into the cute-as-a-button shopping malls. In the early light I counted jewelry stores, all with big signs advertising that they made things to their clients' own design. Gemstones in settings barely out of date, I fancied, were being constantly reset in Florida's resorts to keep pace with fashion and sparkle voguishly out of the crepey skin and liver spots.

Just after dawn the bus pulled into a country depot set far out of town. A well-dressed boy, not much older than my son, who had been sleeping like a baby across the aisle from me ever since Tampa, woke up, stretched, rubbed his eyes.

"Is this Naples?" he asked.

"See it and die," I said.

"Oh yeah," he said. "Totally."

That night I had dinner in a genteel restaurant off Naples's smart main street.

"Don' wan' buh-hurr," said the old woman at the next table. A dry martini was beside her plate; she was drinking it through a straw. She was bleached and lifted, dressed in bright red, and twinkling with real rocks. Her husband tried to keep her quiet by speaking inaudibly himself. With embarrassed apology he looked around at the other tables of elderly diners. "Wh'zat on y'r plate?" she giggled. "Oh, a shell!" She'd had the crab, he'd had the chicken; she had slipped the piece of shell onto his plate in a boozily jokey way. "Hey, that was a goo' one," she cried, and irritably: "Didn't you hear what I said? A goo' one." Suddenly full of wisdom, she leaned over the small table and said: "When you get down to it, wha's the difference between claws and fingers?" The hush, though it was disapproving, gave her words a kind of importance. What *was* the difference between claws and fingers? All the difference in the world to an old broad having her rings reset by a jeweler in Naples. But not much to a crab.

My journey was no longer young. It was swinging back to its beginning with feverish speed. Already I felt homesick for the road, and the bus itself, that dear old Greyhound home of mine. However, at the same time, the instant I let my imagination off the rein it raced ahead with maniacal excitement to put a key in a familiar door, receive news from friends, cook itself a meal, and start to put in order countless glimpses and strange words, every last one of them nothing but American. They were tumbling around my mind like the tesserae of an unmade mosaic.

BUS 61 to MIAMI

Leaving Naples by bus I saw homes more modest than those belonging to what my taxi driver out to the depot called "the

SOBs of the Pelican Club." From Naples to Bayside, Miami, is a glorious run on the Tamiami Trail across the limits of the Everglades. Gradually houses and commerce peter out. Then great flocks of birds, necks outstretched, pass overhead, and basking egrets scatter themselves like white commas over the wilderness of reeds and saw grass. Big irregular patches of dark water prove the whole vast area to be essentially a gigantic lake, and though from the bus it seemed practically deserted, I knew it teemed with aquatic and amphibious life. I was the front-seater, praise be! And once in a while the driver said: "Quick! An alligator!" But I have not been blessed with the gift of game-spotting, and by the time I turned to focus my eyes, ol' gator done gone. Only once, on the surface of a muddy ditch running beside the road, did I see two little dormer-window eyes sending off ripples side by side, and so like their depiction in cartoons and fairy tales I clapped my hands and cried out: "Alligator!" As if the Everglades were the last place on earth to see one.

Near the end of the journey, when Miami was already looming big on the horizon, a young man at the back of the half-empty bus burst into raucous song.

"Whenever trouble comes," said the driver, "you can be sure it's gonna be in the last five rows."

BUS 62 to KEY WEST

The Bayside depot is no bigger than the average filling station, and it was crowded. I sat next to a trim black man of middle age who was waiting for a northbound bus. He spoke to me in BBC standard English with an overlay, or undercoat, of something rich and sticky.

"I have for many a year gone everywhere in the United States by bus, my deah," he told me. "I'm on my way out to New Orleans, where I will be staying with a good friend for Mardi Gras, my deah. I go Greyhound, of course. *Siempre* Greyhound. I am a milliner by profession. Why, certainly in London, my deah. I keep a little flat in Mayfair."

He wore a wide-brimmed hat of black velour, a flowing tie, and
a loose jacket. When he was in London, I'd wager, he would not
dream of taking public transport. But he understood perfectly the
cachet of traveling by Greyhound around America: it was like
doing the Nile on a barge or joining a caravan across the Sahara.
On one level Greyhounding was more then just cheap and efficient; it was authentic, it was the real Yankee Doodle way to
travel, as endorsed by bluesmen in their songs and featured in
chewing-gum commercials. Especially if one did not actually need
to go by bus, it was a grand way to see America, and really very
high style. "My deahs," I could hear the milliner telling his titled
clients back in Mayfair, "*toujours* Greyhound!"

The bus to Key West was a genuine island bus carrying people
lightly dressed for the season, most of them on their way back to
island homes. The well-dressed matron behind me chatted across
the aisle with a bearded hippie in ringlets, and even though the
conversation was mainly about the weather, they were not a pair
who would have anything at all to say to each other in the course
of ordinary continental travel. But islands have rules of their own
and encourage eccentricities: ergo, the Brits, for example, whose
ways are largely incomprehensible to mainlanders. In the front
seat was a girl wearing lots of Guatemalan embroidery and very
little makeup. Her standoffish sexiness had impressed me back in
the depot, and her absolute indifference to the boys who had been
giving her the eye. Suddenly she leaned over to the driver and told
him how she always loved to see the osprey nests on top of the
telephone poles, "like big old straw hats," because that was when
she knew she was back home in the Keys again. At the next rest
stop I saw her out there yakking it up with the boys from the back
of the bus.

Highway 1 strings its Keys into a necklace of odd beads adrift
between the Gulf of Mexico and the Atlantic. Key Largo, Marathon Key, No Name Key, Duck Key, and all the others: a seduc-
tive voice sings out from their weather-beaten holiday charms

lining the highway, but it is also rather doomful on the sly. Any traveler through those flattened drops and droplets of southern-most America must imagine how violently storms have swept them, and that someday a storm will come that sweeps them clean. In spite of the glittering water everywhere, there is an impression of dark practices just out of sight, and old secrets not quite lost in time. Once, I might have lived in such a place and become a local character: Crazy Irma who got off the Greyhound down by Momo's Bait Shop and set up her teepee in the marshes. I thanked my stars I'd had my fling in never-never land a million years before and there was no time or reason to repeat it.

A sturdy lad across the aisle from me began to laugh and tell me how great it was to be going back to "the most excellent Keys." He had just been in Miami, where, to hear him tell it, the streets ran with blood and the news was all bad. He showed a lot of leg and arm, covered with tiny golden curls, and his beard was fair and curly too: he glowed. He said he worked on boats that chartered out of Marathon Key on short cruises and fishing trips. And then he described to me the rafts and open boats he and his crew came across regularly that carried men and women, frequently entire families, fleeing from Cuba.

"And some of them, believe me, from Haiti. Lots of times they've just taken a few, like, tubes and strapped them together with boards on top the way kids do at the beach. We come across 'em pretty regular. It doesn't look like a lot of water to cross on the map, but let me tell you, it is a totally other thing when you're out on those straits with just a little bit of food and water. Totally other. Mostly," he said, "they're dead or dying when we come across 'em. Now, our crew, we always take 'em on board. There's others as figure when they're dead, it's not worth the bother."

It was late by the time I checked into a motel in Key West, and I was hungry. In a darkened mini-mall open on one side to the highway, I found a restaurant set in a parking lot the size of a football field. Inside it was practically empty. "Only one this evening?" asked the hostess, and led me to a table in a dark corner where I could hide my shame. I ordered a bourbon and sat back to look around. Near me a young man with spray-on stubble and a pigtail nuzzled a pretty brunette. Behind them, two slender long-haired blonds, boys or girls, conferred closely across their table. I sipped my drink, ordered local seafood, and hoped I'd have the will to try a piece of Key lime pie.

I was the only person in the place who was not half a couple, and only one woman was older than I. She sat at a table diagonally in my line of vision. Although she was well past the point where time could be bothered to mark her any further, the bones of her face were fine; her neck was slender, and still straight. A long-stemmed glass in front of her held a frothy cocktail, and when she reached for it, lamplight played on a dull, expensive gleam around her wrist and fingers. With her was a man of about my age, twenty years or more her junior. He was balding and plump and dressed in big-city gear. At first I took him for her lawyer in from Miami or Washington, perhaps to discuss her last will and testament, or a property deal. But then I heard the obsequious tone of his laugh, and I saw the tape recorder between them on the table. Hadn't I been in his spot in my time? He was a journalist. And she was his story. By concentrating, I homed in on what she was saying, and her words fell like a blessing on the final turning point of my American journey. "He sent me some dried butterflies once," she was saying. "I had to go down to the post office to get them. And there they were. They'd come from Africa, and they were all dried up. . . ."

Nowhere but here, I thought. Only in America do things occasionally pan out as we imagine they will when we are young. There really are still cowboys to be found in a wildish west, and resident philosophers in North Dakota bookstores. Hollywood is full of movie stars. On Middle American farmlands, religious sects endure as nowhere else against all time and reason. I had met a ruined blues singer in Memphis. And on the northern buses there were big men going after bears with crossbows. Job-hunting was done on a geographical scale that in most other parts of the world would require a new set of papers and the courage of a pioneer. Octogenarians traveled thousands of miles sitting up on buses to see new babies or visit old friends.

"Homeland," I thought.

The waitress was hovering.

"I'm going to try that Key lime pie of yours," I told her.

"He" of course, the one who sent the butterflies to a pretty girl on Key West? There was no other "he" could have been but Ernest Hemingway.

The next night, after a day of sight-seeing in spite of sporadic showers, I joined every other visitor and most of the locals for the trek to Mallory Square. Every evening a crowd gathers there at the waterfront to gawp at the sun, which early risers have already seen that morning batted out of the east, and to cheer when it is driven again into the dove-gray waters of the Gulf. A carnival springs up too on the esplanade to mark the close of day. Teenagers were selling T-shirts and cheap jewelry from stalls. A girl of six or seven stood on a soapbox to sing "Danny Boy," then stepped down and danced a solemn jig while her parents backed her on fiddle and fife. A man in a kilt with a faraway look in his eyes played the bagpipes. An Italian swallowed swords while his girlfriend collected coins in a ten-gallon hat. Although the sun was too fierce to look at straight on, it was beginning to contract and cast off heat and color onto the surrounding sky. At the far end of the promenade I came upon a small crowd formed around an empty space.

"What are you waiting for?" I asked a snub-nosed girl.

"The Frenchman."

"Why?"

"He makes cats jump through hoops of fire."

"He's not gonna come," a gangly boy behind her said sadly. "He never comes when it's rained."

★　　★　　★

The sun had shrunk to the size of something young men could toss around a beach. Puddles on the ground mirrored red. From the nearby aquarium, where the last visitors were being shown around before closing time, rose a chorus of "Oooohs." I had taken the tour earlier and knew that the guide was just then dangling a fish on a line over a tank of sharks, so everyone could see how totally awesome was their appetite, to say nothing of the ghastly pragmatism of those teeth. More and more faces in the mob turned expectantly to the west. Women leaning on men's shoulders, boys arm in arm, were all flushed with reflected rosiness and pink around the eyes. At that moment, I was attacked by a wave of gut-wrenching terror. Without any thought but to get away from there before the sun went down, I turned my back on Mallory Square and ran back to my hotel through the empty streets that were still flickering and faintly lit by the dying fire at the far end of the earth.

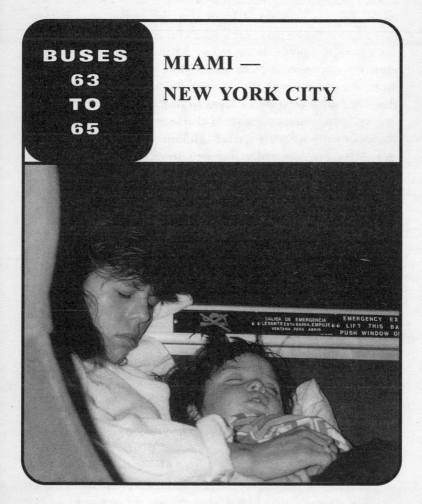

BUSES 63 TO 65

MIAMI —
NEW YORK CITY

*The younger they are, the deeper they
sleep on a bus at night*

BUS 63 to MIAMI

The sun was coming up again as I walked the few blocks to the bus depot. One other passenger waited for the bus to Miami, a man of about my own age, tan and fit, not precisely handsome, but not half bad to look at. Soon he was telling me that he'd retired from business a few years earlier and now followed his true inclination toward boats and sailing. When he wasn't on board his own sloop, he delivered yachts for other people. He was on his way home to Alabama from the Key West regatta, and he had chosen to travel by bus across the Keys so he could have a good look at the starboard side of the causeway and mark shallows, harbors, and channels on a chart he carried with him. As for me, I was about a third of the way into *Moby-Dick* for the first time since 1950, so when we boarded, he took the front seat and I sat behind the driver: thus, we could talk easily to each other, but did not absolutely have to do so.

There were but a handful of passengers on board: a few young men who shambled to the back and fell asleep, and one last-minute boarder who barely made our departure. She was a fat, pretty young black woman dressed in dark cotton suitable to an office, and on her face were traces of a frowning martyrdom I associate with employees of the social services. We were no more than half an hour out of Key West, the Old Salt and I luxuriating in our capital seating arrangements, when suddenly the Social Worker rose from her own seat near the middle of the empty bus, strode briskly down the aisle, and without a word plunked herself into the aisle seat next to me. Had she wanted to join us, or talk to me or to the driver, such a flagrant breach of bus etiquette would have been justified. But she merely sat with her arms folded and a tight, rather righteous smile on her face. Her bulk squeezed me against the window and made a wall between me and the Old Salt, who leaned around her and signaled me to take the aisle seat next to him so we could continue our conversation, mostly about the inland waterways of America. The first chance I had, I squeezed past the Social Worker with apologies and joined him.

"Only a nigra would be that uppity," he said as I settled in beside him. Horrified, I looked back at the Social Worker. She must have heard. But the expression on her face had not changed, her chin was as high and her smile as strangely inward.

By the time we reached the first Greyhound stop at Miami Airport, I knew the Alabama man was divorced, available, sixtyish and in good health, well off, and with time to kill. Admittedly, there was an electric instant as we said good-bye, for I was continuing on to Bayside, Miami, when with the least encouragement he would have offered to spend the weekend with me. But gone were the days I'd change my plans for the whisper of love, so we shook hands and let the kissing moment pass us by.

"Lookin' at you," said the woman behind the desk at the Bayside depot, "I'd judge South Beach is where you'd like to stay." I had asked her advice about where I should go for a day or two in Miami's sprawling complex. "It's arty," she said. "And it's European."

"Have you been to Europe?"

"Nope. But it's probably like South Beach."

Nothing is like South Beach. When I was a child we used to spend our holidays a few miles farther up the coast. But I come from a family of walkers, and I'm sure we must have made it as far as South Beach; if I cannot recall, it's because children have no eye for style, and besides, back then in the early 1940s the classic art deco buildings of South Beach were probably looking old hat and decidedly dowdy. Years later, during my homemaking stint in London, I used to haunt flea markets searching for precisely the sort of thing South Beach is, and I could not shake the feeling as

I walked the sunny streets that I was threading my way among pieces from an outsize tea seat of the 1930s. To have come upon South Beach out of the blue would have been a dream, like an explorer stumbling on a great lost city in the jungle. But many others had been there before me, and with an eye for its production value. Pouting, emaciated girls and hunky boys strutted down the sidewalks everywhere; always a photographer danced backward in front of them, while minions went ahead to clear the way.

Most of the hotels of South Beach have been lovingly restored, but a few are growing derelict around ancient residents who are, literally, sitting tenants. They gather in chairs and wheelchairs on the porches all day long, gaze out impassively at the kids streaking by on Rollerblades, and view all the ballyhoo with indifference from a defunct and receding time zone. I saw one old relic, when he found his passage blocked by a crowd of kids skating in circles for a film crew, patiently maneuver his walking frame into the gutter and work his way around the obstruction without a word of complaint. Only on the beach, where I went to escape the photo shoots and zippy kids, a very old lady was shaking her fist at the ocean and screaming: "Where do you get off pushing me around? You scumbag! Go suck your wiener. . . ." The surf roared back at her and rattled pebbles across the sand.

Somewhere nearby, perhaps even on the spot where I was standing, fifty years or so ago I stood once with my mother after nightfall. A grove of royal palms shot up around us; they are gone now, presumably victims of storms and pollution. Moonlight fell in a tight circle and trimmed with silver the scallops of the noble tree trunks. I wore a blue pinafore with a daisy appliquéd on the pocket. Mother stretched out her arms to the ocean that was rustling in the dark like an audience fluttering programs.

"Irma, oh, Irma, never forget this moment!" she cried.

And I have never forgotten it, though what I remember chiefly is that I was thinking at the time I was going to remember what I chose, thank you very much.

*   *   *

The day was windy and cool; there weren't many people on the beach. Down near the water where the sand was dark and damp were bits of broken coral, small whole shells, and odd fragments the Atlantic had washed up from its fascinating ports of call. My father was next to me in memory, tall, and so deeply tanned from the sun that Mother, or someone, used to joke that soon he would not be allowed on the better beaches, which in those days had a whites-only policy. Miami Beach is where America becomes my father's land. Our winter holidays there were a part of his dream, and an achievement of manhood for a kid who grew up in two tenement rooms on the Lower East Side of New York City. I looked along the shore for the hotel where we used to stay. Wasn't it called the Bancroft? But it was gone. Or I looked in the wrong place. There were others, though, that I remembered from back then: the Eden Roc, the Saxony, the Sans Souci—still with traces of magical splendor, they line the coast like lavish old ocean liners beached for the duration of a war. Only near the ancient unchanging sea had my father been perfectly relaxed and happy. He loved our holidays in Miami. And he loved me then, too.

After lunch, I walked to the far end of the beach beyond the last of the art deco installations, where a bayside park is sheltered from the wind. A young black boy, no more than twelve, fishing from the rocks pulled in a big one just as I was passing. The fish thrashed in the sun and older fishermen nearby shouted out congratulations, mostly in Spanish, to the proud youngster. In the shade of trees lining the path couples embraced, gasping like hooked bass. Women well covered in clothes and flesh, wearing headscarves too, talked on the benches and rocked babies, while their menfolk, jackets off but not their hats, read in the shade and argued in Yiddish. Two pretty girls from Manchester, England, asked if I'd please take a snapshot of them with their camera. On the count of three they smiled; at the very instant I was clicking the shutter, a bearded old Jew in a long coat shuffled into the frame behind them.

*   *   *

Back on the beach I scooped the sand to make a sort of chaise longue, sheltered on the windy side, and I lined it with a hotel towel. Then I took off my shirt. Underneath I was wearing an old black maillot, but I kept my jeans on against the chill. Settling down into my fox hole, I prepared to finish *Moby-Dick*. Gradually, I became aware of a human shadow fallen and fixed on my little pool of sun. I looked up with precisely the quick annoyance of the buses late at night when some wretch takes the neighboring seat even though plenty of others are free. There stood an old, old woman in a print dress and bulky cardigan. The wind had tugged long strands of gray hair out of the bun she wore and was whipping them around her face. Heavy lace-up shoes were no doubt full of sand and must have been uncomfortable—but what's a little more suffering in a long-suffering life? She was holding a plastic container. From the way it was hanging lightly at her side. I could tell it was empty.

"Oy," she sighed. "You should never have arthritis."

I closed my book and sat up.

"Is it very bad?"

"It's making a cripple out of me. The only thing helps . . ." She nodded toward the great Atlantic. "Salt water helps. So every day I'm coming down to the beach looking for someone who will . . ." She raised the empty container and shook it.

Hopefully I looked around for a youngster or a man in a bathing suit. Only a family of Cubans was to be seen, fully clothed and huddling out of the wind next to the lifeguard's station. No lifeguard was on duty—who was going to be fool enough to swim in such a cold, choppy sea? The old lady sighed again: "Oy!"

I sighed: "Ah!"

"Oy!"

"Ah!"

The hard part was keeping my balance against the undertow. After the first few seconds, I was numb to the freezing water.

Filling a container in a rough surf is not as easily done as I had hoped. By the time I finally emerged from the sea I was soaked with spray and the wind stung like a shower of darts.

"You are a good girl," she said when I handed her the dripping container. "May you always be healthy."

"Why, thank you."

But she was already on her way to the boardwalk, and moving briskly too, for an arthritic granny carrying a container full of sea water.

BUS 64 to WASHINGTON, D.C.

In the Bayside depot a Haitian woman in a big black hat, and wearing stockings outside, over her ankle socks, asked for the key to the rest room. Then a skinny black man in a knitted hat had to be shooed into the night for trying to sell gold bracelets cheap to waiting passengers, and a boy in front of me needed a complex ticket. I heard the agent tell him the trip was going to take three and a half days and he'd arrive at 3:25 A.M. When my Ameripass ticket had been filled in for Washington, D.C., I realized with a strange shock, as if it were a surprise, that there would be but one ticket left to go. Next to me in the waiting room sat a young black man with a hissing headset. On the other side of him, another young black man was reading the Bible. "Hey, man," said my neighbor, and without removing the headset he asked: "Is that the King James Version?"

"Uh-uh," said the reader. "No way."

Nearby one man was telling another his marital history. "My first wife, she died. My second wife, well, she was only sixteen. I shoulda known better. That one couldn't last. But my third wife, now, she was a reasonable woman, and that marriage lasted me fifteen years. Then I married again, and that marriage didn't last no time. We just got divorced last March. I guess I shoulda stayed married to number three. But her and I? We got on each other's nerves maybe the last three years. Now I gotta new girlfriend.

She's married to a real bad alcoholic. Her divorce is comin' through pretty soon now. I might try for number five."

The bus to Washington and New York was called. The first empty double seat I found was eight rows back, bus-right. The Bible reader was across from me and one row up. As soon as he sat down he turned on his overhead light so he could continue to read; he had switched to a pamphlet called "The Quest for G-d!" I envied him his ability to concentrate. I had finished *Moby-Dick* that afternoon at a beachside café and brooded for a while over the splendor of the final paragraphs. Since then, I had been too distracted to lock onto consecutive thoughts. There was not one moment of the past three months I regretted, not the most uncomfortable, or the loneliest, or the most commonplace. For days at a time I had wished the journey would never end. Yet, before the next nightfall I was going to be in Washington, D.C., and then, compared to the thousands of miles at my back, it was but a short walk to where I had started out, and my excitement was so intense it was as if a journey were beginning, not ending. A little more of the jitters and I knew I'd be talking to myself. Already I had noticed a few nervous glances from boarding passengers who decided to move on past me and farther down the aisle.

At the Miami Airport stop a noisy bunch of young people boarded. Most of them headed straight for the back rows. Only the seat next to me and three or four others remained vacant. Across the aisle the double seat was taken by a couple speaking Spanish. The woman took upon her lap a boy of about ten, a homely child with an old man's face but big bright eyes that were watching everything. His father laughed and ruffled his hair and his mother locked her arms around him, hugging her good fortune. I wondered how long it was going to be before they realized the boy was of an age that entitled him to a seat of his own. No doubt they had paid full fare for his ticket. I blew up my pillow, stretched out as usual with my head in the aisle, and pretended to sleep. But now mixed with excitement was guilt. Although the people across the

aisle made no complaint, I knew they must be increasingly uncomfortable. When in Jacksonville there was a reshuffling of passengers, I couldn't bear it any longer.

"Excuse me," I said, and tugged on the sleeve of the man across
the aisle. He turned his happy, honest face my way. "Wouldn't
you like to sit here?" I patted the seat next to me. "Your boy is old
enough for a seat on his own." The man shook his head. He had
not understood. In front of me was a handsome young couple who
had boarded in Jacksonville. I'd heard them speaking Portuguese
and I assumed they were Brazilian. Undoubtedly they spoke Spanish too. I leaned over. They were locked in each other's arms,
wide awake. I touched the man on his shoulder, which made him
jump, and I asked him to tell the people across the aisle the good
news I had for them. The mother laughed when she understood.
Gently she kissed her son on his forehead; he had stayed awake as
long as he'd been able, but his head was lodged under her chin,
and his eyes were closed. She slid over into her husband's seat so
the boy could lean against her shoulder. I remembered how that
felt, and what it was like to kiss the top of a drowsy head. The
father moved next to me.

Virtue had to be its own reward. After a few minutes I gave up
trying to sleep. I let the air out of my pillow and folded it into my
bag. For the last time. Outside, the ghost of Georgia slipped past
our windows. Was this not the best of all? This long black ribbon
of empty road, pale trees and grasses, houses with windows closed
up tight for sleep, and clusters of light springing into sight then
disappearing into less than memory. Already the night sky was
taking on its tricksy cast, a practical joker about to spring another
surprise: my last dawn on the road. We slipped into Savannah. A
string of pearly lights outlined a beautiful bridge to the left of the
bus. The man next to me pointed to it, nudged me. "San Francisco?" he asked.

His innocence, or ignorance, touched a chord. He smiled at me,
and I smiled back. My map had been folded and unfolded so many

times it was threatening a continental divide on a massive scale. Very carefully I turned it to the eastern coast and pointed out where we were, then I opened it all the way to the West Coast and showed him San Francisco. He nodded, but I could see he was baffled by the map, and by the sheer hugeness of the United States. Then I noticed the boy was awake, leaning across his mother, watching me with blazing curiosity. My trip was all but over; I knew the stops ahead by heart. Instead of returning the map to my bag (for the last time), I leaned over and passed it across to the boy.

"For you," I said, "to keep."

If I had a thousand maps I'd have given every one of them for a thousand smiles like his. His gremlin face was suddenly all child, glowing with the excitement of travel by night on a big Americruiser. It was a kind of adoption. There was a reshuffling of places, so he and I could sit side by side to study the map and talk in our mix of languages. He was quick, too. In no time he understood how to read the road ahead. He thanked me in English.

For the rest of the morning and until late that afternoon the little family belonged to me. They were from Panama, and out of their country for the first time. They were on their way to Hartford, Connecticut, where an American friend, or perhaps it was a relative, had invited them to stay. I thought the boy was going to swoon with delight when I made him understand there was snow on the ground where he was going. On the entire journey I had not felt more an American than I did then, wanting them to love my country and take back happy memories. My biggest problem was how to keep them safe in the Port Authority when they arrived there late at night, needing to transfer to the Connecticut bus. I knew I'd have to think of a way before we arrived in Washington, where I had to leave them on their own.

As it turned out, I had no time to waste. Not far outside Richmond, Virginia, the driver pulled into a small depot and announced that Washington passengers were to be shunted onto another bus waiting there. Those with luggage in the hold had to claim it; New York–bound passengers were to stay put. I explained to the boy, and he to his parents, that I had to leave. The Brazilian honeymooners were on their way to New York, and before I disembarked, I begged them please to see my little family to the gate for the Hartford bus at the Port Authority. They said they would. I hope they did. The family rose to see me off. I shook hands with the gentle mama and the trusting papa. I leaned down to shake hands with the boy. But instead we threw our arms around each other, kissed, and then both turned away very fast. The bus pulled out and I stood in the cold watching it disappear. For the last time.

"Welcome aboard," said the driver. "No cigarettes. No cigars. No pipes. No crack. And no co-cay-een. . . ."

We pulled away, and my neighbor in the window seat behind the driver turned to me, wild-eyed.

"You know, wherever they send me, it don't matter where, that's where I gotta go. If they tell me Alaska or somewhere, hell, I gotta go. My dad said, 'Recruit her! For God's sake, take her!' He was in the army, too, about my age. My family's broke up. I won't miss my family none." Her voice was loud and piping. On the aisle across from me a young woman holding a baby on her lap set her face resolutely the other way. "Hey, James," my neighbor said. She leaned forward to tap on the glass behind the driver. "How you doin', James? What time you wake up this morning, James?" If the driver heard, he paid no attention, and people nearby avoided looking our way. "Fredericksburg," said the Army Girl, "is just one historical place after another. They have reenactments all the time."

"Is that where you live?" I asked.

"I haven't caught a cold yet," she said, not to me or anyone special. "A whole year and I have not caught one cold yet. I have a theory. I do not have a cold or any other sickness during or after my period. But before, that's different. Before, I am so-o-o-o sick. I hadda have my physical for the army. That doctor poked and prodded me, and took my blood. It was disgusting. But I passed. So I must be healthy. They're gonna call me in a couple days to let me know if I have some blood disease or something. I had real good beef for dinner. Taxpayers paid. I bet they give me a gun to shoot and everything. Pow!" She whirled around with her fore-finger pointed at me. "If I hadda kill somebody I'd shoot him in the forehead. Ambush. Pow! Pow! I know this guy had real small fingers. Small guy. Small fingers. He could break somebody's neck, you know? Kee-rack! Pow! I don't know where he come from. Somewhere." She pounded on the glass. "James! Hey, hey, James. See that little shack of a bus station up there? That's where I gotta get off."

"My name ain't James," the driver grumbled.

The bus door opened to let her out and closed behind her. "Bye-bye, crazy girl," I thought. For the last time.

The woman on the aisle gasped as the Washington Monument and all the lights of the city came into view.

"Oh, look! oh, look!" she said to her baby and pointed out signs: "To the Capitol," "To the House," "To the Senate." Tears were rolling down her cheeks. But the sign that thrilled me so I wanted to leap up and shout "Eeee-haw! You betcha!" was the one over the highway directing traffic: "To New York."

Washington is a one-industry town. And it's a man's town. Women outnumber men there, I was told by my tour guide, but I suspect that's because men still need secretaries, wives, mis-tresses, manicurists, one or more of each per man, according to his status. It's a very fifties, short-back-and-sides sort of place, at least around Capitol Hill and outlying Georgetown.

"Somebody has just taken over that house," said the guide on my tram tour. Aside from me, there were two mink-clad women and a pair of Amish boys. He was pointing to an imposing man-sion on a residential street. "There's been Secret Service guys hanging around it, so it's a good guess it must be someone im-portant. Don't know who. But you guys take this tour again in a couple a days, and I promise I'll know by then. D.C. is gossipsville par excellence."

Farther along he told us how to recognize lawyers who had practices around Dupont Circle: they always wear dark suits, white shirts and red ties.

"Look! There goes one now!"

Amish boys, dowagers in mink, and yours truly turned in our seats and craned our heads to watch a Washington lawyer scamper across the street.

Somewhere along the line I'd lost my toothbrush. At the entrance of the drugstore where I went to buy a new one was a young black woman with two babies. She was begging, and I gave her a dollar. When I came out again, all hell had broken loose in the street. Blue lights were flashing everywhere and two policemen stood by a car pulled up at the curb. The woman driver of the car had her head cradled on her arms on the steering wheel. There was intense police activity across the street, where a very thin, tall black man was plastered face first against a mesh fence, being frisked by officers. It was the first occasion of overt violence I had seen on the entire trip.

"What happened?" I asked the panhandler.

While I was in the store, she told me, a street peddler had pulled a knife on the woman when she refused to buy a gold chain he was hawking through the window of her car.

"She looks awfully upset," I said.

"Well, of course she upset," the panhandler said. "Man, I be upset too, wouldn't you? Big black man comes at you with a knife."

BUS 65 to NEW YORK CITY

I heard myself talking normally to fellow passengers at the gate, just as if I were not faint with excitement. There was an ex–transit cop who commuted one day a week for classes at NYU; a German student and his friend from Texas who were both visiting New York for the first time; a young Japanese woman holding a beautiful child; and a crowd of noisy young black men dressed in gorgeous colors, who went straight to the back of the bus, where they enclosed themselves in headsets. The sun was pale enough to look in the eye; the day was clear and very cold. Brooks and lakes we passed were crisp around their edges, and icicles were hanging from the eaves of houses. I was remembering an Indian tribe I'd read about that used to send its youngsters out alone for a spell in the wild before they were accepted as adult members of the community. In a perfect world, every American boy and girl would be lifted out of the ghetto, or the suburbs, or the farm, and on their eighteenth birthdays each of them would be given an open ticket to go out alone and take a good look at their astounding legacy. And yes, you bet, they would have to go by bus. Even if not many Americans flying from city to city for fun or profit appreciate the fact, the real source of their importance in the modern world lies thirty thousand feet beneath the wings of their airplane: it is the country itself, the extreme westerliness of its place on the globe, and most of all its incredible beauty—an inheritance so stirring that to see it from the window of a bus was enough to make me wonder if perhaps I had a soul after all. And was the world created by an artist God?

Most of the stretch of road between D.C. and Manhattan must appear to a newcomer as repetitious and nearly featureless. But I spent a lot of my childhood in just such country; it too has its charms and its comforts. My brother and I used to peel the silver birch bark so we could scratch messages with a twig on the soft inner lining. And in the bony gray thickets of winter we found bits of china, sometimes whole cups from dolls' tea sets, that had been lost in summer, and hunters' shell cases, snakes' skins, and the skeletons of field mice, all uncovered by the brittle cold stretches of the year, and ours for the taking. As the countryside effaced itself more and more, then was sacrificed to the onslaught of Baltimore, Philadelphia, New York, I felt I was returning not to a place, but to a time gone by when a little girl always knew where her home was.

We pulled into a rest stop on the Jersey Turnpike barely five miles from my mother's house. I could have gone to one of the public telephones and called a neighbor to come and fetch me in a car. I could have walked. But over my head an invisible bow was being tied and it had to be finished neatly, or it would not hold. Eagerly I reboarded the bus as soon as we were called.

"Is that it?" the German boy asked the Texan. He was pointing over the Jersey marshland to the Newark skyline. "I think that must be it."

"No, sir," said the other. "That's not it. Or maybe it is."

The road continued through the long grasses where rats and mosquitoes breed. Off in the distance was the ruin of what had been an active local radio station when I was a kid. We used to pass it every week on our drive to and from the country. It marked the point where my brother and I began agitating for junk food— "Torrid K9, Torrid K9 [hot dog, hot dog] . . ."—until my father lost his temper, or gave in. Not much longer, hardly any time at all, and there it was before us like a brand-new island shaking free of reeds and water.

"My God," said the German. "That's it!"

"Manhattan" and "Out of Town": that was how our files used to divide the United States during my stint of working in a New York office. And it still happens often that when I mean to say "America," I say "New York" instead, though not much could be further from the facts. I grew up under Manhattan's skirts. Practically everything important I ever learned, good and evil, I learned in New York City. When I left, it was to go east. And even though I'd returned many, many times in my years abroad, not until I arrived there with the immense spaces of America and the whole of out-of-town at my back did I fully understand the enormous vitality of my great city. I stepped off the old gray dog at noon on a cold, bright day and smack into the big time.

*   *   *

No wonder New Yorkers are so crazy for the ballet: the pedestrian needs to choreograph a path through solid humanity on the streets. Only Far Eastern cities have such a seething on their sidewalks, and they lack the variety of New Yorkers. I did not tap-dance down Forty-second Street only because I'm a klutz and I don't know how. Inside my head, the little gray cells were all lit up and jiving. O, New York, New York. If America were battery-operated, you would be its power source. And if ever you decide to cut yourself loose from the continent to which you are moored, you could do very well sailing the seven seas and selling all manner of goods and services to natives everywhere at knockdown prices.

Three months, ten days, and four hours after I had set out from New York City, I returned to its Port *of* Authority and went upstairs to Gate 421, where I was going to tie the knot.

THE LAST BUS

The author, cleverly disguised as a middle-aged woman in a funny hat

Fourth row, bus-right, on Suburban Transit, I braced myself for the end. The year had changed since I'd last passed that way. Old leaves were gone and branches were beginning to swell, though a residue of blizzard still glinted on the ground. Newark Airport, where I had arrived from London once upon a time, lay to the right; a plane swooped in low as we were passing. "Mommy, Mommy," whined a little girl near the back of the bus, "when are we gonna get there?"

Passengers read newspapers and books, some of them looked over files from work, and a few were dozing lightly, not seriously trying to sleep. At the back of the bus were some very old people. Not a can of Mountain Dew in the crowd.

"Are we there yet, Mommy?" cried the child.

No warnings about cigarettes, cigars, or crack co-cay-een; the driver had nothing special he needed to say. Exit 8A was just ahead and none of us was going to be with him for long once he left the turnpike.

"Mommy, Mommy . . ."

"Oh, honey, please be quiet. You're nearly home."